The Red Chair Experience
Chris W. Michel

The Red Chair Experience

Copyright © 2022 by Chris W. Michel

Printed and Electronc Versions
ISBN 978-1-956353-16-7 / ISBN 978-1-956353-17-4
(Chris W. Michel/Motivation Champs)

Photo Credit: Cassie Rae
Cover Design: Laura Edgerly

All rights reserved. No part of this book may be reproduced or transmitted in any form or by any means, electronic or mechanical, including photocopying, recording, or by any information storage and retrieval system, without permission in writing from the copyright owner.

The book was printed
in the United States of America.

Special discount may apply on bulk quantities.
Please contact Motivation Champs Publishing to order.
www.motivationchamps.com

Introduction

Reading for inspiration with intention.

I have wanted to write a book for years, but I was not sure what I wanted to write. I had been reading books that inspired me daily. It was part of my daily meditation routine that I had found over the past few years. I started this book because a friend of mine sent me a meme that challenged me to find my passion during the pandemic. It inspired me to move ahead with my dream of writing if for no other reason than to write. This book was also inspired by the death of my younger brother, which helped me to see that the life I was living was not where I wanted to be, and it was starting to shift. Certain things no longer held value as they did in the past and other things started to become more valuable.

I had my red chair sitting in my master suite and I was sitting in it to do my daily reading. Then it was time to start writing some of my own experiences that could inspire others. The journey of writing this has been one of discovery, acceptance, forgiveness, and of course love. All of these were and are for me and others. I wrote this because I needed to talk and learn about these topics. I needed to listen to the experiences around me and within me. Some of the things I share in this book were in the past, but many of them were happening as I wrote them. This book has helped me to feel feelings that I only read about or saw in the movies. It has helped me to understand that feelings are an important part of life when we discover them. They can help us and not hinder us.

My intent for writing this may have been therapeutic and cathartic with the off chance that someone else may find it helpful. I wanted this to be something that could be read daily, not necessarily consumed in one sitting. Some of these days will strike a chord and others may fall flat on the day that you read them. Like the books I read daily, I hope that these daily reads provide a gentle reminder to you of how things can be.

My hope for you, reader, is that you will find inspiration for your daily life. We only have the day in front of us to work with, though we can make plans for the future, and we should learn from our past. You may be struggling with something today that you want to focus on, so jump to the index, find a particular topic, and read that page or pages for your heart and mind. I hope you find peace, inspiration, challenge, and even thoughtfulness in yourself while reading this. Maybe you could take some notes and start your journey of writing to inspire yourself and others. My hope is that this book may help you find your own red chair experience!

Red Chair Experiences

"What I saw was that no matter who we are, life is going to put us through the changes we need to go through. The question is: Are we willing to use this force for our transformation? I saw that even very intense situations don't have to leave psychological scars, if we are willing to process our changes at a deeper level." – Michael A. Singer - The Surrender Experiment

I am the proud owner of a red leather reclining chair. I say proud because it has a deep, special meaning to me, and it is my favorite color. Its first owner was my stepfather, and he was my business mentor that I would call about my career path. I valued his thoughts and opinions above anyone else because he had some similar experiences in his life, and he had my best interest at heart. He and I both played college football, he at Alabama and myself at Illinois. He passed away in the spring of 2016. Its second owner was my younger brother, who was one of my best friends. My brother had developed issues with his hip and needed to have a comfortable chair where he could sit and occasionally, he would sleep in it because it helped to relieve the pain. My brother died in the fall of 2019. My sister-in-law, along with my niece and nephew, struggled with what to do with the chair as it meant the world to my brother, and to them, it was a reminder of him. She asked if I would like the chair and without hesitation, I said yes. My red chair sits in my master suite, and I use it to have my mindful time of the day, reading, meditating, just sitting to feel feelings, and sometimes, I even have conversations with the previous owners. My red chair is special because it has a depth of meaning to me and in someone else's hands would mean something completely different. Do you have your own "red leather chair?" This kind of place may not work for you, but do you have a place to sit and read, to contemplate life's challenging questions, to meditate, or to just feel the feelings in your life? I hope you do and if not, find what works for you because we all need a place to have our red chair experiences.

Today, I will spend time in my place of experiences or even find a place of experiences that works for me to be present and mindful and take in the opportunities that life has to offer me today.

Dedication

This is dedicated to everyone that is looking for a better version of themselves, waiting to be released.

Acknowledgment

I want to say thank you to the following people that helped me in some way shape or form to put into words the things that needed to come out and create the red chair experience. Thank you, Mike "Biggs" Dixon for the gentle nudge to get started writing the book. Ron Stryker for being the inspiration and a best friend, you are missed. Thank you, Peni Roberts, and her late husband Bill Roberts, for their support over the years and for allowing the red chair to come into existence physically and metaphorically. Thank you, Stephanie, Solange, and Johnny, for entrusting the red chair to me. To The Red Chair Council, Harry, Kathy, Mike, and Scott, you have inspired me over this past year, and I am very grateful. To Kiersten, Devon, Dalton, and Katie, you all inspire me! To John and Cathy, Jeff and Kelley I am grateful for you and your influence. Thank you, Trina Labenski for all your encouragement and support. I love all of you very much!

January

New Beginnings   January 1

"I think in terms of the day's resolutions, not the years." – Henry Moore

Starting a new year is always a time of reflection. What did you do last year, and what do you want to accomplish this coming year? Do you make goals that are just for the year, or do you break them down to quarterly, monthly, or even daily? As you spend time with family and friends do you take the time to discuss your accomplishments, the things you learned, and how much you have grown, emotional, physically, and even spiritually? Hopefully, you take the time and encourage your heart to see the growth that you have made. In this past year, I have learned about my health and how I need to control my diet so that I do not have to deal with gout which I have been dealing with for over twenty years. I got to start fulfilling one of my life goals: writing a book. I also started my own business. I have started having regular video meetings with my family and as a result, I have gotten to spend more time with them. I have learned how to take better care of myself mentally, physically, and spiritually. It has been a challenging year with a lot of change, but I look forward to what growth will happen over the next year. Hopefully, you can find the growth opportunities and take a step toward a better life for yourself and your family. What happens when you look at your goals from a daily perspective and not as a whole year?

Today, I will look for ways to make progress towards my daily and annual goals.

You Can Never Go Back   January 2

"No man ever steps in the same river twice, for it's not the same river and he's not the same man." – Heraclitus

I used to think I could always go back to things, maybe it was a relationship, a job, or even a chore around the house, thinking they would be the same as before. The reality is you can never go back! You have changed, they have changed, and maybe the situation has changed. Things around us, victories, losses, especially death, change who we are. I have walked away from puzzles and returned hours or days later to find the solutions staring me in the face. It took separation from some relationships for me to realize this truth.

I have friends from my youth that I still keep in touch with. I am able to connect with some right away and with others, it takes a while to get back on track because so much has changed in myself or with them. I found that with some people, I changed and the things that brought me and this other person close are no longer there, or I did not have the same beliefs I did when I was younger and less experienced. I wanted to go back to the way things were and the perceived comfort or familiarity of that relationship, but I could not, and I did not realize it until much later.

I was getting frustrated by the lack of emotional connection that I was having because I was looking for a feeling or positive memory from the past that was no longer there. Every day we are making steps forward or backward whether we want to or not, we never stay the same. I heard this when I was in my late twenties or early thirties, and it has always stuck with me. At times, I can/could see this clearly and not so much at others. What are you doing to make steps forward every day and do you see when you are stepping backward?

Today, I will look for ways to return to familiar relationships, jobs, or even chores around the house, without the expectation that they or I will be the same as it was before.

TIME TO EXPLORE   JANUARY 3

"Kids should be allowed to break stuff more often. That's a consequence of exploration. Exploration is what you do when you don't know what you're doing." – Neil deGrasse Tyson

Have you traveled? Have you gotten on a bus, or train, or plane to go somewhere you have never been before? Do you get excited about the idea or opportunity to see someplace new to you? A mountain, lake, sea, ocean, crop field, forest, or river, can bring different sights, smells, sounds, thoughts, and emotions. Those then become new memories that you get to have and possibly share with a loved one or a friend. I went on a cruise ship that traveled to the Northeastern United States and into parts of Canada. I got to see things I had never seen before. I got to visit places that filled me with awe. I saw mountains, battlefields, and other landmarks. What do you want to see or experience? What stops you from making the trips? Can you make your plans and see those plans through so that you can explore what is important to you? Sweet is the memory that warms the heart and brings a smile to your face.

Today, I will be open and look for the next inspired exploration.

SALES AND SPORTS   JANUARY 4

"When the going gets tough, I'm not always sure what you do. I'm not saying that I know how to fix everything when the going gets tough, but I do know this: when the going goes tough, you don't quit. And you don't fold up. And you don't go in the other direction."- John Madden

I was blessed to grow up and play sports and those sports taught me several lessons, probably most important was resilience. There is a mental toughness that can be learned from playing sports for a length of time. You develop the ability to work through, tough and uncomfortable situations. Sales can require a similar type of mental toughness. You hear "no" a lot and rejection is not something that most people can handle on a regular basis. If you are in sales, you were probably built for this! Not many people can do sales effectively. There are many people who try but some succeed because they were born for this. Some people are born to be scientists, astronauts, medical personnel, trainers, motivational speakers, and some were born to be in sales.

If you are successful in the sales world, then you likely understand what it takes to sit with someone and understand how to find their needs and wants and apply your knowledge about your product or service to help meet those needs and wants. Sometimes you do a good job and sometimes you fail, then you learn. You learn because you are resilient. You have a mental toughness that pushes you to find a better method, a different or better solution.

Today, I will learn from the "NO" responses and find a better solution and find my resolve to be a better salesperson. Learning to work around or through the obstacles or objections is what good salespeople do consistently.

The Path   January 5

"Every time I've strayed from the beaten path, I've never regretted it."
– Tori Murden

Too often we can get caught up with staying on the path, whether it is life, work, exercise, or even a diet. We beat ourselves up for eating this or taking a day off. Sometimes we need to have that break and as long as you get right back to your normal then you will be fine. If you choose to stay off the path, you have created another path, which is not necessarily bad but at that point, you have made a conscious decision to stay on your new path. I have been going through a journey of health, trying to figure out, with the help of professionals, how to heal my body of sickness and inflammation. At first, I was given a very restrictive diet that was really hard to stick with. This diet removed all the things I really liked and if I stepped off the path, I would feel it for days. Then I kept getting better and better and the longer I stay on the path the less frequent and less intense the flare-ups happen.

How can you find the path that you need to be on and how can you sustain that path? What do you need to learn, what do you need to change to help you find your path?

BE PRESENT   JANUARY 6

"Do what you can, with what you have, where you are." – Theodore Roosevelt

Too often we miss the final statement in that sentence. We have no issue with doing what *we* can with what we have. When asked to be present, I have struggled with this over the years. I used to tell people that they need to keep moving forward so that the bad stuff in their life would not catch up with them. I believed that we could outrun the garbage from our past. That is not true. The change in scenery was deceptive and misleading. When you can be present and sit with the discomfort of just being, you will learn a valuable lesson. There is an inner peace that comes with being still with your thoughts and yourself.

Being still can be difficult and uncomfortable for some. It means that we must listen to the voice in our head that has been telling us to just sit and relax. It means that we must let go of the counter voices that tell us to keep moving otherwise we are not making progress or growing. Staying still is growth.

Today, I will look for opportunities to sit and be still in the stillness and peace of where I am. I will learn to grow in being present.

LOOK AROUND   JANUARY 7

"Life moves pretty fast. If you don't stop and look around once in a while, you could miss it." – Ferris Bueller

When was the last time you stopped to look around and take in the scenery, the smells, and the sounds? Do you intentionally enjoy the meal you are eating or your conversation with friends, family, or colleagues? When I play golf, I make it a point to stop and stand on the tee box of a picturesque view and take it in. Being thankful for the peace and serenity that I am feeling at that moment. To take in the beauty that I see and forget all that may be going on around me or happening in my life.

Where is your personal tee box? Is it the ocean? Is it in the mountains? Is it in a big city with tall buildings? Is it in the peace and quiet of your home, meditating or praying? Maybe it's on your five-minute walk to the bus. If you need to get away to do this, then do that! Have you ever smelled a young puppy's breath while they are licking your face? Smelled the skin of a baby as they lay in your arms? Smelled the rose garden that your grandparents have outside their house? Awakened to the smell of fresh coffee being made? Smelled the aroma of the food being made by your favorite chef? Pause and look around, otherwise, you could miss the very thing that you are looking to experience, or feel. Do you play golf, hike, run, read, watch movies, play video games, etc. just for the competition or to really get away from the hustle and bustle of our lives? Unplug yourself from life by shutting off your phone, computer, tablet, etc. Life moves pretty fast. Do not let it pass you by.

Today, I will find ways to stop and find the experiences in life that I want or need. It could be a simple view, smell, or taste that makes all the difference.

FAIRNESS   JANUARY 8

"Fair play is primarily not blaming others for anything that is wrong with us." – Eric Hoffer

"That is not fair!" I have said that a few too many times in my life. I was trying to express how I did not like the way I was treated or the outcome that I received. Life is not fair we have all heard that. But what makes it fair for me is not what makes it fair for someone else. Fairness is subjective and yet it seems to offend every one of us when it is not directed in our favor. What can you do when life is not fair? Accept it and make the most of what you can with ethics and morality. That seems odd to say, with ethics and morality. To overcome your disposition, you should not resort to undermined, or underhanded tactics to get the scale tipped back in your favor or even back to level. Sometimes you will lose because life was not fair to you, but that does not mean you need to "make it right" by your hand. This is a different message than life being equal for everyone. We all should have the same opportunity no matter who we are. But sometimes life is not fair, because your customer has a predisposed view of what they want, and you cannot offer that. You may have to walk away from that situation and say, that was not fair, but I could not have done anything else to make it so. When you have no control over the fairness of a situation sometimes you can do nothing but walk away. If it is something that should be fair, a national contract, or something with "rules attached by a governing body" then you should do what is possible to make it fair.

Today, I will look at fairness differently and find ways to overcome the lack of fairness with ethics and morals, that I can control and not worry about those that I cannot control.

ANGER   JANUARY 9

"Be patient and calm — for no one can catch fish in anger." - Herbert Hoover

I am sure we have all felt anger because of someone else's actions, or maybe it was because we did something to another. I have heard that there is nothing wrong with feeling angry. Actions that follow the feelings of anger are tricky. You may have heard that you should not act in anger and that is sound advice, however, can you tell the difference between anger and righteous indignation? Righteous indignation is attacking the problem *not* the person. If you felt that you have been unjustly accused or wronged, then your anger towards that accusation or wrongdoing can be justified by righteous indignation. But if you are attacking the person that has accused or wronged you then you are reacting with anger. It is hard to be calm when you are angry. But being calm is the best way to see the truth of the situation. Again, there is nothing wrong with feeling angry, however, it is how you deal with it that makes all the difference. Are you able to feel the anger and move to how to fix it pretty quickly or do you stay in your anger for a while?

Today, I will recognize anger and how I can make it about the problem and not about the person.

BEING DIRECT   JANUARY 10

"Direct confrontation, direct conversation is real respect. And it's amazing how many people get that." – Penn Jillette

Being direct or straightforward can be hard for some and yet so easy for others. Regardless, being direct is and should be respectful in that you are not trying to hide something from someone that you care about. Being direct can help to resolve a lot of issues before they become issues. If you have ever been talked to directly it may have stung at first, but I bet you understood things a lot quicker and were able to move on faster as well. Being direct can and needs to be a normal part of our daily conversations. I am not saying that you should drop all your filters and start going around being brutally honest with people about things that are petty. It should be a part of your daily conversation when you see something that is important to you and deserves to be addressed right now. Too often, we can let things go that bother us and as time goes by it festers into something far more than what was said or intended. So, bring it up and be direct. It is probably not personal, but if it is, you can hash that out as well. Being direct will bring the freedom to you that you deserve. Do not be afraid to be direct. You will get better at being direct over time too. Like riding a bike or making a presentation, the more you practice it the better you will get at it.

Today, I will find ways to be more direct and not shy away from conflict.

GRIEF   JANUARY 11

"No one ever told me that grief felt so like fear." – C. S. Lewis

Grief is a tough emotion to define, let alone experience. I have felt grief over relationships, lost jobs, lost opportunities, and the death of a loved one. Grieving the end of a relationship can be difficult, especially if you were not ready for that relationship to end. It may have needed to end for the other person and you so that you could move onto something better, for both of you. The loss of a job and loss of an opportunity is difficult when it is not your idea, though you probably needed it to be over and you could not see it. Though hard to see we get the chance to start anew or jump to the next level because of this ending. The death of a loved one has been the most challenging to me over the years because you do not get to move on to something better. Though the death may have been understood, due to age or illness, it does not make it any easier. You have a place in your heart/life where this person took up space and held it for you and you held it for them. There is no shortcut on this one. There is not an easy step-by-step process that you can do to help you get to the next level or move on. That person will always be a part of you and your past. Grief has helped me as I have allowed it to wash over me, and I have been able to sit in the grief and not push it aside. This may sound strange, to sit in the grief, but there is no other way to describe it than to sit in it and be still. Like standing in the shower and putting your head under the water and letting it wash over you. You feel the coolness or warmth of the water as it covers you. Grief has been like that for me. It washed over my entire person, head to toe, fingertip to fingertip. This too shall pass but you are now a different person. Grief is good, and necessary to help us to make the next step. Whether the career move, relationship or just being able to get up the next day after the death of a loved one you get the chance to take the next step however small it may appear to be.

Today, I will see grief for what it is and allow it to flow over me when needed to be able to take the next step whatever that may be.

Fear vs. Understanding   January 12

"Nothing in life is to be feared, it is only to be understood. Now is the time to understand more, so that we may fear less." – Marie Curie

Courage and fear are at opposite ends of the emotional spectrum. I have courage when I speak in public, or train groups of people, whether large or small. It does not mean that I have do not have butterflies before I do my presentation, but I do not fear the situation because I know the material. When you are afraid of something you more than likely do not understand it. I am not making light of your fears, like a fear of heights, or a fear of water, because there is something deeper behind those things. If you want to overcome them, you must get help from someone trained to help you overcome that fear. But a lot of our day-to-day fears can be lessened by taking time to understand what is behind the fear. Fear can grab a hold of us and not let us be who we are supposed to be. If you are afraid of getting on a plane, you may not get to see the places you want to see. If you are afraid of speaking in front of large crowds, you may not be able to do stand-up comedy. Those things may not speak to you or be a desire of yours. What do you want to do that you are not able to do because of the fear in your life? Do you want to sell a million dollars worth of goods or services for your company? Do you want to make six figures? Do you want to have deeper relationships? What fear is holding you back from becoming what you want to become?

Today, I will look at my fears and see how I can overcome them. If I need to get help from someone to overcome my fears, then I will take steps to make that happen.

Focus   January 13

"You will never reach your destination if you stop and throw stones at every dog that barks." – Winston Churchill

Do you find yourself easily distracted by the things that are going on around you? When you have a task to do or a place to go, do you find a bunch of other things that need to be done along the way? Maybe you are avoiding tasks because you are not focused or simply not ready to do what needs to be done? It is easy to do things that we like to do. When we have to do something, even though it is the right thing or something that needs to be done, our hearts may not be ready to do that chore. Focus on doing what you need at the time you have to do it and you can focus on other tasks. You waste time when you stop to throw rocks at dogs.

Today, I will focus on the task that I need to do and not allow the barking dogs to distract me from my task.

SIMPLE LIFE   JANUARY 14

"A simple life is good with me. I don't need a whole lot. For me, a T-shirt, a pair of shorts, barefoot on a beach and I'm happy." – Yanni

Are you happy with a simple life or do you prefer to have a certain level of complexity? Most of us know this as adding drama to our lives. Some people do not like to add drama to their lives, yet they are constantly stirring the proverbial pot. So, how do you complicate your life? Do you push your friendships, romantic relationships, siblings, parents, children, or coworkers? I am not talking about letting things go that need to be discussed or compromising on something that you feel very strongly about. Some people have a difficult life because they were raised that way and have yet to be able to work themselves out of that life.

Being an adult, I get to make choices that affect me and those around me. I can further complicate my life by making poor choices, similar to the ones that got me where I am, or I can choose to make choices that will simplify my life. The choices may not be easy and the path to get out of our situation may be very difficult. You may think that it is easier to continue down this path than to make those difficult decisions and ride out those waves for a while. When you look at the bigger picture of your life are you happy where you are, or would you like your life to be simple?

Today, I will look at how I can make my life simpler and start making decisions that will lead to that simpler life.

GAMBLING   JANUARY 15

"Life consists not in the holding of good cards but in playing those you hold well." – Josh Billings

The number of risks you are willing to take is proportionate to the amount of value you find in that situation. Some things we value a lot, friends, family, a job, and others we value less. There are some among us that are huge risk-takers, and they will normally not think twice about the risk involved because they are high on the dopamine their body is producing just thinking about the challenge ahead of them. Most of us will look at a situation and assess how valuable the situation is and what the payoff will be regarding that value and figure out if we want to take the risk or not. Some of us need to take more risks. Others of us need to *learn* how to take more risks so that we can find a better way of doing things, find what we like to do, find the person to be in that once-in-a-lifetime romance with. What do you want to do, run forward, or shrink back? These are the tough questions when we are in the moment, and we need some guidance. Find your inner voice, listen, decide, and be ok with whatever your choice is, just decide. Sitting on the fence is no way to live either. Once you decide to move forward, you can look back and decide if adjustments need to be made for the future.

Today, I will learn to gamble with decisions I make so that I can make the most of the situation.

LOVE   JANUARY 16

"Me: Why do nice people choose the wrong people to date?
Teacher: We accept the love we think we deserve.
Me: Can we make them know they deserve more?
Teacher: We can try."
– The Perks of Being a Wallflower

We are all capable of giving and receiving love. Sometimes you may feel like you are getting all that you can from a relationship. I have found that you are loved not because of how good you are but because of how good others are to you. Love is a funny thing in that, some of us grow up learning how to love through great examples from those around us and yet others of us get to learn how to love from seeing how bad others around us are at showing their love. There are things to be said for both methods of learning, but nothing beats the former, learning to love from great examples of those around us. They can be family or friends or neighbors or even coworkers. They do it without conditions, restrictions, or hesitations. We all have the opportunity to love like this whether we grew up this way or not. We *can* learn to love. What kind of love do you want? Only the best, but what do you think *you* deserve?

Today, I will look for ways that I can love others not because of who they are but because of the person that I want to be.

COLLABORATION   JANUARY 17

"Individual commitment to a group effort - that is what makes a team work, a company work, a society work, a civilization work." – Vince Lombardi

We can do things by ourselves and can do them well. They are creative in their own way. Some can write, others can speak, others sing, lead people, organize others, and the list can go on. We all have been part of a team at some point in our lives. We had to work with others and get along with people so we could do something together. Create something as a team instead of just as one person. Could we do the project or work by ourselves? Maybe.

Too often we think that we want to be alone and not have to work with others. We are seeing a shift in the workforce as I write this, where people want to work from home. Apart from their coworkers. Working alone has some advantages and disadvantages but the key question is, can we work together? I have been an individual contributor most of my career. All that means is that I was there to sell it to the client. Someone set the appointment after taking the call, that was placed by a customer that saw an advertisement, that someone created. I can go out and sell on my own, but I need someone to make the product, I need someone to deliver the product or even install the product. I will need someone to account for the transaction that I help create as well so that everyone can get paid. Also, someone needs to write the checks to pay everyone. This could be a small company and all those jobs are held by one person. Most of the time, we need to focus on what we can do well and let others do what they do well. When we collaborate, we can bring different strengths to the table and accomplish so much more. We can work on a project together and the ideas that flow are multiplied because someone said something that sparked you to think of something else, and so on. I believe this is what spawned the saying the whole is greater than the sum of its parts. What has collaboration done for you? Have you been able to work with others to create something? We have the chance to work with others, but we get to choose who we collaborate with.

Today, I will find ways to collaborate with others and create something much bigger than I thought possible.

All the Small Things   JANUARY 18

"Enjoy the little things, for one day you may look back and realize they were the big things." – Robert Breault

We are taught to not sweat the small stuff and yet we need to focus enough on them to get them done. We can let them slide if we are not careful. Sometimes the little things become big things. A dish in the sink becomes a sink full of dishes when we continue to think it is only one dish. The little pain in our back puts us in bed for a couple of days because we did not listen to our bodies. That little problem we did not take care of at work becomes a lost sale all because we did not respond to the email. When we take care of the little things, we are freed up to do what is important to us later. We also will find that maybe they were bigger than we thought at the time. To the person we saw and smiled at every day for over a week, who later tells you that it saved their life. The kind gesture that your coworker did for you allowed you to see your kid's recital or game. That day your child made a breakthrough in confidence because you were in attendance. We all have seemingly small things in our lives that we can gloss over or simply forget. Those small things can lead to big things that have an impact on you and others. Whether now or in the future the small things will make a difference. Give them the attention they need but do not dwell on them so that you lose focus.

Today, I will remember to do the small things because they do make a difference and they will lead to bigger things.

Healing   JANUARY 19

"You can't heal in the place that hurt you." – Anonymous

I think we can all agree that healing is a good thing! How we got there to need the healing is another story. Trying to heal in a place that has hurt you can be very difficult, and you may not completely heal either.

Sometimes, we cannot get out of the situation that is harming us quickly enough. Maybe you do not have the money or the resources to leave the situation. Start working on a plan to get the healing that you need and get to a better place. It may not be popular or easy, or maybe it just requires us to make a move and we can begin the healing process.

Looking for happiness in the place we lost it in is also a bad idea. I got hurt, emotionally. I tried to return to the things that brought me joy and happiness. But I did not leave the situation, I buried my head and my emotions and tried to work harder thinking that would fix my problem. The problem was I was not dealing with the problem. I was dealing with the symptoms. Once I was able to figure that out, I could start the healing process. As I write this, I am still going through the healing process and I continue to grow in ways that I did not think were possible anymore because I was hurt, damaged but not irreparably damaged. I had to make a move to get out of that emotionally damaging situation. Part of the healing was finding my part in the situation and changing that. Another part was seeing what I *allowed* to happen. It was time to set boundaries. When I was able to set the boundaries, I could walk away. Look for the way that you can change your situation so that you can start the healing process.

Today, I will find a way to start healing and moving toward finding my new happiness. Not happiness in something or someone but truly finding the happiness that I have within me.

TRIALS   JANUARY 20

"Consider it pure joy, my brothers and sisters, whenever you face trials of many kinds, because you know that the testing of your faith produces perseverance. Let perseverance finish its work so that you may be mature and complete, not lacking anything." – James 1:2-4

This has long been a favorite verse of mine because of the way it is worded. Perseverance *must* finish its work so that you *may be* mature and complete. Going through trials is not easy especially when you do not want to go through tough times or want to learn something. I have learned the value of seeing these as opportunities. I have come to accept them and look at them for what they are learning opportunities.

When we are younger, we look at these as roadblocks or stumbling blocks to getting where we want to go. We miss out on the chance to get it right and our true lessons get put off until a time when we can be made mature and complete. Complete is not the end all be all, it is a way to define what happens to us when we become mature. We are more complete when we learn through trials. I look at this as not just faith in our lives but in our characters overall. Because the testing of your *character* produces perseverance. What are you going through now that needs to be developed to maturity or completion? Look at the trials happening around you? Maybe you have a few things to work on right now, pick one and work on it until others see the maturity coming around in you.

Today, I will look at the trials I am going through as opportunities to take steps toward maturity.

Reputation   January 21

"It takes twenty years to build a reputation and five minutes to ruin it. If you think about that, you'll do things differently." - Warren Buffett

We tend not to think a lot about the consequences of our actions until we see the repercussions of those decisions. We want to be the best, smartest, fastest and if you are willing to do anything to get those dreams, it can cost you in the long run. Do you think about your words and actions and what they will mean for the long term? As you work to create your reputation, whether you know it or not, you are creating your persona daily. How you act with friends, family, coworkers, and even strangers, is developing who you are and how you are perceived. As we get older, we can see this more clearly but sometimes we hit that stage where we can think, I am who I am and I cannot change, or maybe will not change. You can always change and grow if you want to. You can always build and shape your reputation.

Today, I will look at ways that I can build my reputation.

Take a Chance   January 22

"If you get a chance, take it. If it changes your life, let it. Nobody said it'd be easy, they just promised it would be worth it." – Dr. Seuss

Take a chance they said. It will be fun they said. Do you look at taking chances as fun or exciting? Most people do not look at it that way because it is uncomfortable. It is outside of the norm, and we like being comfortable. Some people are adrenaline junkies and need to change their situation all the time. They are willing to take a chance at every turn. If things do not change for them, they feel sad. They are used to the rush they get when things change around them. Some people fear change to the extent that they will do everything in their power to not allow the change in their life. They like the status quo. They like the predictability of their lives and their situation. For the rest of us that are not looking for change all the time or never want to change, there is a certain level of anxious excitement that happens when we are faced with change. It could be a simple change or monumental change. The bigger the change the more anxiety that comes with it. Maybe you met someone today that piqued your interest. Maybe you were contacted about a new job situation. Maybe you get the chance to move into your own home. Life is full of opportunities for us to take a chance.

In sales, this happens most days. Will they take a chance on me and my product or service? I do not consider myself to be an adrenaline junkie by any means. I am not averse to risk-taking, but I also tend to overthink things. I am a fan of the risk-reward systems that are in my life. I took a chance and started my own business. I had been in the corporate world for most of my career and had worked for a couple of smaller businesses, but I never had my own business. It has been scary at times, wondering where will the next client come from, or what do I do next? Through it all, I would not change a thing.

What do you want to do? You have a choice. Do you want to stay in that apartment? Do you want to stay in that job or career path? Do you want to stay single or in a relationship that is not moving in the direction you want? What do you want to take a chance on today? We all have the opportunity at one time or another. Sometimes, when we ignore the opportunity long enough the door will close, and we do not get the chance ever again. That can be a good thing or a bad thing, but you get to decide.

Today, I will get to decide if I want to take a chance. The opportunities are there, but they may not be the right ones for me at this time, and it is ok to pass on those. But when you take a chance, remember it may not be easy, but it will be worth it.

CHARACTER   JANUARY 23

"Show respect even to people who don't deserve it; not as a reflection of their character, but a reflection of yours." – Dave Willis

Character is who we are when we are alone, and no one is watching. If you are gentle, kind, forgiving, giving, gracious when no one is watching, you are likely to be like that when you are around others. Our character can show through at the best and worst of times. It can reflect our integrity. It shows through when we generously give to someone and when we angrily cut someone off in traffic. It shows when someone is disrespectful to us, and we do not respond in kind. When you play games, like cards or golf, your character can come out as well. Your character can be all the difference when you are trying to win the sale or get that job.

I have had plenty of opportunities to see my character in full bloom. I have been in situations where I let my impatience and lack of compassion get the best of me. I have also been in situations where I found empathy and compassion to give to people that were in need. What do you want your character to be like? Your past does not define your character, you still have a decision in how it gets formed and presented to others. When we take the time to work on the things that are important to us, we can change our character. We must spend the time to make the changes though. Character is not something that is easily changed most of the time.

Today, I will look at my character and see if I want to make changes. If I need to make changes, I will start with some steps to make corrections where needed.

RULES   JANUARY 24

"I follow three rules: Do the right thing, do the best you can, and always show people you care." – Lou Holtz

Have you ever noticed how many self-imposed rules we have in our lives? Do you feel like things just keep getting more complicated because we have so many rules? Rules are great and useful when applied properly to our lives but can become a hindrance when we get caught up in them, or when we let them rule our actions. We can fall into the trap of making a rule for everything we do in life, every decision we make. History has plenty of people that came before you that made rules for every little detail in their life. It can make living easier because you are not having to make decisions about all the little things any longer but making rules for every situation can be tiresome and overwhelming. If you live by fewer rules, then you can have a simpler life.

Today, I will learn to live more simply by doing the right thing, being the best I can, and showing people that I care.

Results   January 25

"I've always believed that if you put in the work, the results will come."
– Michael Jordan

A sales job is a lot like any other job. It takes work to perfect your craft. If someone tells you that they do not need to work at it then they will be passed by. The best salespeople understand that you must take time to understand the product or service. They also understand that the customer needs to be heard, listened to, and understood for you to do your job properly and close the deal. I know several salespeople who do not like to role-play and think that their time with the customer is enough practice. If that is the way that you look at the leads that you run, then you need to readjust your thinking because you are wasting those sales calls. You can make excuses and say they were not ready to buy or any other excuse but if you put in the work, you will make the sale. Good salespeople know that they must practice away from the customer in order to be ready to meet any objections that they may have or to prevent them in the first place because they were prepared. You must put in the time to get the results you want. Do not be the salesperson that goes to the customer unprepared and then makes all kinds of excuses for not closing the deal.

Today, I will prepare for my sales calls as much as possible with others before I get to them so I can see the results sooner rather than later.

Legacy   January 26

"So many people think about their legacies at the end of their lives. When they face their own mortality, that's the problem! Only when they face their own mortality do they start thinking about legacy and giving and giving to charity and giving it all away. Why not do that when you are twenty-one? Why not do that when you are eighteen? Why not live your

entire life thinking about your legacy, meaning what impact will we have on the lives of others?" – Simon Sinek

What is your legacy? What if, heaven forbid, something happened to you today? What would you be remembered for? What would your impact be on the world? Maybe that does not mean much to you right now. Maybe you are living your best life possible, and you would not change a thing. Over the years we get opportunities to see our mortality, when a loved one, friend, or even ourselves are in an accident that puts our lives on pause. It is times like these that we get to think about what my impact on this world is that I live in going to be. I had a friend that died when I was about thirteen, a family member passed when I was about nineteen, that same year I was in a car accident where I fell asleep at the wheel. All these situations were opportunities for me to look at my mortality. Maybe you have not had these in your life yet, or maybe you have not seen them as opportunities. If you have not, then maybe it is time to start looking at ways for you to have an impact on your world.

As Simon Sinek says, why wait, why not live your entire life thinking about your impact on the world? It does not have to be a global impact, or it could be. It could mean that you made the world a better place when you left. What does that look like? What stirs your soul? I am inspired to spend most of my Saturdays, using my abilities, doing charity work that helps others have a better life. What inspires you to make an impact on those around you?

Today, I will figure out what kind of impact I want to have on the lives of those around me and what my legacy will look like.

NEGOTIATIONS   JANUARY 27

"Never split the difference." – Chris Voss

In sales, and in life, we run up against situations that require negotiation. You are not getting exactly what you want/need, and they are not getting exactly what they want/need. This is where it is important to understand that you do not always have to compromise on what you want/need. Splitting the difference is not always the answer either. I learned this while in sales that when a customer asked me to split the difference I would purposefully say, I cannot do that but here is what I can do. If you are in a sales call and you are negotiating the final details of the sale, do you give them a split the difference offer? If you do, then do you believe that you are worth X amount more than your competition? Are you not better than the person that they are pitting you against and if not, why should they give you the business? If you have truly done your job and built the value of you, and your product or service, then you should expect more for your offering. People will always ask for a lower price because if you do not ask you will not get it. If you can show the value of what you are offering and the benefit it will bring to the customer, then why are you still negotiating? One of two things will prove to be true, either you are meeting with someone that always asks for a cheaper price, or you have not done your job. When you prove the value of what you are selling and close the deal, then it probably is the latter. If they only want to negotiate price and they will not listen to you then you may be dealing with the former.

Today, I will look for ways to build my negotiation skills and continue to build value.

EARNING TRUST   JANUARY 28

"Men are socialized to trust women until evidence to the contrary surfaces; women are socialized to be suspicious of men until an individual man earns trust." - Warren Farrell

Our society is built around trust and trying to find out whom we can trust. We have natural defenses built into our psyche and then we have the ones that are taught to us by those we are supposed to trust. We are taught things by those in leadership positions in our lives like parents, teachers, other adults, and extended family members. Too often we see those in the teaching roles extending their own fears and misinformed understandings to the younger generation. We grow up with this belief system that was given to us by other's experiences. There is something powerful about being able to teach others to avoid our own failings or our shortcomings. It is something else to teach people to not trust another simply because they look like someone that hurt you in the past, without knowing the person themselves. This theory can best be seen in people's trust or lack thereof in certain professions. There are people that we automatically distrust simply because of what they do for a living. When I mention lawyers, police officers, politicians, and salespeople, what are your first thoughts? Do you think about someone that you know in each of those roles and automatically make a judgment on the whole of the profession or do you think more openly? We can get caught up in not trusting people because of what they do but that is not the way you want people to look at you, is it? Men are viewed differently than women. Is it because the men have acted a certain way with consistency and therefore every one of them is to not be trusted? Has every woman acted in such a way that they should be trusted without verification? We are too quick to judge and not quick enough to ask the right questions, then verify with follow-up questions. I am not saying you should blindly trust everyone, but you should not distrust everyone either. Eventually, we have to make our own decisions and be responsible for those decisions. How do you treat others and what are you teaching those who come behind you or follow in your footsteps?

Today, I will find ways to unlearn some of the mistrust I have learned over time and learn to ask the right questions. I will no longer look at certain professions and cast a dark cloud over them just because.

Live Deliberately   January 29

"I went to the woods because I wished to live deliberately, to front only the essential facts of life, and see if I could not learn what it had to teach, and not, when I came to die, discover that I had not lived." – Henry David Thoreau

Do you know how to live with intention? Do you go through your life with a purpose? It took me a while to figure this out. When I reached college, I felt like I was wandering through life and just rolling with the punches that life continued throwing at me. I did not know how to live with a purpose. When I learned that we can and should have a purpose in our lives then I was able to feel more a part of things. When you go to sales calls you have a purpose, an intention, that is placed upon you. You are to get the order and succeed! But wait there is more! There is a lot more than just getting the sale. Now you can pay your bills, fulfill your dreams, buy that house, go on that trip, send your kids to that school, and so much more because you are living with a purpose. When you live with intention, you are more focused and able to get more things done. You also feel more accomplished because you *are* more accomplished.

Today, I will look at how I live my life and find my intention and my purpose.

Transparency   January 30

"A lack of transparency results in distrust and a deep sense of insecurity."
– Dalai Lama

Transparency is something we want from leadership. We want to know that they have our best interest at heart and that they are not holding a separate agenda that goes against what we believe. But as individuals, we may not want to be transparent with others because we do not want them to see the "ugly" side of us. We do not want them to see the imperfections and flaws. Why the difference? We want people to be open with us and yet we find it hard to be that way with others. If you struggle with being open with people or being transparent then think about why you find it hard. Think about why you are afraid of sharing this side of you. For some, it is about shame. Finding ways to be open and transparent can be a challenge. Finding ways to not overshare can be a challenge as well. Not everything is to be shared. You have a lot of thoughts that run through your mind every day and not all of them are good. You should not feel the need to share every thought that comes to your mind. Part of transparency is the discernment of what and when to share things. If you are at a business meeting it may not be appropriate to share what your kids said at dinner last night. Then again it might, depending on what they said and what you are talking about. What about your customers? What should your share with them and how transparent should you be with them? Do not be afraid to be transparent with your customers because they, like you, want to know that you have their best interest at heart.

Today, I will look at my own transparency and find ways to be more appropriately open in all my interactions.

CURIOSITY   JANUARY 31

"The important thing is not to stop questioning. Curiosity has its own reason for existing. I have no special talents. I am only passionately curious." – Albert Einstein

Have you ever played the "WHY" game with a three-year-old? It seems to never end. Why? Why? Why?

When was the last time that you asked why until you were told *exactly* why, and it met with your curiosity? If you have a passion for something you will find the answers that you need, and maybe a few more. We are all curious about something or some things.

I grew up playing all kinds of sports but never play organized volleyball. When I finished school, I knew some people that played and even went to several games to watch my friends play. Then I wanted to play. I read books on strategy and learned about different plays, etc. I became passionate about it and would play whenever I could. I went out and bought a ball so I could practice. I had to find some more friends that I could play volleyball with as my immediate friends did not play, nor were they interested. Later in my life, I was asked to help coach volleyball teams.

My career in sales was like that for me too. I knew a little about it and when I finished college it was my first job. I was not very good, but I was willing to learn. Over the years, I went to seminars, read books, watched videos, and learned from people that could teach me about sales. Eventually, I was asked to help develop training classes and mentor other salespeople because I had achieved some awards and was viewed as someone that could help others. Where is your curiosity taking you?

Today, I will find things that I am passionate about and show my curiosity by asking the right questions and not stopping until my curiosity has been satisfied. That may take some time.

February

CAN YOU SPEAK METAPHORICALLY?   FEBRUARY 1

"Metaphors have a way of holding the most truth in the least space."
– Orson Scott Card

Sometimes it is hard to get our message across and we seem to be at a loss for words. If you spend time reading and studying people you will find that the best way to explain things can be by using metaphors. When you are in sales, you need to learn how to speak in ways that your consumers will understand what you are trying to say. I have been in an industry that has very technical terms and it was easy to talk technically and not speak on the customer's level of understanding. When you do this, you can make the customer uncomfortable and not want to work with you because they do not understand what your product or service can and will do for them. Effectively communicating is critical when in sales and using metaphors and anecdotes can help you get your point across and help you get the sale.

Today, I will look for ways to simplify my message with customers and use metaphors and anecdotes, when possible, to help effectively communicate with them.

EXPERIENCE   FEBRUARY 2

"The value of experience is not in seeing much, but in seeing it wisely."
– Oscar Wilde

Are you able to gain the experience that you need, or does it take several times for you to truly gain the experience? Sometimes we are not ready for the experiences presented to us and we must do it again to learn properly. I am a fan of the movie "Groundhog Day", *spoiler alert*, Phil must go through the experience of the day again and again until he sees it wisely. At first, he is an arrogant person who thinks highly of himself. He sees that he is not getting out of "today", so he starts to live life without consequences. Starting with the whole idea of getting or taking things to make his life easier, money, food, overindulgence in everything imaginable, and without contentment. Phil even comments to Rita, "I'm a god — I'm not the God, I don't think."

After a time, he realizes that life is not about what he can get out of it but rather what he can give to others to make their lives better. When you have an experience are you able to learn from it or does it take you a few times to see it wisely? Are you seeing the things you need to see and putting that in your memory bank so that you will be better next time you run into a situation like this? Experience, like wisdom, takes time to develop. You must be willing and able to go through the uncomfortableness of learning to gain wisdom. Sometimes it is easier than others. But make sure you are looking wisely at the experience so that you can truly gain the wisdom that you desire. Otherwise, you may get stuck seeing the same lesson over and over and over.

Today, I will look more intently at the experiences I have to see more wisely the things I can learn from them.

FAILURE   FEBRUARY 3

When a reporter asked, "How did it feel to fail a thousand times?" Edison replied, "I didn't fail a thousand times. The light bulb was an invention with a thousand steps."

How do you act when you fail? Are you discouraged? Do you beat yourself or others up when you have not succeeded? The real question is, will you get up the next time and try again? We look at failure as a bad thing, however, without failure, we would not know how to succeed. We must fail in order to find our way at times. It can hurt when we fail, and it is not fun, but it can be exciting when we learn something new. Learning can keep us honest and, on our toes, creating a path we did not see before. Edison did not see failure as something that set him back. It was another way to learn. It was an opportunity to get it right this time. How do we change our thinking about failure and the idea that it can be a good thing? It starts with us believing that we are not perfect and knowing we will have opportunities to learn a new way of doing something.

Today, I will allow myself to learn from my failures and see what paths are opened up as a result of my optimistic and positive outlook.

SMILE   FEBRUARY 4

"We shall never know all the good that a simple smile can do." – Mother Teresa

Sometimes, I forget what a simple smile can do for a person. When you greet someone with a smile, it softens them and can warm their heart if they know you are genuine. You never know what others are going through or what kind of a day or week that person has had. What kind of a day or week are you having? You cannot put on a smile if you are going through some rough times yourself. I have coached some salespeople that think that the personal stuff in their own lives does not affect their sales. Can you separate your personal and professional life to the point where people have no idea what is happening behind the face you are presenting to them? People are usually smart enough to see through the cracks in your armor and can see through your eyes. That is why you need to be genuinely happy/smiling when you enter a sales opportunity. People will see that and feel that when you speak to them. How do you respond to a happy salesperson versus a not-so-happy salesperson? Can you feel the difference?

Today, I will look for opportunities to show a genuine smile to the people that I get to interact with throughout the day and see how that impacts me as well.

Patience   February 5

"Patience is the companion of wisdom." – Saint Augustine

For some of us, patience is a difficult concept to master. We want to get to the next sale, we want to win the fight, we want to overcome the next obstacle. If you are patient, you can learn a great many things. You can learn what your customers really want, what your boss is trying to communicate, what that person really fears. You can hear things that are important to know for you to get that next sale, win the fight, and overcome that obstacle that is keeping you from the next level. Learning to be patient is something that can take time and lots of practice. We live in a microwave world, and we are used to instant results or near-instant answers. Nothing can replace the process that needs to take place for us to learn the lessons.

It is not too late to learn the lesson of patience. Waiting out the lesson will provide you with far greater joy than if you rushed into it. We want the answer now and in sales, we want to push that too. That is what some people need our help with, making decisions, but sometimes it is necessary to let it play out. If you have ever had a bottle of fine wine, a great bottle of bourbon, or even a great meal, they all take time to develop. There is a reason that a great chili tastes better the day after it is made, because the flavors take time to come together, and a good lasagna takes about an hour or more to make. Patience can be a wonderful thing if you allow it to be.

Today, I will look for ways that I can be patient and learn to enjoy the wisdom that will come as a result of my patience.

Healing Words   February 6

"The words of kindness are more healing to a drooping heart than balm or honey." – Sarah Fielding

Have you ever been the recipient of healing words? There is nothing like the kind of truth that comes from a loved one when you are hurting. It is like drinking cool water on a hot day, it brings relief to your innermost parts. There is something about this feeling and relief that removes any tension and stress that you may have at the time. There is a difference in things that come from the inside versus the outside if you understand what I mean? Healing, peace, and love when internalized can make all the difference in your life. Can you do this for others as well? Do you know how to help someone with your words? Can you find the proper words, that are from the heart and true, to share with someone that will help heal them from the inside out? You can become thoughtful and kind and find the right words if you spend time reading and learning from those around you. Hearing the healing words is one thing, being able to share them with others is pretty good too.

Today, I will look for ways to find the proper words to help myself and maybe others heal. I will also look for ways to just maybe say nothing but be there for someone else because sometimes no words are the right words to use.

KINDNESS   FEBRUARY 7

"Kindness in words creates confidence. Kindness in thinking creates profoundness. Kindness in giving creates love." – Lao Tzu

How kind you are? I am not sure a lot of people spend time thinking about this unless they are presented with a situation where they must think about being kind versus unkind. If you spend time working on yourself, internally, emotionally, and spiritually, then you will be confronted with being kind. Some will have to work on this more than others, but we all have things we need to work on. When you focus on being kind you will see a change in who you are, internally and externally. When I was younger, I struggled with being kind to people. I did not understand how to show kindness specifically. I could be kind to people but when left to my own devices I could be a real jerk. I had to learn that I was not the center of the universe and that everyone around me had their own story. We each have things that are not exposed for the world to see. This is where kindness kicks in. You show people grace and gentleness because you do not know what they are going through or have been through. Besides, kindness costs us nothing.

Today, I will find ways to be kind in words, thoughts, and actions, so that others will benefit.

LEARNING LESSONS   FEBRUARY 8

"I have never met a man so ignorant that I couldn't learn something from him." – Galileo Galilei

Sitting at the feet of someone with more years and more wisdom is an easy thing to do. If you are someone that enjoys learning, especially from those that we admire or look up to in our line of work or school, then we can sit and learn. Have you ever tried to learn from someone that you thought was not as smart as you? If you humbly listen, then it is easy because you are looking for ways to hear them and the words that they are saying. It does not mean that everything they are saying is gold but listen and you will hear the jewels. How many times have you heard a child say something very deep or honest and it made you think, "out of the mouth of babes?" We do not have all the answers and though it may seem troublesome at times to listen to people that are not as well-read as you are, you can still learn something. If you gain nothing else, you can learn how to listen well.

Today, I will take opportunities to listen to people and see what I can learn no matter the person's age, education, or status in life if only I may learn.

What Do You Deserve? February 9

"I don't deserve this award, but I have arthritis and I don't deserve that either." – Jack Benny

Have you ever been on the receiving end of something good, and you knew you did not deserve it? Sometimes we get something because we worked hard, and that hard work paid off. Sometimes we get lucky, and we get something we may not necessarily deserve. We end up in the right place at the right time and that results in a reward that we may not have had to work very hard for or at all. That goes for the good and the bad. Sometimes we work hard, and the results do not pan out for us but for someone else. As we all know, life is not fair, and we do not always get what we deserve. That is ok too and we must learn to be ok with that at times. We win some and we lose some and they seem to balance out. Some feel like they get less, and others may feel like they get more but for the most part, we get what we deserve. I had shingles at age nineteen and was diagnosed with gout in my early thirties. Those two things are usually found in older people, but I got to experience them early. Life has a way of throwing things at people at different times so that we can change, adapt, and grow.

Today, I will learn to accept things that come my way, deserved or not.

Timing February 10

"Timing has always been a key element in my life. I have been blessed to have been in the right place at the right time." – Buzz Aldrin

There is great wisdom in being silent and waiting for the answers that you seek instead of giving your customers the answers you want to hear. You may want to go back and reread that. It is all about the timing. When you do not wait in silence, then you give the customer an opportunity to let you tell them what to say. That is *manipulation*, not selling. Sometimes you need to help people to see the answer but that will come if you build value through the sales process. This is also important in our personal lives as well. There are many different opinions on how much time you should listen versus time spent talking on a sales call. Most people will tell you to listen more and talk less. It also depends on what you are selling and the part of the sales cycle you are in among other factors. However, everything I have found says that listening more is the right thing to do. Timing is very important to any sales call, process, or cycle. Do you listen to be understood or for understanding? Know the difference and you will do well. Listening to understand is the ability to hear holistically what the customer has to say and respond when appropriate to all that was said. When you are listening to be understood you are probably cutting off the customer when you think you have something important to say and you may have missed the importance of what they are saying to you. When you listen for understanding, you hear everything that they are trying to tell you and you can ask important questions like, is that important to you? Just because the customer says they "want" something it may not be important to them. They may have heard about it and are telling you what they know.

Today, I will look for ways to pause and listen to the conversations that I have. I will learn the value of timing.

Advice is Just That, Advice! — February 11

"To advise is not to compel." – Anton Chekhov

Do you feel frustrated when someone does not follow the sage advice that you gave them? Do you feel like you are compelling someone when you give them advice? Years ago, someone told me that advice is just that, advice. You can take it or not. You cannot expect someone to take it either. It is just advice and nothing more. Being a parent, I got to see first-hand how giving advice becomes a lesson for the giver as much as for the receiver. Being an early parent, I wanted my girls to heed all the wisdom that I had. I had lived many years more than them and they should want to listen to me. That type of mindset does not bode well for raising your children in a helpful, loving way. When I did that, I found that my girls were almost more defiant because I took away their opportunity to choose. When you have your ability to choose removed from you, no matter how trivial, it can put you on a defensive path.

If you go into a situation where you are seeking advice it is different. You can get frustrated because you give someone some great advice and they do not take it, they still do what they want to do, for whatever reason. Our minds can be developed to believe that we are great advice-givers and not great advice-takers. Hopefully, you learn that advice is just advice, and it has nothing further to give, especially if there is no one to receive it. You cannot be ready to give the "I told you so" speech when people do not follow the advice you gave them. Have there have been times when you have chosen not to listen, or maybe you did not truly hear when someone shared their wisdom and advice with you?

Today, I will look at how I give advice and what my expectations are that come with my advice. I will remember that my advice is simply advice and comes with zero expectations.

COURAGE   FEBRUARY 12

"Courage is knowing what not to fear." – Plato

Courage is the ability to stand up when everything in you wants to stay down. A lot of times it is a lack of knowledge that keeps us fearful. Knowledge comes from previous experience and that can produce the courage to overcome the fear from the situation. One of the first times I got to lead singing in the church I was attending years ago, I was leading a song called The First Noel. Almost everyone knows the first verse and it is easy to sing. Do you know the second verse? I did not and when we practiced it beforehand, I had a hard time getting the cadence and the wording right. When we went to sing it during the service, I tripped over the second verse at least twice before I stopped the song and sang the first verse over again, then we ended it. That really bothered me because I was embarrassed, and it was hard to focus on the rest of the service, but I found the courage to get back up and finish the song leading. I have sung that song and that verse countless times since then because I practiced it over and over and over. That practice gave me the courage to sing it again in public, without fear. What can you do to find the courage to overcome fear in situations?

Today, I will look for ways to build courage through knowledge so that I will have less to fear.

ROUTINES   FEBRUARY 13

"As we go about our daily routines, our internal monologue narrates our experience. Our self-talk guides our behavior and influences the way we interact with others. It also plays a major role in how you feel about yourself, other people, and the world in general." – Amy Morin

Setting up routines for your life can be helpful to make the little daily tasks easier. Knowing that you will get up and read, meditate, workout, then make breakfast, then get cleaned up and ready for work or school is a good way to start your daily life. It can give you the opportunity to prepare for the day and get your mindset for the day. It can help you with a challenging conversation that you need to have or a presentation you are giving that day. Routines can help us develop our character and maturity because they can be like the foundational blocks for the day. If you do not pay attention to the base of your walls your building will collapse.

Today, I will look for ways to develop my morning routine to start my day off with the proper mindset.

LOVE THE ONE YOU ARE WITH — FEBRUARY 14

"Never worry about numbers. Help one person at a time and always start with the person nearest you." – Mother Teresa

Some people think that life, like a career in sales, is all about numbers. That statistically speaking if you do the work the numbers will play out and you will be successful. We will statistically live to be a certain age, and so on and so forth. What happens when we live according to the stats? We meander through life and miss all the good stuff because all we think about is the numbers. We think or even say, "I am playing the odds." We forget about the work that people go through to make the statistics happen. We are naïve to think that we can just go through life and all this good stuff will happen because that is what the statistics tell me. In sales, if you are not focused on the client, you are in front of, then you will miss out on that opportunity. Too often we can get caught up in how many calls we need to make that day and not love the one we are with at the present time. This is true for a number of professions and not just sales. In sports, if you are thinking about the next play or the next time you get an opportunity then you are not doing your job presently. In management, if you are focused too far down the road and not looking at what is happening today with your team, you are going to set yourself up for a fall in the near future. When we take care of things one client, situation, or relationship at a time then we will be successful. We have to give our focus, love, and attention to what is right in front of us. The rest we will work on when it is time.

Today, I will find success in being present with the client or situation I am with and not trying to get through this meeting to get to the next. Each one will have its own time.

FINDING FAULT — FEBRUARY 15

"Never find fault with the absent." – Alexander Pope

How do you feel when you make mistakes? Do you try to save face and avoid responsibility? I still struggle with this but when I see the issue for what it is, I can more easily admit my errors and take responsibility. Taking responsibility is a step toward fixing the problem. When we can start moving towards a resolution then we are making progress. Sitting on a problem and fighting over whom is to blame never gets us closer to the answers that we need it only serves as a way for us to feel more superior than someone else. It can be easy to blame others for things that go wrong, even more so when they are not present to defend themselves. Humility makes it easier to take responsibility where we need to and move towards resolution.

Today, I will look for ways I can take responsibility for my actions and start to move towards a resolution instead of trying to place blame.

DENIAL   FEBRUARY 16

"Nostalgia is denial. Denial of the painful present." – Midnight in Paris

Nostalgia is the wistful affection for the past. How many times have you caught yourself thinking about how wonderful things were way back when? Hopeful of things gone by or things that may have made your life easier today? I have been guilty of this line of thinking myself. Wishing for a kinder gentler time when I did not have to worry so much or work so hard on my personal stuff. Yet, when I really looked at the past it occurred to me that I was not seeing things as clearly as I remember. The movie Midnight in Paris speaks to this theme.

The main character has the opportunity to visit the past and is in love with the idea of what it would be like to have lived in Paris in the 1920s. So much so that he is in denial of the painful present surrounding him. I will not give any spoilers on this one but suffice it to say that we too can get caught up in wishing that we were in a different time and place because what we are dealing with personally may be too much for us to handle.

Sometimes, we are somewhere else because we do not want to be where we are at the present. When you learn how to live in the present you will not spend so much time living in denial and being nostalgic about things that you cannot relive or be a part of again. I have nothing bad to say about remembering the past with great fondness. That does not mean you are wanting to live in that moment again. There is a difference between remembering fondly the past versus denying the present to live in the past memories.

Today, I will remember the past with fondness but will not live in the nostalgia that may keep me from living in the present.

RANDOM ACTS OF KINDNESS   FEBRUARY 17

"Carry out a random act of kindness, with no expectation of reward, safe in the knowledge that one day someone might do the same for you."
– Princess Diana

Have you ever been the recipient of a random act of kindness? Maybe someone paid for your meal, or a stranger gave you a gift without an opportunity to return the favor. We hear about these things and maybe even you have done it once or twice. If you have done it, do you remember what that felt like? We all can perform acts of kindness whenever we choose to do so. It does not have to be some grand gesture. We think of giving money to people but what about time? Can you find someone that needs a mentor? Someone that needs an upper hand that you can give. Start with something small. Let your heart be compelled to give out of compassion and empathy. Look around and you will find opportunities when you open yourself up to them. If you act on it privately, not on display for the world to see, you will find greater joy. When you do it for your personal gain you rob yourself of the heartfelt joy of giving.

Today, I will open my eyes and my heart to random acts of kindness. You know them when you see them. You have something you can do for others without any expectations of a return gesture.

HONESTY WITH ONESELF   FEBRUARY 18

"The best measure of a man's honesty isn't his income tax return. It's the zero adjust on his bathroom scale." – Arthur C. Clarke

Being honest with yourself can be a challenge. When we lie to ourselves, do we really think it works? Are we really that gullible? I know when I have eaten too much and why I gain weight. I know why I do not want to exercise regularly. I do not have to lie to myself about why I do or do not do things. I used to set my clocks in my home or my vehicles ahead five to ten minutes so I would be on time. However, I almost always would calculate out the time that I know I had and would still run-up to the last minute or even be late. Why not be honest with yourself and say I have to get up at this time and I have so much time to do what I want to do before I have to exercise or go to work or school? If you cannot be honest with yourself about something as simple as time, how can you be honest with yourself, or others about bigger things?

Today, I will start by being honest with myself so that I can be honest with others.

FAME   FEBRUARY 19

"Showing off is the fool's idea of glory." – Bruce Lee

What is it that motivates you toward the prize? What do you seek to find at the end of your journey? Is it fame and fortune, or recognition? For those of us in sales that are driven, it is usually something along these lines. We like to be recognized for our achievements and held in high esteem amongst our colleagues and/or competitors. Too often, we see someone that has that confidence that is overflowing, yet is lacking the experience to have such confidence, and you may want to show them the error of their ways. Fame is not easy and not for everyone, because some of us cannot handle it. If you have ever played king of the hill, you may remember that being on top means that everyone is always coming after you and trying to bring you down. Fame can have many forms but most of us will only see local or regional fame and that is enough for our egos. Can you find joy in success without recognition? You are the one that needs to find satisfaction in your accomplishments. No one can give you the joy that comes from your own accomplishments.

Today, I will look for ways that I can find the satisfaction and joy that comes from achieving my goals.

Your View   February 20

"People are not disturbed by things, but by the view they take of them."
– Epictetus

When you share your opinion with people, they tend to do one of three things. Either they agree with you, they disagree with you, or they are ambivalent toward your view. It can be something as simple as the crust on a pizza or your favorite drink. However, when you mention something like politics or religious beliefs people tend to get very polarized very quickly. Why do those topics bring such stark responses? Pizza is a personal choice just like politics, and your favorite beverage is like your religion, is it not? Some of you just said no very loudly in your head. Your taste buds are more fickle than your religion or your political beliefs because it is at the core of who you are. You must take time to figure out what you genuinely believe and that should not change easily or quickly. It is simply your choice, not someone else's. Your view is your choice, and you get to decide how you view things. That may be right or wrong but that is also for you to decide. Before you make a choice and decide to take a hard stand on it you should take the time to do some research and try not to let your feelings get in the way. Look at all sides, the ones you might agree with and the ones you might disagree with so that you can hear all sides before you decide where to take your stand. Then remember that it is your view and may or may not work for others, as much as you want them to be on your side.

Today, I will look at my views as only mine. I may share them with others but will drop the expectation that others will see things as I do.

ABILITY TO LOVE — FEBRUARY 21

"It is sad not to love, but it is much sadder not to be able to love."
– Miguel de Unamuno

When we think of "love" it can be about many different things. It can be EROS, a romantic type of love, PHILIA, which is a brotherly type of love, and AGAPE, which is considered universal, charitable, or even altruistic. When did you think about loving yourself? I mean genuinely loving yourself by taking care of yourself, what you eat and drink, exercising, sleeping, etc. You cannot love others if you do not genuinely love yourself. If you are giving to others and do not give to yourself then you are robbing yourself of the love necessary for yourself to give love to others. This can be a foreign concept to some of us that were never really taught to love ourselves. You think you are taking care of yourself, but you are just doing enough to keep yourself moving forward. Do yourself a favor, and others too, stop and look at the sunset, appreciate the breath that you are taking. Savor that wonderful meal you cooked. Go to bed early enough for you to wake up early enough to do the things that are important to you, reading, exercising, meditating, etc. Love yourself so that you can have the capacity to love others. This will show through in all that you do, even sitting across the table from your client as you make your sales pitch.

Today, I will look for ways that I can love myself first so that I can have the ability to love others.

MIRACLES   FEBRUARY 22

"Miracles do not, in fact, break the laws of nature." – C. S. Lewis

Have you seen a miracle in your life or the life of someone around you? It could have been as simple as watching someone change the way you never thought they could change. It could be more complex than that. I am not talking about a magic trick or sleight of hand. Can you see the traces of a loved one that has passed away in something as simple as a feather in a location that a feather should not be? Have you heard the inner voice that told you to go a certain way home or to your location only to find out that had you gone the way you planned you might have been in the middle of a horrible accident? Miracles can happen when you walk down the street and catch yourself when you trip and do not plant your face on the concrete walk. They also happen when a woman becomes pregnant for the first time, or a child speaks their first words, or you get that dream job.

Miracles can happen in different ways for different people. None of which is yours to determine whether or not it is valid or meets your standards of truth or magic. You may have a warped sense of truth or standard for truth. Why do we find it necessary to knock down someone else so we can feel better about the lack of miraculous things that we see happening in our lives? Are we that special? Miracles are happening all the time and some people choose to see them, others do not or cannot see them. Why does it take a bunch of college-aged hockey players, playing for the first time together, to beat a group of more seasoned athletes, that have played together for years, in a game of hockey in 1980 for us to understand that miracles do happen, if only we will open our eyes?

Today, I will be open to the possibilities of miracles happening around me or for me.

How do You See Things? February 23

"The optimist sees the glass as half full. The pessimist sees the glass as half empty. The engineer looks at the glass and says it is the wrong size glass."
– Unknown

Or maybe the bartender simply reminds you that the glass is refillable. We can be optimists or pessimists in this example, but I would rather be the other person that sees the bigger picture. Looking at things differently is a gift that some of us can ignore. When you are able to see things with a bigger perspective you tend to have a gentler spirit and more of an even keel towards them as well. A lot of us see things through eyes that are tainted with our past experiences and understanding. Instead, we should look forward with a fresh perspective of the bigger picture. There is nothing wrong with using your past to gain understanding. It is wise to do so. However, when you use it to predetermine how something will go, that is where you can go in the wrong direction.

Today, I will use my past experience to help guide my vision of things in front of me but will not allow it to determine the outcome. I will try to view things anew and with a view that gives me a better understanding of the whole picture.

Simplicity February 24

"Life is really simple, but we insist on making it complicated." – Confucius

Often, we think that life is hard, and we get stressed out by the things that we have going on in our lives. Have you ever stopped to consider how it got that way? How did things get so hard and stressful in my life? We generally make it that way. We can overcomplicate things because we would rather have a challenge than an easy road. We do not do it on purpose, but we do not prevent it from happening either. We can overthink the situation and it gets messy. Then we are in so deep, we feel overwhelmed and stressed out. It is hard to see the forest for the trees and this can be one of those situations where you cannot see where you are adding stress to your life because you are too involved. Sometimes we need to take a step back to look at how we can simplify our lives instead of making them more complicated. When you do this, you will find the amount of stress and complications in your life will be significantly reduced.

Today, I will find ways to simplify my life instead of complicating it. I will look at people and situations around me and figure out which I have control over and react accordingly.

HELPING OTHERS   FEBRUARY 25

"Life's most persistent and urgent question is, 'What are you doing for others?'" – Martin Luther King, Jr.

We all have agendas that need attention, and we may have work or school that needs attention as well. How are you at serving others and making sure that those around you get a chance to have their needs fulfilled? How do you feel when you give your time to others? Is it a burden or is it something that brings you joy? I kept looking for something to fill a gap in my life. That gap could only be filled by serving others. Aside from charitable events or fundraisers, I found that I needed to be of service to my community. We can give money to charity and that is important but doing for others is better than just giving money. Learn to use your time for others too. We can think I have too much going on in my life to stop and help others for hours a week. I have kids and a family to spend time with. My folks, or my in-laws, are older and I need to spend time with them. I would encourage you to do that while you can and need to do that type of service.

Being of service to others is not just about some big corporation asking you to help them. It can be your neighbor who is no longer able to cut their lawn or afford to pay someone to do it for them. It can be helping coach your kid's athletic team or supporting your kid's other endeavors. We all get the opportunity to serve others in so many different ways that can benefit us as much as it does them.

Today, I will look for ways that I can serve others and not neglect what needs my attention in my life.

EDUCATE YOURSELF   FEBRUARY 26

"A person who won't read has no advantage over one who can't read."
– Mark Twain

When I was growing up, I did not like to read, and I do not remember it ever being encouraged except when we had to write a paper or do a book report for school. I started to enjoy reading in college when I found a topic that interested me, and it made me dig deep into books. I had a thirst for knowledge. Learning how to educate yourself after schooling is finished is invaluable. I enjoy reading books now and truth be told I enjoy listening to books even more as I am not a fast reader. I have been able to gain a lot of wisdom over the years from reading books. You can expand your world when you read. They can be fun for business or even self-development. Reading can expand your vocabulary, increase your understanding of others and yourself, increase your intelligence, and can actually bring joy into your life.

Today, I will find ways to broaden my life through reading more than just a social media feed or text.

ANXIETY   FEBRUARY 27

"Between saying and doing, many a pair of shoes is worn out."
– Iris Murdoch

What keeps you up at night? Many times, we can worry about what will happen if. We can get caught up in the constant battle that wages in our minds and prevents us from doing what we should be doing. Anxiety can stop you in your tracks. Anxiety can make you someone that you do not want to be. Your stomach feels like it is in knots, and you stop eating or doing things that you would normally do. When you face the thing or things that are causing you anxiety you can get back to what makes you confident and full of life. Serenity is the opposite of anxiety. What makes you feel serene and calm? Is it the sound of the ocean as you watch the sunset? Is it some type of music like classical or jazz? Find the peace that is within you during times of anxiety to help you overcome the effects.

Today I will find the calmness that is within me instead of the anxiety that lurks around the corner.

True Friendship   February 28

"Try to be a rainbow in someone's cloud." – Maya Angelou

Have you ever noticed how a true friend can just brighten your day? I have some friends that just bring a smile to my face and when they do, I text them or call them and just let them know I was thinking about them. That is why you thought of them in the first place was it not? Take the time to reach out to your friends or family when you think of them. You never know what is happening in their life and they might need to see a rainbow to cheer them up or put a smile on their face. True friends look out for each other, care for each other, think of each other. You want a true friend, then you need to be a true friend. Some of us struggle with this concept because we want the results without the work. If you are willing to do the work, you will get the results. Be a friend and you will have a friend. Know that sometimes, you will try and be a friend to someone and it just does not work out. They cannot be a friend for you or vice versa just because one of you is not ready. We have to be emotionally available for friendships too. We can develop that over time, but we have to be available on some level to begin the relationship too.

Today, I will look for ways that I can be a true friend to someone.

WHERE DOES THE TIME GO? — FEBRUARY 29

"You must remember this, a kiss is still a kiss, a sigh is just a sigh; the fundamental things apply, as time goes by." – Herman Hupfeld

Some things mark time in our lives. New Year's, a birthday, an anniversary are all things that we might be nostalgic about and reminisce about. Some of the things that come up can be a hindrance or may help the next chapter or year of our lives. If you do not take time to reflect on a regular basis, then you might miss out on all that has happened, or changed, and you will find yourself asking, where did the time go? When I ask myself that question, it is because I missed out on all the good stuff. I missed the memorable moments. I try and take time at each of the significant and appropriate times for me, to reflect on the recent past. I want to see what has changed and what I have to look forward to. What goals do I need to set or ideas that I want to make happen? Make time to sit and reflect at these times, maybe even make a point to do this quarterly so that you can have a regular check-in time with yourself. Make time so that you can take it all in. Sometimes we need to make time so that we can reset ourselves. Maybe we have gotten off track and we need to get back on course. Whatever the reason, make time so that you do not lose time.

Today, I will look at the time I need to reflect and start to schedule that so that I do not miss out on the good stuff and can make sure I am staying on track.

March

DIFFICULT TIMES   MARCH 1

"It always helps to have people we love beside us when we have to do difficult things in life." – Mister Rogers

We all have times in our lives when we go through difficult things. Some catch us by surprise like a relationship break up, change in job, or even the death of a loved one. Some we see coming and they are still difficult to deal with. I have found it is more comforting to have a loved one that can help, listen, and even commiserate with us if need be. The comfort comes in someone lending an ear and showing love in a time of loss for us. I have seen a few difficult times in my life and for a while, I thought that I could shut down emotionally and cover up the pain by being strong for others and it made it worse. It compounded it when I did deal with it.

I recently lost my brother, but this time I allowed myself to feel the feelings and allowed myself to talk through all that I was going through, and it made a huge difference for me. I have lost grandparents, a stepfather, and even friends but nothing compared to this. I had loved ones that I could talk with and help me. I have lost a job before and when I had supportive people around me that cared and loved me through the difficult times it made all the difference in the world. They allowed me to talk about how I felt, and work through the difficulties I was having as a result of the loss. There is nothing wrong with going through difficult times and the emotions that come with that.

Today, I will remember that difficult times call for loved ones. Whether I need them, or they need me.

STRUGGLES   MARCH 2

"Life isn't about getting and having, it's about giving and being." – Kevin Kruse

Why do you want more? Do you believe that the person with the most toys at the end wins? We struggle with things in life because we focus on the wrong things. We want to get or have something, and we do not think about how we can give to others or just be present. You can feel the tug and feel the turmoil that is presenting itself. What tugs at you and wants you to receive instead of giving? We are taught and trained to get all that we can with all that we have so that we can be successful. I am not talking about being the best person that you can be with the talents that you have been given. You should pursue that with all that you have. But do not forget to give to others and enjoy the life that you have been blessed with. You have special places in your life that can only be filled by the intangible things in life.

Today, I will find ways to let go and give. Learn how to be present and enjoy the life I have been given.

HUMILITY   MARCH 3

"An actor should always let humility outweigh ambition." – Anna Kendrick

We all face the opportunities daily that we get to act with humility or not. Most people think of beating their chest and telling people how awesome they are but that is not the only situation that shows our lack of humility. Humility can be shown in several different ways, not the least of which is letting others share their thoughts and opinions without comment or criticism from you. Growing up with a competitive mindset, being in sales and an athlete most of my life, I was taught to be the best at all costs. Unfortunately, I thought that being the best meant I had to be better than others and in a way that was not humble or graceful. Losing caused me to turn to anger and bitterness rather than turning to humility. There is nothing wrong with losing and turning that into a fuel that drives you to be better, but not if it purposefully involves another person's painful demise. Winning is good but winning with humility or losing with self-imposed humility has its merits as well. I have heard the saying that winning does not teach you anything but losing can teach you a lot. Humility in business is important as well. When you win a job in sales do you gloat about it, or do you see what you could have done better? It is harder to see the things that could be learned when you win but you can always learn ways to improve.

What are you doing to be humble or remain humble today? Where can you be humbler at work or at home with family and friends?

OWN YOUR DECISIONS   MARCH 4

"I've made a decision and now I must face the consequences." – J. Michael Straczynski

Growing up you may not have been held responsible for the actions or decisions that you made. For example, as a child, you may not have had to pay for the window that you broke, because someone else paid for you. As we mature, you get the opportunity to see the consequences of our actions and decisions and you get to own them as well, literally. I am not speaking only of the physical things, like breaking a glass or a window, we can impact the emotional side of self and others as well. We get to make decisions every day and most have positive outcomes. Sometimes, we make decisions, and the outcomes are less than ideal. They can have a negative impact on ourselves and others. Some people go through most of their lives and never see or refuse to see the consequences of their decisions and or actions. When we mature, we see things clearer and we get to take responsibility for those decisions or actions. Eventually, through trial and error, we can predict the outcomes of decisions, with more certainty. It is why we gain counsel when we are posed with life or business decisions, that will affect more than just ourselves. This is part of growing and gaining maturity.

What decisions will you make today and what will the impact be on yourself or others?

WHAT ARE YOU WORKING FOR?   MARCH 5

Build your own dreams, or someone else will hire you to build theirs."
– Farrah Gray

We all have dreams and things that we strive for in life. When you do not act on those dreams you end up working on someone else's dreams. If you want to write a book, start writing your book. If you want to start your own business, start your own business. Sometimes we think we need to wait for this or for that to happen for us to start building our dreams when in fact, we are scared. Sometimes we need someone to push us over the edge so that we can get on with the experience. I needed the loving push of a friend to start writing this book and he did not even know he was giving me the push. I told him how he encouraged me to begin my book and it encouraged him. If you are not ready, then plan so that you can start effectively building your dream. Start building for you!

Today, I will find ways to start building on my dreams so I will not have to build on someone else's for much longer.

YOUR BEST   MARCH 6

"Doing the best at this moment puts you in the best place for the next moment." – Oprah Winfrey

Do you know when you are doing your best and when you are not? I'm sure you do. Maybe this is when you put your heart and soul on a project at work or doing a project at home, or in a relationship. Why is it that we feel that there are times when it is ok to not give our all? I have been in situations where I am not one hundred percent, physically or emotionally, and when I can see I am not being effective or helping out the situation but instead hurting those around me then I have to step back and get better. An injured athlete is only able to do so much for their team until they become a hindrance. Being mentally, emotionally, or even physically injured can hinder your performance at work, and you do not have to be an athlete to see that. Sometimes sixty percent of you is better than none of you. But you know when that is the case, and you can feel it from the others around you as well. I do not like being less than one hundred percent because I like most of the things that I do. Some are just things that need to get done, but even those I want to give my all, like cleaning the house or a report at work. I have been on a team when I realized I was not happy, and it started affecting my performance. I was not able to give one hundred percent of myself and that hurt the team, not just me. I had to make it right or stop being a part of the team and I chose to not be a part of the team because my performance was not going to improve. The team was better without me, and I was better without the team.

When you find you are not able to give one hundred percent, how do you handle it?

Perseverance   March 7

"You must tell yourself, 'No matter how hard it is, or how hard it gets, I'm going to make it.'" – Les Brown

Looking ahead to the finish line is easy when you are in a sprint. When you are running a long-distance race, it can be hard to find the finish line. Life is a long-distance race. You are somewhere along the road and not sure how far out the finish line is. Too often, I find myself looking for the finish line and it is nowhere in sight, which is good and bad. Good in the sense that I have a long way to go before I am finished here, bad because I can lose focus and wonder what am I doing here? When I find myself wandering, it helps to touch base with friends, family, or a good read that can help me hone back in on what I am doing here. Life can throw you a bunch of curveballs. I have gotten better at seeing the curveballs when they start to approach and then I can make the adjustment. This can be as simple as a change in plans, or as traumatic as the death of a loved one. I find it becomes easier to run the race when I am focused on what I am doing right now and the impact that I am making now, living in the present. That focus keeps me running and facing forward, looking ahead to see what other obstacles may be headed my way, and I become more content and more effective.

What helps you to keep focused and looking forward so that you can find your path and avoid the obstacles?

LIFE EVENTS   MARCH 8

"Life-changing events can be very dramatic and, by their very nature, disruptive. You are literally not the same person on both sides of a truly life-changing event." – The Surrender Experiment, Michael A. Singer

Life has a way of showing you what is and what is not important. I have found that you and I have the opportunity, and almost on a daily basis, to see what things we can change in our lives, yet we sometimes choose not to see that thing we need to correct. Then, when it is more important for us to make that change, things happen in our lives to show us the importance of the need for change. I am not saying that bad things happen so we can change. I am saying that sometimes it takes a life-changing event to wake us up to the need for change. Have you ever felt the tug in your life to do something different than what you were doing, and you decided not to do it? Maybe you had a chance to take a job that would stretch your abilities, discovered that you wanted to write a book, or found a relationship worth fighting for? What held you back? Was it the discomfort of not knowing how it would go, or was it that you had stepped out on "faith" before and it did not end the way you wanted, and your feelings got hurt? I have had these types of events happen in my life and I reacted differently at different times. I have gotten better at recognizing the need for change in my life and am still working on making the changes in my life.

What changes do you need to see in your life now and how will you react when the life-changing events come along?

SELF-RESPECT   MARCH 9

"The funny thing is, when you don't let people disrespect you, they start calling you difficult." – Tom Hardy

How much do you respect yourself versus how much do you respect others? Do you let others treat you differently than you treat yourself? Loving yourself is hard to do sometimes. We are our own worst critics. We see and hear things that others do not because we live inside our heads. We have a different perspective than others and sometimes that is good and other times that are not so good. We hear all the negative comments that our inner voice makes, and the criticism can be brutal. Yet, when others say things that are similar or worse, we let it go and, like the voice in our head, we do not address it because we think we deserve that verbal lashing. Respecting yourself must start with loving yourself. Caring for yourself is paramount! I learned this much later than I would have liked to but, I have gotten better. I am healthier both mentally and physically than I have ever been.

When I was younger, I did not realize that I was not mentally healthy, I struggled with a healthy self-image and self-awareness I struggled with self-respect, and I did not create proper boundaries for myself and others. When I was able to understand the importance of a healthy mind and body, I was able to find true contentment.

What will it take for you to respect yourself so that others can respect you?

WHAT DO YOU KNOW?   MARCH 10

"The secret of business is to know something that nobody else knows."
– Aristotle Onassis

A lot of people seem to have something that they want you to know about business that will *make you succeed*. There is one thing that rings true and that is that you have talents that you need to use. You have something that others may not have. What do you know that someone else does not know? What can you do that someone else struggles to do? I can listen to people and hear what they really want and make what I do relatable to the person that I am talking to. It does not matter about their level of knowledge about the product or service that I am representing. Some people are inherently good at sales. Others are meant to defend laws in a courtroom, and others are meant to comfort you as you are in pain. You have a talent that others cannot match. If you do not know what it is, you need to find it and develop it so you can use it. Once you do you can become invaluable to whomever you work for, but most of all to yourself. If you are talented enough you will be able to truly know something that no one else knows. That may mean that you have a business of your own.

Today, I will look for things that I am good at and take steps to focus on the thing that makes me different in business from others.

The Heart   March 11

"The best and most beautiful things in the world cannot be seen or even touched - they must be felt with the heart." – Helen Keller

I had a discussion with someone that reminded me that over the past year or more, I have become more in touch with my emotions. It took a major life-altering event to help me find the ability to understand my feelings, but I now have the beginnings and can work with them. My brother died about a year ago, and that had a profound effect on who I am. I have learned to listen to my heart more than I ever have in the past. I am able to sit in the present and let my heart decide things that I would not have trusted before. I find that things that I gave no attention to before can knock me back on my heels, and things that I used to focus on have lost their luster. Simply watching a movie now that has some emotional twist to it, someone dies, or love lost, can cause my eyes to swell with tears. Seeing the beauty in things that held no beauty for me before. Listening to a song or reading a book has new meaning. My heart got a wake-up call, and for that, I am thankful. I have learned that though we can see, hear, or even touch things, the heart may see, hear, and feel on a whole new level. The heart wants what the heart wants.

What do you believe your heart is telling you? Are you willing to listen?

Music for Your Soul   March 12

"Music is a higher revelation than all wisdom and philosophy." - Ludwig van Beethoven

When I was in college, I learned that I could sing and sing well enough to be in an acapella group. I gathered some friends, and we formed an acapella group. The music moved my soul. I found that singing gave me a love for God, people, and peace that was beyond what I could ever imagine. I was able to connect spiritually with the music, the harmonies, and the words that we sang. To this day, I love to listen to and sing acapella music. It can bring chills and raise the hairs on my arms. The harmonies of people singing can bring joy to my heart like nothing else. It speaks deeply to me and moves me to the depth of my person. Do you have something that can do that for you? Whether it is music or something else, can you find that thing that moves you enough to get chills? Do you enjoy rock, classical, jazz, or blues? Maybe it is poetry or reading books. Maybe it is watching a sunset, sunrise, or even the moon as it rises in the distant sky. Find the thing that makes your heart sing.

Today, I will find things that can stir my soul and sit with it until it satisfies my heart and calms my spirit.

PERSPECTIVE   MARCH 13

"Some people are always grumbling because roses have thorns; I am thankful that thorns have roses." – Alphonse Karr

I grew up working in the landscaping industry for several years of my youth because my dad owned his own landscape company. I got the opportunity to learn how to appreciate how to take a blank canvas, aka a yard, and create a beautiful yard with grass, trees, and bushes. I was blessed with seeing a project from beginning to end. For a long time, I did not want to landscape let alone do yard work at my own house. I had the ability, but I did not have the desire. I have been doing some charity work on the weekends for some time now and I keep getting the opportunity to do some landscaping for this charity. I found myself complaining, mostly internally, about not wanting to landscape. As I began listening to myself talk about my disdain for landscaping, I did not like this version of myself. I thought that if I do not like listening to me, then who else wants to hear this? No one was the resounding answer. I decided to stop complaining and start doing with an open heart and closed mouth. I now enjoy the chances that I get to make a difference with someone's lawn. Maybe you have something in your life that you had to do for a number of years but now you no longer want to have anything to do with it. Maybe it is as simple as me and landscaping but maybe it is more complicated. I had to change my heart so I could change my actions. I was able to see the roses and not just the thorns.

Today, I will look at the things I do not l like to do and decide if the disdain is warranted or if I am simply looking for something to complain about.

THE PRICE OF LOVE   MARCH 14

"Grief never ends, but it changes. It is a passage, not a place to stay. Grief is not a sign of weakness nor a lack of faith: it is the price of love."
– Elizabeth I

The price of love is truly an expense we cannot understand the depths of. When you love someone unconditionally, you find out what you are willing to do and pay for love. You do almost anything because of the love that you have for that person. You do things that scare you and things that bring such joy that you can hardly describe the fullness that you feel. When you lose that loved one it can feel like your heart has physically torn. I have felt that, and maybe you have too. I was speaking to a friend of mine, and they said, grief is your expression of love for someone that is not returned.

I was able to understand that statement. It is not saying that the person we lost did not love us, but that they are no longer here to show or give that love back to us. Grief is hard not to stay in but when we learn it is a passage, that comes and goes when it wants, we can sit through the feelings. We can let them wash over us as we remember them and all that they were and meant to us. Then we can come out on the other side and not stay stuck, paralyzed by the grief. I hope you do not get scared by this but rather are able to find this kind of love. It may sound strange to search out the pain, but it is not the pain you are seeking. Rather it is the depth of love.

Today, I will look at the grief I may have in my life and start to understand that it comes and goes. I will feel what I need to feel and accept that it is the price of love.

ADAPTATION   MARCH 15

"The real menace in dealing with a five-year-old is that in no time at all you begin to sound like a five-year-old." – Jean Kerr

If you have ever played sports, you will understand the concept of playing to the level of your competition. This concept can be the same in sales, in fact, you need to be at least conversing at a similar level to your customer. I had to learn this when I got into heating and air conditioning and found it invaluable throughout my career. I worked in a technical environment but most customers that I dealt with, were mostly non-technical. Speaking technically to someone that is not technical will frustrate them and you. When I met with an engineer, I had to be able to speak the "tech talk" with them as well. This is part of adapting to your environment, much like a chameleon you will thrive not just survive in your surroundings.

Finding common ground for you and your customer can help you build trust and build value in you and your product or service. When you do not build this type of trust or rapport you lose a good chance to win the customer over. Experience has shown me that those who can adapt to their environment are usually the more successful. You cannot fake this. People will see right through you, and this is a terrible way to establish trust. Find out how to be sincere with your adaptation and not just try to do it to get the sale. There is a difference and once you find it you will never want to lose it.

Today, I will look for ways to work on my sincere adaptation to my customers and be more relatable while maintaining authenticity.

ENTITLEMENT   MARCH 16

"Don't go around saying the world owes you a living. The world owes you nothing. It was here first." – Mark Twain

Do you think the world owes you something? Were you wronged at an early age? Did you get passed over for a promotion? Did you not get the job you wanted and the voices in your head told you that you were perfectly qualified for that position? Did you get hurt in a relationship and they should have been nicer to you even though you may have been hard to be around? What is the reason that you believe that you deserve the things that you do not have? Most people have worked to get a position or relationship that they have in life. Some people are in the right place at the right time. That does not mean that you deserve to get what they got.

You may deserve more, but are you willing to accept the results regardless of what you think you deserve? You can set yourself up to be successful by doing the work. You can hustle and make yourself available for when it is your time to receive the blessings of this world, instead of waiting for things to come to you. I have found that when I am not looking to get something out of someone or a situation that things seem to appear that benefit me more than I thought I deserved, if they appear at all. If they do not come around, I am not disappointed because I was not expecting anything to begin with. If they do come to me, then I am grateful.

Today, I will look at the ways that I can be more lenient with myself and others, knowing that I am owed nothing in this life.

WORDS OF LOVE   MARCH 17

"A woman can be anything the man who loves her would have her be."
– James M. Barrie

Some of you may find this quote to be offensive or sexist. I find this quote to be powerful and interchangeable, between men and women. If you have someone that loves you and believes in you, then you are able to conquer the world. When you are encouraged and believed in and someone shares that with you, you are capable of doing far more than you thought possible. Positive encouragement from someone that loves you is like sweet nectar. The opposite is true as well.

Constant nagging or negative comments can weigh on the heart and mind to the point where you doubt most of what you do. I have been on the giving and receiving end of both situations. I have felt the love through encouraging words, from my mouth, and from others. You can do whatever you want, and I will have your back. And I have felt the sting of the negative comments. You are not like someone else, which can translate to you are not good enough. Subtle words can cut you to the very core of your person. Hopefully, you can see past the negative comments and understand that words, like actions, can be powerful both in the positive and the negative.

Today, I will find ways to positively encourage my loved ones and find the encouraging words from loved ones.

Delayed Dreams   March 18

"You pile up enough tomorrows, and you'll find you are left with nothing but a lot of empty yesterdays." – Meredith Willson

You have an opportunity sitting right in front of you and you are afraid to make a mistake or step off the proverbial ledge. What are you waiting for? Maybe you've been hurt or burned in the past and now you do not want that to happen again. You were down for the count way too long and you cannot afford to make the same mistake. Maybe you learned what you needed to last time. Maybe you tried to take that step and you were spared from a whole lot more than just some character building on your part. I can remember a time in my career that I had some leadership opportunities, and I had some good experiences but then they were followed by a couple of bad experiences due to poor leaders, mostly. But it hurt and caused me to question if I was a good leader or if I ever wanted to lead people again. I said out loud, explaining how I did not want to do that again. I was speaking to my mom recently and she reminded me of that statement that I made years ago. I thought more about what I said and when I said it and how I felt when I said it. I then thought I can lead! I said those things when I was hurt, and I did not want to get hurt again. Pain is what causes us to grow if we let it. I have become a better person and leader because of those situations. Your dreams are delayed only by you and the steps that you do not take.

Today, I will look for the ways that I will no longer delay my dreams and put aside my hurts long enough to see what lies ahead and how I can step out on my dreams.

FRESH START   MARCH 19

"With the new day comes new strength and new thoughts." – Eleanor Roosevelt

Dawn means a new beginning, a new start, and a fresh perspective. You get the chance to begin every day like new even though you may have something that needs to be finished from the day before or weeks before. All this means is that you get the chance to start from scratch today and make new decisions. If you made a decision yesterday that yielded negative results, then you can make a better decision today. If you made a good decision yesterday or last week, then you can make that same decision with more confidence. You get the chance to have a new outlook on a new day. You can have more confidence and more peace of mind. You can and will be stronger because you are building on the decisions of yesterday. You can also have a fresh perspective on things because you slept on it, or maybe you walked away from the situation to get some clarity. When I work on puzzles, I will sometimes move to a different side of the table to get a different perspective. That can help me to see things that I could not see when sitting in the same place for hours before. What else can give you a new view on the thing or things you are working on?

Today, I will find a fresh perspective of the new day. A chance to be more confident and gain new ideas with the new dawn of the new day.

COMMON SENSE   MARCH 20

"Common sense is genius dressed in its working clothes." – Ralph Waldo Emerson

You may have heard that common sense is not so common. Have you ever been in a situation that looks simple and yet the person or people you are working with do not seem to be able to use common sense to figure it out? It seems to be missing from the interaction. I have found that a number of my really smart friends, tend to be lacking in common sense. I am not sure why that is the case other than their intelligence has overshadowed their ability to see things practically. When you can see things practically it can help you in situations. Intelligence is great but sometimes you need to use common sense to see things from a practical perspective. Education is great and necessary, but so is common sense.

Today, I will look for ways that I can apply sound judgment to practical matters.

CHILDREN   MARCH 21

"Teach your children well... and know they love you." – Crosby, Stills, Nash, and Young

Most people I know who have children want their children to have what they did not when they grew up. Usually, they think about physical things or educational needs. They want their kids to have more opportunities or a better life than they had. We teach our children and try to give them what we think is best for them and yet we miss the opportunities to listen to what our kids want. I am not talking about giving our children the opportunity to make life decisions at age five. However, do we listen to them enough to hear what they want or need? I have found that my kids need my love and support to become greater than me. That will manifest itself in other things but starting with the simple things makes a big difference. Loving my kids can make them more confident, more loving, and more generous. Supporting them can make them stronger, more confident, and give them the opportunity to take chances when they do not think they can do something. Most of our parents did not have a book on how to raise a child. Neither did we, though some books have been written about how to raise kids and I am sure that they are helpful. Did you read all the books on how to raise a child and how did you do with that? I am hopeful that you did not make the mistakes that I made.

I got help and advice while raising my children and later gave advice on how others could raise their kids. My kids have done a great job despite the inadequacies that I may have provided as their father. They did not always want or need my direction or advice, they needed me to listen and love them. While I learned that, my children grew into the strong ladies that they are today. I have also learned that they still want and need my love and support, even as adults.

Today, I will find a way to love and support my children the way that they need and want to be loved.

TOLERANCE   MARCH 22

"Sooner or later, if man is ever to be worthy of his destiny, we must fill our hearts with tolerance." – Stan Lee

What is your ultimate goal and what are you willing to do to get there? If you have not taken time to think about where you want to end up, then what are you shooting for? Are you wandering around aimlessly? We often think of working hard, long hours, or taking actions that will help propel us to the next level and get us closer to our desired goals. What about your tolerance? Do you see how your level of tolerance can keep you from getting to your desired goals? If you are curt with people then you need to work on being patient. Likewise, if you are lacking in maturity then you need to develop your level of maturity so that you can reach your desired goals. Are you seeing the opportunities that will help you develop mentally, physically, and emotionally? The more you work on developing those characteristics the more prepared you will be to reach your destiny.

Today, I will find what I can do to build my levels of tolerance in different areas of my life.

Urgent Versus Important   March 23

"I have two kinds of problems, the urgent and the important. The urgent are not important, and the important are never urgent." – President Dwight D. Eisenhower

You may have heard before that there is a difference between urgent and important. Making that distinction in our minds can get tricky. We can think that because our boss asked for a report by the end of the day that the report is somehow important. It may not be to you, but it is to your boss. What is important to you is usually different than your boss. Though you have the same company goals in mind you have different things that are important to you, family, friends, hobbies, even personal goals. When you can discover the difference between what is urgent versus what is important, it can help you to prioritize and actually get things done. This has been a constant struggle for me. How do I determine what should take priority? When I put thought into it, I can see what needs my attention and what does not need my attention. You need to work at this to make it part of who you are. You can build your character to be able to discern urgent versus important.

Today, I will start to find what is urgent and what is important.

Planning   March 24

"Planning is bringing the future into the present so that you can do something about it now." – Alan Lakein

Planning is important to success. If you do not plan for success, your chances significantly decrease. Sometimes it is hard to sit down and figure out the direction you want to go and the things that you need to do to be successful. Sometimes, we just are not inspired, or we lack direction on where we want to go. Sometimes, we feel uncomfortable sitting alone in silence contemplating our future. All these things are just stumbling blocks on the path to success. Things that will slow you down and get you off course. Allow yourself time to plan, contemplate, and make decisions about your future and how you can and will be successful. Start with something as simple as writing all your plans, goals, and ideas down. Then you can prioritize them and move forward.

Today, I will find the time to make plans for my future days, weeks, months, and years.

What is Your Value? March 25

"Self-respect is a question of recognizing that anything worth having has a price." Joan Didion

Often, we think about what we can do to build the value of the product or service we represent. But how often do you think about the value within you? What are *you* worth? What is something that you said you would never do, and have you done it yet? If so, what price did you settle on for something that you said you would not do? Self-respect is something that has no price. You should be willing to forego anything for your self-respect. However, if you have no self-respect then you will give into anything at any price.

I found that one way I showed myself disrespect was in the ways I took care of my body. When I was in college, I was an athlete and was in the best shape of my life, thanks in part to people around me. When I left college, I still enjoyed working out and playing sports. When I got in my forties that took a turn. I stopped working out, I was not in very good shape and had gained about fifty pounds. I had to start respecting myself again. I started by looking at what I was eating and how much I was eating. Then I started looking at what this was doing to me and my mental health. I found that once I started respecting myself, I raised my self-worth, to me and others. I had to work at how I view my body both mentally and physically. Today I continue to look at the ways that I can raise my personal value through reading, giving my time to others, and to developing my spirituality.

Today, I will find ways to build my own personal value.

WORDS SPEAK VOLUMES   MARCH 26

"Three years he said that. 'Good night, Westley. Good work. Sleep well. I'll most likely kill you in the morning.'" – Westley, The Princess Bride

The movie quote above always struck me as funny but odd. Funny because it was said so matter of fact. Odd because there seemed to be a solid relationship with some depth to it. When you are in a relationship you should choose to speak with kindness and care. Some relationships are hard because one or both parties do not know how to effectively communicate. What kind of relationship do you have if you were to hear the words, sleep well, I will most likely kill you in the morning? Not very good, right? But what do you tolerate in your relationship? What is your communication like with your significant other, your close friends, or your family?

I have been in a long-term, romantic relationship where I was told regularly, from the beginning, I do not need you. At first, I thought how sad and how can I fix this and make her need me? I learned that it was not something I could fix because she really believed that, for various reasons, she did not need me. She did say she *wanted* to be with me. I found that hard to wrap my head and heart around. In an intimate relationship, I want and need the other person to want and need me. Likewise, I want and need the other person in my life.

The words we speak and hear can have a major impact on how we act and live, and how others will act and live with us. This kind of communication in a relationship is like a riptide or undertow of the ocean. It goes unseen or unnoticed on the surface but can tug at you and even pull you under the water so you cannot breathe or come up for air. We would talk about this on several occasions and how it made me feel that she did not need me. It did not and would not change and would be a dividing piece for me, of our relationship. That was not all that was wrong with that relationship as I said and did things that were not healthy either. What do you mean when you say things whether thought out or off the cuff? As Luke 6:45 says, "out of the overflow of the heart the mouth speaks."

Today, I will find ways to listen to my words before I speak and choose them carefully.

Saying and Doing — March 27

"Faith without works is like a song you can't sing. It's about as useless as a screen door on a submarine." – Rich Mullins

Watching a submarine going down into the water and seeing the water roll right into the ship through a screen door, sounds ridiculous right? That visual is like someone telling you one thing and their actions are telling you something else. It just does not make sense. When you realize your actions speak on your behalf, it makes it hard for you to contradict those actions, unless you are a really good liar. You may be able to lie to yourself for a little while, but your actions will always expose you. When I played sports and was defending someone, I was always taught to watch the person's midsection because that is their center. They cannot go anywhere without that. You cannot be faked out if you focus on the middle of a person, much like focusing on the actions of a person.

Today, I will look at my actions and my words to make sure that they are in line with each other.

Basic Needs — March 28

"You are rich if you have enough to meet your most basic needs. You are rich if you have access to clean water, food, shelter, love, a roof over your

head. You have to count your blessings to see that you are richer than you think." – Michelle Singletary

We all have basic needs in our lives. When we mindlessly go about our day, most of the time we take care of the basics. This is how we survive. But can we run on autopilot and be effective? Probably, but not for very long. But what happens when we forget the basics? What happens when we forget to get a haircut and our hair is out of control? How do we react when our stomach is growling because we have not eaten for most of the day? What about some other basic needs like security/safety, and love? When was the last time you got a hug from a loved one? When we neglect these basic needs, we are neglecting ourselves. If we are not taking care of the little things, are we able to take care of the bigger things? The bigger things may be getting done because they are bigger and more visible. Are they getting done as well as if we were taking care of the little things first? The little things lead to bigger things.

Today, I will make time for the basic needs in my life and make sure that I am taking care of them first. Then I can focus on the larger things.

LOOKING AHEAD MARCH 29

"Keep your face always toward the sunshine - and shadows will fall behind you." – Walt Whitman

What are you focused on? Where are you headed? If you are constantly looking behind, you will get tripped up and fall. If you are focused ahead of you then you can see the obstacles ahead and avoid them. Looking ahead is more than just a couple of steps. They say that a safe driving technique on the highway is to look about twelve seconds ahead of you. Do you look that far ahead or are you short-sighted? You cannot look too far ahead, or you will miss the very things that are right in front of you. Find the balance in looking ahead. Can you see the things in front of you? Your day, your week, your month are they in focus? Are you looking at this hour, or this minute, and cannot see what later this morning or even this afternoon will hold for you?

When I focus too much on the immediate or the distant future then I lose sight of the things that I need to focus on when they come around. I know I am doing well when I have the next couple of weeks planned out with some meetings, training sessions, and I am also adding in a few meetings that need to happen because of more immediate needs that appeared recently.

Today, I will look at my schedule, this week and month to know where I am going and still focus on the things that need my immediate attention.

OPPORTUNITY   MARCH 30

"If opportunity doesn't knock, build a door." – Milton Berle

Some of us know how to wait on opportunities and capitalize on those opportunities when they arise. Others know how to make opportunities happen by knocking on doors or in some cases building the door so it can be knocked on. In some sales careers, cold calling is absolutely necessary and not so much in others. I have worked in a call center making several calls an hour. I have been in sales roles where ninety percent of the leads were handed to you due to the nature of the business. What do *you* like to do? I found out that I am not a good call center, telemarketing kind of person. That did not fit with my personality, so I stopped applying for those jobs quickly out of college. I thrive in a consultative type of sales role. Where I get to help people find what they are looking for versus pushing people to buy the product or service that I offered. When I learned that about myself it made finding my niche in sales a lot easier. What do you like? Be honest with yourself because you will find yourself in a job that does not work for you or your company? If you do not know, there are plenty of personality assessment tests out there for you to take so that you can be aligned with who you are. Find the opportunity that fits you best and work towards your success in that area.

Today, I will ask myself what I really like and then find ways to do what I like so that I can find the right opportunity for me.

The Scattered Pieces Will Come Together   March 31

"If you are curious, you'll find the puzzles around you. If you are determined, you will solve them." – Erno Rubik

I like to work on jigsaw puzzles. There is something soothing about taking a scattered mess and putting it back together. Sometimes, I have to remind myself that life can be like a jigsaw puzzle. You have to put some things together to see the bigger picture so that you can work on another section. You have so many pieces to the puzzle in your life that it can get messy. You have your family life, professional life, friends, and recreational life. Any one of those can feel scattered and out of place at any time. Looking at the puzzle from a different angle sometimes can help you see how things will fit together where you could not see them before. Sometimes we can get frustrated when we look at all the pieces scattered about. I usually start with the edge pieces, then I will work on a color or a pattern that is clearly defined and toward the outside and I can build from that. We need to focus on putting things together a little bit at a time instead of trying to fix the whole puzzle at once. Find all the pieces that look alike and start working on that. What are the easier sections that you can put together and build upon? When you start building a little at a time you can start seeing progress and the puzzle will come into view.

Today, I will find the pieces that I can put together and start building from that. I will turn the table sideways if needed to get a better perspective.

April

Draw Without an Eraser   April 1

"Life is the art of drawing without an eraser." – John W. Gardner

Time is a funny thing. Funny in that we cannot rewind it so we can correct a mistake or do something over again. We can repeat things over and over until we get them right. That is called practice. However, every moment we live, we cannot get it back. Every word that leaves our mouth cannot be removed from our history. Have you ever had to draw something without an eraser? When I was eleven years old, the VCR had just come out. I do not believe we owned one until about five years later. It was our first experience with being able to stop and rewind a movie or a sporting event in our homes. Before this time, we just lived life in real-time. I remember when I was a teenager trying to learn the lyrics to songs. I would record them on a cassette tape and rewind them again and again so I could hear them again and write them down to get them right. Today, we have advanced in our ability to record ourselves and replay what we said or did and then correct it, or even edit the video or recording to cut out the mistakes. Most of our lives are not recorded, thankfully. Life is messy! It is not perfect nor are we. We do the best we can and sometimes we make mistakes. That is called life. Put your phone down, put down the recording device and just live for a moment or a few moments. Draw without an eraser and see where it goes. We can learn so much by making mistakes. Using your device to help you to improve is a great tool but sometimes we need to put them down and live our lives at that moment.

Today, I will find ways to live my life without trying to constantly erase the mistakes I make. Life is meant to be lived as if I were drawing without an eraser.

Change   April 2

"Change before you have to." – Jack Welch

Are you afraid of change? I have known several people in my life that the very idea of change causes them to get anxious. If you look at the life before you and think about what it will look like if you do not change, does that scare you? Life is full of change and without change, we would be nothing more than infants that never grow up. It may sound extreme but think about that possibility. When we decide not to change, we are saying that where we are at currently whether spiritually, emotionally, or physically, will get us through the rest of our lives no matter how long or short that may be. What we may not realize is that the statement says I refuse to change. I do not want to be any different and I want things around me to stay the way they are because they are comfortable.

We want the type of change that is convenient and does not cause pain, or we do not want change at all. Change is part of life. We cannot escape it. The day turns to night and night turns back into day. Rain comes and goes and even snow will fall if you are lucky enough to live where that is possible. We change clothes daily, or we should. This is all part of the change that happens daily. I know when I was growing up, I had some growth spurts, periods where I grew a lot in a short period of time. It hurt! My knees and shins hurt the most, or at least that is where I felt it the most. When we grow spiritually or emotionally it can be the same thing. It can hurt! The pain produces the growth that we need to be a better person, more experienced, or more emotionally fit to handle what is to come. Do not let the fear of change, or the pain associated with that change, in your life keep you from growing into the person that you can and want to be.

Today, I will find ways that I can change in the ways that I need to before it is thrust upon me.

FOCUSED PLANS   APRIL 3

"The absence of alternatives clears the mind marvelously." – Henry Kissinger

Do you have a clear vision of where you are going and how you are going to get there? Sometimes we can have plans and yet the options for those plans can be numerous and that clouds our vision of where we are headed. When you have a clear plan of how to get from where you are to where you want to go you have a focus that can rarely be deterred or altered. I have been on sales calls before where I felt like there were so many options it became difficult to focus on how to get to the solution for the customer. It usually led to confusion on the customer's part and too many options for them. I am all about giving the customer the proper number of options that they can then choose to find what fits them best. If I did not ask the proper questions to help me narrow the field of options, I was not effective at all. When I asked the proper questions and narrowed the options in my head, I was much more concise and was able to effectively give them the options necessary and they made the decision to move forward with us. How do you handle the vast amount of information that you have about your company and your product or service? If you were to share with the customer everything that you knew, it would overwhelm them.

Are you paralyzed by the number of options you have at your disposal? Take the time to ask the right questions and funnel down the information that you have to provide, and you will succeed. Not just in sales but in life. Sometimes I can feel overwhelmed by the simple things that need to be done because everything has a priority. Laundry, dishes, making meals, cleaning the house, all have a priority. When you realize that taking one step at a time can help eliminate the numerous options before you. Do one thing then move to the next item. Make a list if it helps you to clearly work on a thing that you can then cross off to show yourself progress.

Today, I will remove the excess of alternatives that are available to make my decisions and the decisions of others easier.

Freedom   APRIL 4

"To be free is to have achieved your life." – Tennessee Williams

What do you believe freedom looks like in your life? Are you truly free in your life or are there things that hold you down and keep you captive? Many of us think that we are free and yet we cannot explain what that truly means to us. Freedom comes in many forms, but true freedom is found in not being controlled by other things, people, or even situations. We allow our jobs to control us, yet we claim we must work late to finish the project and miss family time. We are consumed with a relationship that pulls us away from family, friends, or even our work. We are consumed with making enough money so we can go on that vacation or get out of debt. If you are free, you know what it's like to have peace of mind.

Have you been in a place where you are nearly overwhelmed with the peace and joy that comes from freedom? It is not easy to achieve this type of freedom but we all can if we are willing to see our lives for what they are. Meditation has enabled me to find some of this peace and freedom. What are you willing to give up in your life to find the freedom that you desire? Most of the time it is merely time, but sometimes it may be something that we think we enjoy, our job, playing sports, or grabbing a drink with friends. Can you spend time finding the freedom within you?

Today, I will look for ways that I can find the freedom that I desire for my life.

Imagination   APRIL 5

"Imagination does not become great until human beings, given the courage and the strength, use it to create." – Maria Montessori

Are you able to dream big about things in your life? Some of us are out of practice because we do not dream as we used to years ago. We have lost the inner child that learned how to dream big. We get told too many times that we cannot do this or that and the next thing you know everything you do has no imagination to it. We have negative conversations with ourselves, and we think of all the stuff we messed up and not the things we did right. We can gain our ability to dream again but like everything else in life, we must make time to make it happen. Spending a little time imagining what it would be like to make that sale, get that promotion, or get into that perfect relationship.

When I played college football, one of the things that we would do is positive reinforcement exercises. Imagine a room full of college athletes laying on the floor in a nearly dark room totally relaxed and focusing on the moves that we will make that week to perfectly execute the plays. There were no mistakes because we could play it out in our heads the way we intended it to go. It meant we could determine the outcome, so why would anything go wrong in our minds? The interesting thing about that is, it worked! You can do the same in your life with your thoughts and actions by using your imagination to see yourself doing the job properly, saying the right things for every objection that comes out. Better yet, say the proper things ahead of time so that there are no objections. Imagination can help you succeed if you spend time developing it.

Today, I will find ways that I can work on imagining what my life can be like.

CUSTOMER SERVICE   APRIL 6

"Southwest Airlines is successful because the company understands it's a customer service company. It also happens to be an airline." – Harvey Mackay

When was the last time you went to a restaurant and things went so well you could not wait to tell your friends about the experience that you had? Everything was amazing! What about the time you went to that restaurant and the service was poor the food was cold and tasteless, and you will never give them your time or business ever again? We tend to remember extreme situations really well. Can you remember the name of the place you had lunch at today or dinner the other night? When we give mediocre customer service people tend to forget your name, the company, and maybe even what they purchased. While I was working in heating and air conditioning, I learned about the importance of going the extra step for my customers. I wore shoe covers, removed old filters or trash from the attic or crawlspace. I changed light bulbs and looked for other appropriate ways that I could serve them as an invited guest to their home, aside from helping them with their heating and air system replacement. I respected their homes beyond my expectations, which usually was more than they expected from me. In that business, I was an invited guest not someone to sell them something. I knew that would take care of itself if I did my job properly and one of those things was to provide them with amazing customer service. How are you at providing customer service?

Today, I will look at how I can provide better customer service and it can start with a simple smile.

CHARACTER VS. REPUTATION   APRIL 7

"Be more concerned with your character than your reputation, because your character is what you really are, while your reputation is merely what others think you are." – John Wooden

Understanding the difference between character and reputation is important. If you are worried about what people think then you will do whatever you can to please people and not focus on who you really are. You will be constantly chasing the value of yourself from others instead of building the value of yourself from within. You can build your character with humility towards yourself and others. Not looking for ways to tear people down but encouraging them to be better. Choosing your words carefully before saying them. These three things can carry you a long way if you take time to practice them daily. You do not always have to be right and if you are, you do not have to tell everyone.

I was with a colleague at a customer's house. The customer was pretty smart and was able to figure some things out with his HVAC system, but he knew enough to be dangerous, as the saying goes. My colleague is a very smart man when it comes to HVAC systems and how they work, and the customer said something that we both knew was wrong and I looked at my colleague with that look of please do not tell him he is wrong. Unfortunately, my ability to send my thoughts to him was not good enough and he proceeded to tell the customer of his transgression. The customer got upset and for the next couple of minutes, I was looking for a way to diffuse the situation. We were able to get things back to calm and I asked my colleague if he could help me with something outside the house, the old I need to talk to you outside move. I asked my colleague if it was important to tell the customer that he was wrong in that situation because what he had said was rather harmless. My colleague is a humble enough man to realize what had happened and he was able to smooth it over with the customer to the point that the customer would only call him if he had a problem going forward. My colleague had the character to do the right thing, albeit a bit late, with the customer. He could see the mistake he made and was able to correct it. That takes character.

Today, I will work on building my character through things like humility, building up others, and mindful speech.

EXPECTATIONS   APRIL 8

"When one's expectations are reduced to zero, one really appreciates everything one does have." - Stephen Hawking

Expectations are a tricky thing to master; you can have super high ones and it propels you to great things or you can have low expectations and truly appreciate all that you have. Nothing is wrong with either one of these views. You need to set high expectations of yourself so that you will be motivated to do great things. You will need those to get you over the next hurdle and continue to grow as a person. Low expectations can be used to understand that all you have around you is a blessing, a gift that needs to be appreciated. You may have worked hard in your job to get where you are and to have the things that you have. Do you walk around your house and admire all that you have? If you have moved more than once or twice in your life you gain a better appreciation of how much stuff you really need to admire. I have been learning about setting expectations for my work and personal life, which in turn has influenced my contentment. I am learning that through proper expectations I can be content no matter what the situation. This is not an easy thing for me to figure out. I have been working hard with high expectations for a good portion of my life and I have been able to do and see a lot of things in my life, good and bad. Now instead of buying that next thing for my house that I will also have to move the next time I move in life, I am able to give more of my time and money to things that are becoming more important to me, like my community. What are your expectations for you and your life and how are you currently managing them?

Today, I will start to look at my expectations for my work and personal life and the impact that it is having on me and others.

GIVING   APRIL 9

"No one has ever become poor by giving." – Anne Frank

Have you ever been alone after you have given to someone? I do not mean something simple or something that you do regularly. I mean if you see someone in need and no one is around, and you give something of value to them. When someone is doing a charity event and you privately give to that event. Not for others to see. How do you handle giving situations? Do you find ways to give of your time, your money, or your talents? Do you manifest the things that are needed by offering them up to God and/or the universe? Does that ever cross your mind? Too often we think that we must work harder to manifest things in our lives. Have you ever thought I was in the right place at the right time? Giving can be like that too.

The other day I was looking at my bank statement and something looked off. I had three large credits where there should have been a debit. I did some research and found that I was given the refund, not because of an error but because it was given to me. I checked it before I spent it, but it was correct. It happened to be almost the total amount needed for something else that came up and was unexpected. I try to be more giving with both my time and my money. I have been blessed being in sales and as a result, I get to share that with others. How do you feel when you give? Is it with angst or trepidation? Is it with fear that you will not have enough? Learn to give to people with little or no expectations. If you give someone something, do not expect it back. If you do expect it back, then you probably should not have given it in the first place. It can cause you and others unnecessary tension.

Today, I will look for ways to give to others, whether with money or my time. I will find the joy that awaits me and others.

METHODOLOGY APRIL 10

"What methodology do you follow as a salesperson?" – Unknown

Some people have some sort of methodology that they follow, either for life, work, or relationships. While in sales, we learn different ways to help out our clients. We develop a methodology of our own. At least that is the way it should be. Some people follow Zig Ziglar, Brian Tracy, John Maxwell, or any number of other sales leaders, and you should have people that you look up to and admire for paving the way for you to grow. But if you just repeat everything that they wrote in a book or said in a seminar, you are nothing more than a robot. People can see a robot. They know when your heart is not a part of what you do or what you say. Don't get me wrong, we have all been duped by someone that could lie very well. But that is not your true self, is it? If you are lying all the time and feel like you can keep getting away with it in sales, you might want to rethink that. When finding your way in sales, it is good to find some tidbits that you can cling to from others. But we must make them personal. Add your seasoning to what you are saying or doing.

I love to cook, and I struggle with just following recipes all the time. When I make something the first time, it generally will be different from that point forward. I will change it a little bit here or there until I find the right taste for me that day. Read plenty of books, listen to plenty of speakers to find your voice. Find what works best for you and your clients on that day. It will be different with the next person, or the next day. Build your foundation, *then* be flexible. You can be consistent and still change. Your core is not changing. Your foundation is not changing. Your methodology may not change. You will figure out how to help the most people.

Today, I will find ways to learn how to add to the foundation that I want to build. Then I will be flexible to learn how to help others.

GRACE   APRIL 11

"I do not at all understand the mystery of grace - only that it meets us where we are but does not leave us where it found us." – Anne Lamott

Grace is receiving things undeserved and unprompted. It means you are getting something you do not deserve. You cannot work for grace. You can only receive it. How do you feel when you receive something you do not deserve? Is it humbling to you, or do you feel a sense of self-righteousness? Grace is one of those things that makes me feel very humbled. I do not deserve to have the life I have because I have done things to screw it up.

I have been a college athlete and able to eat most anything most of my life and had no allergies to my knowledge. In the last few years, I started finding that I was allergic to almost everything. My doctor wanted to put me on allergy shots every other week. I started looking into what was happening and I was able to find a doctor that helped me understand why my body was rejecting everything I had been doing for years. By grace, I am healthier today because I was able to find someone to help me understand the whole picture, not just cover the symptoms. I do not deserve this because of the way I have done things for years.

Today, I will find the grace that is being presented to me and accept it for what it is, an undeserved gift.

COUNTING THE COSTS   APRIL 12

"Better remain silent, better not even think, if you are not prepared to act." – Annie Besant

Actions speak louder than words. When I would study the bible with people, there was a specific lesson on counting the costs. If you are not familiar with that phrase, it means that you need to sit down and decide if you have what it takes to see this decision to completion. Back in the New Testament times, this was a very critical step in becoming a follower of Christ because their lives were being threatened on a regular basis. If you were not willing to die for the cause, then you might want to think about that before you start along the path of being a disciple of Jesus. This is something that you should do with the major decisions in your life. Sit down and take the time to count the costs of your decision. If you do this then be prepared for this, this, and this. We do that with marriage, buying a house, buying a car, or even when we are looking at taking a job. Counting the costs is an important thing to do when looking at the major decisions that we face throughout our lives. What about the lesser things in our lives? Do we count the costs on those as well? We do this more often than you may think, and we should. Life is not just flying by the seat of our pants and hoping that things will work out. Though I do know a few people like this and for the most part things do work out for them. However, some consequences come with those things that fall through the cracks as a result of the seat of the pants mentality. This should not take a lot of time and effort unless the decision is larger and has a larger impact on you and those around you. When you take the time to sit down and count the costs, you are ready to move forward with the decision that you have made. You may not need to answer to others as to why you chose the path you did unless they are directly affected by your decision.

Today, I will look at how I make decisions and if I am counting the costs for the decisions that warrant it.

SPIRITUALITY   APRIL 13

"When I have a terrible need of - shall I say the word - religion. Then I go out and paint the stars." – Vincent Van Gogh

What does spirituality look like to you? Is it hypocritical? Is it restrictive? Does it cause you to feel the warmth of love and gratitude? Being spiritual is different from being religious. Being religious has a lot of negative connotations. It smacks of self-righteousness and is more concerned with being right than loving, forgiving, or even gracious. We are all spiritual beings and can improve our spirituality by reading, praying, or meditating, and learning how to think of others before ourselves. When I was younger, I was involved in a religious organization that taught me a lot of great things and how to become more spiritual. I also taught myself how to become more religious and I did things and said things that were less spiritual. Much like most of the experiences in my life, that taught me a great deal and I am the person I am today because of that experience. I am now able to be more spiritual. I am able to act and say things that are far more loving and filled with grace than I did in the past. Part of that is maturity and part of that is understanding the difference between religious and spiritual. Being spiritual attracts people and being religious pushes people away. Customers, friends, and even family are drawn to those that are spiritual. Look at the people that you are drawn to or attracted to. More than likely, they are spiritual in some capacity.

Today, I will find ways to be more spiritual and less religious.

Mind Control   April 14

"Do not get upset with people or situations, both are powerless without your reaction." – Unknown

Are you quick to speak and quick to anger? Each of those can get you in trouble by themselves but when you combine them, they can set you back quite a bit. Situations can upset us and people even more if we let them. We can allow them to get inside our minds and work their magic so that we are powerless. Being able to control your thoughts is a powerful thing, yet few of us understand how to do that. It is not something that comes easily for most of us, but it can be done. I tend to stay inside my head. After reading *The Surrender Experiment* by Michael Singer, I learned how to allow myself not to listen to all the negative chatter that happens in my head. I also learned to prepare myself to surrender to the things introduced to me by the universe/God that can provide a positive storyline for my life. Too often we can let the negative thoughts cloud our mind: Why did she say that? What did he mean by that? Why do I always do or say that? The negative storyline can be overwhelming if we listen for any length of time. Being able to stop that negative tape from running and finding the positive things that are happening or about to happen can open a whole world of new ideas for you and your heart. I do not know that you can stop the first thought that comes to your head but what do you do after it pops up? Can you take control and not allow the negative things to overwhelm you?

Today, I will see how I handle the first thoughts that come to mind and start to focus on the good that can come from changing my mind.

WITHHOLDING   APRIL 15

"You cannot receive what you don't give. Outflow determines inflow."
– Laozi

When we hear the word withholding, it usually revolves around taxes, the truth, or information if you are watching a police show. When we hold something back, it may be because of how we were treated in the past. It may be because of a certain belief that we have developed over our lifetime. Sometimes we can hold back information because of a lack of knowledge, or it never crossed our mind. Withholding feelings and money usually follow the same pattern. Do you look at your life and ask yourself, why am I holding this back? It could be something simple or something you think is super complex because of all the feelings that are tied to it. When I have withheld things in life, it usually revolved around my emotions that were tied to that thing. It also revolved around my fear of looking a certain way, mostly stupid or inexperienced. When I am afraid of being honest or want to hold something back, I can usually catch myself now. It took a while to let go of the fear that was in my head. We usually have to move past the fear to get to the heart of matters.

We can only hold on to so many things. When we hold on to something it takes up space. Maybe that space is needed for something else that we need to carry, in our hands or our hearts. We may need to hold space for others, and we cannot do that if we are holding on to something that blocks that space, emotionally. What are you holding on to that is keeping you from giving to others? What are you withholding today that is taking up space physically or emotionally?

Today, I will let go of the thing or things that I am holding that are not allowing me to give to others.

MATTERS OF THE HEART — APRIL 16

"It is a fool who looks for logic in the chambers of the human heart."
– The Coen Brothers

Sometimes we look for things that are not there. The human heart can be full of emotion and not lend itself to being logical. When you are dealing with matters of the heart things get very emotional very quickly and logic is hard to find. You are talking to a spouse, significant other, or even a co-worker, and things get emotionally charged. Most of us *tend* not to be able to be logical at this time and we say or do things that defy logic. We want to be right! We want to win! Yet we forget about the truth of the situation. We want our way to be the truth. If you go look for a white piece of sand on a black sand beach you will be searching in vain. I want people to be good-hearted and act similarly to me in terms of being nice and thoughtful but that does not always happen. I can be selfish and insensitive and that does not go along with the previous sentence either. Thinking like this can be a little naïve but it does not mean that you should not look for the good in people. It just means you might have to adjust your reaction to that person if you find that they are not aligning with how you want them to act. Being able to see people and situations for what they are can be difficult. Being able to step back from a situation can help you to see clearly what you need to see. Add logic to the situation and remove the emotion. Ask yourself if your expectations are appropriate for the situation, if not, adjust for that as well.

Today, I will look at situations with more clarity and not expect a heartfelt situation to be filled with logic.

INSPIRATION — APRIL 17

"You can't force your will on people. If you want them to act differently, you need to inspire them to change themselves." – Phil Jackson

Have you ever worked for someone that felt like they were constantly pushing their ideas on you? Worse still, have you been the manager that forces people to do things that they do not want to do? Few things feel worse than being on the receiving end of such requests or demands. I had a boss that was very oppressive and tried to make me do things that made me feel like I was lying to my customers. I was asked to not tell the full truth and manipulate the situation so I could get the business. I know it showed in the results and it did not accomplish what they wanted. I have also worked for someone that encouraged and inspired me to the point that I would run through a wall if they asked and with an attitude that reflected the inspiration.

The difference between the oppressive and inspiring leader can be and is refreshing to the soul that receives such encouragement and inspiration. We often think that we have to wait for our manager to tell us what to do. We can get frustrated with the lack of direction and inspiration that our managers give to us. Sometimes, we must be the leader that we want or need because leadership is lacking in our lives. It may be at these times that we find that we are our own best boss. What can you do to inspire yourself and others to do great things?

Today, I will look for ways that I can inspire myself or others through my actions.

GAINS   APRIL 18

"One reason people resist change is that they focus on what they have to give up, rather than what they have to gain!" – Rick Godwin

We all like to gain things in our lives, especially when they come easily or with little effort on our part. Sometimes we have to work for them though and this is the struggle. We want a six-figure job with little to no experience. We want the management position when we have only a couple of years of industry experience and no leadership experience. We want a nice house, a nice car, a nice family without all the work. We do not want to give up our time, our family life, our fun time, or the sacrifice to get the things that we want in life. If you do not want to sacrifice, then do not expect the gain. It could come to you as an undeserved gift, but you should not expect it. Not often do we get things in our lives without the work to achieve them. Stop looking at the future prize without looking at the work to get the prize. It should inspire you and give you the determination to do the work needed for such a prize. The prize would be worth nothing if everyone could get it. Remember that everything worth gaining is worth the work to get it.

Today, I will look at the gains that I want in my life and set a plan to do the things that will help me achieve them.

MISTAKES VS. WISDOM — APRIL 19

"If you could erase all the mistakes of your past, you would also erase the wisdom of your present. Remember the lesson, not the disappointment."
– Unknown

Too often we can be embarrassed about things from our past. What we fail to understand is the wisdom that we may or should have gained from those situations or events. I can remember going to a high school reunion and I felt guilty because all I could remember was how many mistakes I made and the way I acted back in high school. What I found was that I was probably the only one that remembered all my failures and everyone else seemed to be there to have a good time reconnecting with old friends. When I look back on that event, I was not able to enjoy it as I should have. I had some great conversations and was able to reconnect with friends from the past, and I still talk to a number of them years later. Later, I was able to see that I have changed so much since high school, and I am not the same person I was back then. You should not be the same person you were in high school either. You should have grown and matured since then and this is a chance for you to do so again. Take the time to reflect on what you have changed and how you are different. You may still be embarrassed by your past decisions, but you can also be proud of the person you have become as a result of your growth.

Today, I will look at the situations from the past with a proper perspective and see the wisdom learned from the mistakes.

PASSION   APRIL 20

"The only time I waste is time I spend doing something that, in my gut, I know I shouldn't. If I choose to spend time playing video games or sleeping in, then it's time well spent, because I chose to do it. I did it for a reason - to relax, to decompress or to feel good, and that was what I wanted to do."
- Simon Sinek

What are you passionate about? Is it a cause, a charity, or something that you do for work or for pleasure? What do you spend time thinking about? Most of us know what we are passionate about because it is the thing that brings us the most emotion. They can be highs or lows, good or bad. We can be passionate about work or a relationship. When that passion drives us to the point of obsessing over that job or that relationship or that sport, etc. is when it becomes a problem. Passion can make you successful and happy. Passion can also make you a tyrant and controlling.

People throughout history have been passionate for the right reasons, inventing things or developing things for the betterment of mankind. Some people have been passionate about things they believe are right and yet so wrong for themselves and mankind. Figuring out what you're passionate about is a good place to start. Then you develop it into something healthy that helps drive you towards your goals and your desire to help others? You should work at your passion regularly so that you can manifest it to what you really want or desire from it. Passion for a relationship, a career, or a sport can make you the best you have ever been.

Today, I will look for ways that my passion drives me and search for ways to develop it, in ways that are productive and helpful to myself and others.

Motivation   April 21

"People often say that motivation doesn't last. Well, neither does bathing, that's why we recommend it daily." – Zig Ziglar

What helps you get through your day? Is it a significant other, children, parents, or pets? When you are having a rough day or feel down during the day, what helps you turn it around? Sometimes, it is a song, a speech, a conversation with a friend or family member, or the memory of some victory. We all need something to keep us moving throughout the day. There is nothing wrong with feeling the feelings of a situation. But then we need something to pick us back up so we can move on to our next thing. When my brother died, I would find myself wandering during the day. I understand this is normal and expected.

Sometimes, I just needed something to help me get motivated. Listening to certain songs helps me, going out for a walk, or just getting out of the office for a few minutes to take some deep breaths. When I played football in college, I used to listen to a certain playlist filled with rock songs that helped get me in the proper frame of mind for the game. Find what it is that motivates you and helps pick you up. Have the list at the ready when you come across a situation that requires that extra boost. I have created a playlist on my phone that I can play when I need it, and it is called Change the Mood. It is filled with songs that are a little fun, quirky, or that can get me out of my own head. What can you do to help change your situation and help motivate you?

Today, I will look for things that help motivate me and push me in the right direction.

GROWTH   APRIL 22

"Research is creating new knowledge." – Neil Armstrong

What are you doing to grow, whether it is your maturity, your spiritual well-being, or your business acumen? You are making steps going forward or going backward daily. If you aren't growing, you are dying. Growth is something that you get to control every day. I found that I enjoy learning things, whether it is reading books or listening to podcasts, or watching documentaries, there is something to be learned. When you spend time doing research on something you are making progress in the knowledge of that subject. If you want to learn about business, you will read business articles, books, listen to podcasts, or even watch movies about how businesses have grown or failed so that you can learn. If you want to know more about sales, you will read about how to be a better salesperson, listen to podcasts about being better at sales, or even watch movies like Glengarry Glen Ross, The Wolf of Wall Street, or The Pursuit of Happyness. I have seen people do the opposite too. They do not want to read, listen to podcasts, or even watch movies to better themselves. They are content with who they are. What you decide to do today will impact tomorrow.

Today, I have the opportunity to take a step forward or a step backward. Very rarely will I be able to stay in the same place day after day.

LISTENING   APRIL 23

"A good listener is not only popular everywhere, but after a while, he gets to know something." – Wilson Mizner

Do you listen more than you speak? Are you able to enter a room full of people and engage by actively listening to what is being said? Listening is hard work because we want people to know who we are and what we know. When you listen, you get to understand more about people and what they want. You get to learn about people and places and things when you listen. You cannot learn when you are talking. Active listening takes time to master. We think we know how to listen. Listening to learn or to understand is about others and hearing the words in your head and making note of the special things that were said. Watching their body language while they speak about certain things will tell you if they are serious about it or making light of it. Listening to learn is an art form that some people have learned how to do very well. I had a conversation with a church leader, and it was the first time that I had spoken to him. He knew how to listen to me and focus on just me when we were talking that made me feel like I was the only person in the room. There were thousands of people in the room at the time, and several were waiting to talk to him. Learning how to make someone feel listened to like that is a skill that has to be learned. Learning how to do that will make you a better listener and will give you wisdom into people that you cannot learn otherwise. Another side effect of listening more than talking is that people will find you more attractive and wiser than if you talk all the time.

Today, I will learn to focus my listening attention to help understand others and what they truly want or need.

PERSONALITY   APRIL 24

"I have an unfortunate personality." – Orson Welles

How would you describe your personality? How would others describe you? Why is this important, especially in sales? If you have a goofy personality, then people will not take you seriously and that will be good for some sales positions but probably not for others. If you understand what your personality is like, then you can do something about it. Sometimes we need to understand what is keeping us from getting the sale and sometimes that thing is simply *us*. Sometimes we can do something about it and sometimes we cannot. If you find that your personality is offensive to more people than usual maybe it is time to do something to change that part of you. On the other hand, it could be time to find something else that you enjoy that does not put you in front of a lot of people. Finding the right career path to fit your personality can be hard at times and easy at others. I know people who think they enjoy sales, but they cannot stand people. It makes it hard to be good at sales if you do not like people.

Today, I will look at how my personality may be affecting my job and will make changes where necessary.

Gratitude   April 25

"Silent gratitude isn't much use to anyone." – Gertrude Stein

We can forget what it feels like to compliment someone and how it feels to receive a well-placed compliment. When we forget, we rob that person of the joy and the confidence that comes from the words that you speak. You know what it is like to hear those words from someone that you respect or admire. The satisfaction that it can bring to your heart. When we do not say anything to the person who went above and beyond, we are hurting ourselves and those that can benefit from the kind words. We are not letting someone else feel the joy or satisfaction that we feel. It may not be our intent but that is what happens when we say nothing to someone that has done a great job. There have been many times when someone could have said something that may have seemed trivial to them at the time but would have meant the world to me. You are doing a good job, you are doing a great job, I really appreciate you for taking on that project and doing it well. Those would have made a difference for me or for others. You have the chance to let people know that they are good, great, and special. If you fail to do that then you are robbing not only them but yourself of the joy that comes with the expression of gratitude.

Today, I will find opportunities to let people know that they are doing a great job and not keep it to myself.

Accepting Change — April 26

"In order to accept change and the suffering it brings we need to find meaning in it." – Mary Norton Gordon

Sometimes change can come easy to us. We simply change direction by turning left or right and there you have changed. Other times it is like pulling teeth. I mean that literally. I had my wisdom teeth pulled in my mid-twenties and I remember the dentist having a difficult time with one of my teeth because it was wrapped around the bone, at least that is what he told me. His knee was in my chest and tears were streaming down my cheek as he did what he needed to do to remove that tooth. We can be like that tooth and not want to let go of the way we are doing things. Yet, when we change sometimes it is such a relief and things go a lot smoother than we anticipated. In fact, our lives get better, our jobs get easier, our relationships blossom.

When we learn to accept that life is full of change and that staying in the same place, way of thinking or patterns of our lives is not an option. If you find yourself stuck in your ways or refusing to change you must ask why? As a salesperson, we are constantly adapting to the people, places, and situations around us. If you are losing deals and you do not change, you might lose your job. If you are not changing the way that you are trying to do things in your life you could lose your friends, your family, and even your life. Learning to accept change is a necessary part of life because without change you will lose a lot.

I have met a number of people that say they are too old to change their ways. I know some people that will not change because they do not see a need to change, they have always done it this way and I am not going to change now. Maybe you are saying that you find the change to be too difficult. No matter what you are telling yourself or others, change is a part of life. The sooner we learn to accept change, the sooner we get to learn or experience new things.

Today, I will look for ways to accept the change that is coming and needed in my life. I will learn to set aside my old beliefs that I cannot change no matter what the reason.

PERSONA   APRIL 27

"I refuse to join any club that would have me as a member." – Groucho Marx

Are you known as hardheaded or sarcastic? Are you quiet or verbose? Are you thoughtful, pensive, or someone that flies by the seat of their pants? What kind of person are you? People are looking at who you are and, like it or not, they are sizing your up. You may be up for a promotion, but they do not think you have the character for the next level. You may be in a relationship, but your significant other does not think that you are ready to settle down. Your customers may think you are great to hang out with but not someone that they can trust with the million-dollar deal. I struggled in my life with being too haughty and sarcastic and I found that people, especially employers, would like me for certain projects or positions, but not the important ones, in my eyes.

I took it upon myself to become the person I wanted to be in order to achieve the things I wanted to in my life. I had to make the character changes that I had been putting off or not seeing as important. I had to learn about humility. I had to learn how to handle things with less importance on me and more on the team or others. I had to start being less sarcastic, less of the funny guy because I was not going to be a comedian for the rest of my life. I wanted to be someone that could be taken seriously and left in charge. Changing your persona is not an easy thing or something to be taken lightly. If you want to be the funny guy, be the funny guy. If you want to be a serious leader, be that. If you want to enjoy life and be great at sales, then be that. What is it that holds you back from being the person that you want to be?

What is my persona? Do I need to it make changes to it? How can I make the changes in my character today that will help me be a better person with a better persona?

LEARNING THROUGH OTHERS　　　　　　　　APRIL 28

"Learn from the mistakes of others, you can't live long enough to make them all on your own." – Eleanor Roosevelt

I was a teenager once and I am sorry that I put my parents through that pain. I knew a lot and was not able to listen to others and learn from them because I knew a lot. When you realize that you may know a lot, but you do not know it all, then you are capable of listening and learning from others. When I got older, I felt that I had lived long enough to give everyone advice too! People do not always want to hear your thoughts or input on how they ought to do something. Maybe they want to figure it out for themselves.

When my daughter was about three or four, we were teaching her about the stove and how it can be hot, especially when we are cooking on it. She did not want to hear the wisdom that we gave and chose to see for herself if the stove was hot. We did not allow her to touch the stove. To prove her point, she made the choice to touch the stovetop and was quicker than us at this particular moment. She found out and was able to teach herself about stoves. Thankfully, she did this when we could help lessen the damage. Some things may be obvious for us to learn from others.

I found this quote was quite profound to me. I had not thought about all the time it would take for me to learn from all of life's lessons. Thankfully, I do not have to and neither do you. You get the opportunity to learn from others, whether through books are conversations, we get the chance to learn from others.

Today, I will learn from other's mistakes so that I can make my life easier, and I will not have to make so many on my own.

ACCEPTANCE   APRIL 29

"Acceptance doesn't mean resignation; it means understanding that something is what it is and that there's got to be a way through it."
– Michael J. Fox

Too often we think that acceptance equates to resignation. We can accept things or people's ideas/beliefs and not compromise ourselves or our beliefs. Acceptance is just being able to let go of the idea that we have to control that situation or person. I spent a number of years studying the bible and felt like I needed to make sure that others believed the same way I had come to believe. I learned to accept that there is more to life than being right and "forcing" that belief on others. Acceptance has taught me patience and love.

Often in sales, we want people to come around to our way of thinking or beliefs because we could not be wrong, and we have the best ideas and solutions to their current problems. Though your ideas are good and helpful they may not work best for someone else in their situation. It does not mean you do not work hard at your craft and get better at learning how to sell but it does mean that you learn how to accept others and their ideas to make you a better, more well-rounded person. In the movie Miracle on 34th Street, Santa Clause is not afraid to say that his store did not have an item or that it was offered by the competitor down the street for a better price. People looked at that as being wrong because it drove business away from Macy's, his current employer. Turned out to be some of the best advice he could have given to people because it showed he cared more about the person and gave them the proper solution to their situation. Have you ever done that? Have you ever advised someone to go with your competition, not out of spite or because of the job, or because the customer was going to be difficult to deal with, but because it was the best for the customer, and they actually had a better solution? That is *true* acceptance!

Today, I will look at things for what they are and find ways to either improve what I can or accept the difference.

Adversaries   April 30

"Every character needs an adversary - one who is both challenging and a contrast for the hero. The best adversaries reveal something about the character they're contrasting." - Greg Rucka

Who are your adversaries? In business, we have competitors/adversaries that we get to work against quite a bit. If you do not have any adversaries, you are doing something wrong. Adversaries are good and helpful if you maintain a healthy relationship with them. Adversaries help you get better and can spark the right competitive juices to help you learn about yourself and how you can improve your process, pitch, or even your character.

I had a couple of regular characters when I was in HVAC sales. I would see them when they came out of a customer's home, or I would see them at regional meetings. I spoke to some of them as they were friendly competitors, and others not at all. It helped me to constantly ask and answer the questions, what did I do right and what could I do better? My customers would help me understand who my competitors were if I asked the right questions. Like Sherlock Holmes and Professor Moriarty, they needed each other. You need your adversaries, and you need to learn how to work with them to improve lest they always win, and you cannot have that.

Today, I will seek out ways that my adversaries can teach me how to improve.

MAY

Affirmation   May 1

"I'm an artist; affirmation is like catnip to me." – Andrea Riseborough

Are you someone that feels the tug and need for affirmation? I am that type of person. I can be left to do a job and when I am finished it is not enough for me to know that I have done a good job. I like to hear that other people think I did a good job as well. Once I hear that I can move on but if I do not hear that I start to wonder if they think I am doing a decent job. That can lead to too many conversations in my head that usually do not end well for me.

Now, I do not need affirmations all the time, but it helps me and my psyche to know that I am on the right path. You may find this to be true for you as well. We all need to know that we are doing a good job, not a parade or big celebratory type of party in our honor. We just need to hear the words, "well done!" It has been said that you should do unto others as you would have them do unto you. Sometimes we do not get because we do not give. We do not give praise or affirmation to others and therefore we do not receive it ourselves. Can you be that person for someone today? When we start to do this for others, it is amazing to see how things come back around to us in the same form as we give. If I am sincere in my praise or affirmations to others it seems to come back to me from places that I would never expect it to come from.

Today, I will look for ways that I can give praise or affirmations to others and be open to the affirmations I receive.

You Can Be Vulnerable   May 2

"You can't base your life on other people's expectations." – Stevie Wonder

At times, it can be hard to be genuinely you when you are with other people. We want to compete or show others our good side. Growing up we are usually taught to be tough and to hide our feelings. Being vulnerable can be hard and feel very awkward. Being vulnerable means being teachable, moldable, and willing to learn. We are not afraid if someone sees our faults. We welcome the correction so we can be better than we were yesterday. Are you willing to be wrong? Are you willing to make the correction, even from someone that you may not like, respect, or get along with? Can you see the truth even when not everything they may be saying is not true? We want to defend ourselves for the "right" things we have done and forget the truths, no matter how small they are. Vulnerability is a strength, not a weakness that we get to possess.

Today, I will look for ways that I can allow myself to be vulnerable and see it as a strength, not a weakness.

ANSWERS   MAY 3

"A good teacher isn't someone who gives the answers out to their kids but is understanding of needs and challenges and gives tools to help other people succeed." – Justin Trudeau

When I was given the opportunity to be a leader for a company, I was not one to give people the answers straight away. I was the person that helped them to find the answer. I was not trying to be cruel, but I want people to have the ability to find the answers they need themselves versus having to get the answer from someone. There are some that like to be lazy and only get the answers and not do the work to find the answer. These were the ones that were frustrated by my way of answering them. Sometimes it is ok to just get the answer, sometimes that is all we want. A simple yes or no, or one-word answer so that we can move on with whatever it is that we think is more important at the time. When you take the time to find the answers it can be more satisfying or even helpful for you. Simply relying on others to give you the answers does not make you smarter, but only makes you look smarter for a time. Depth of knowledge comes from digging deeper than just the answer.

Today, I will not just ask for the answer but will look deeper into the answer to gain knowledge beyond what I was looking for.

CAN OR CANNOT, DO OR DO NOT   MAY 4

"If you hear a voice within you say, 'you cannot paint,' then by all means paint, and that voice will be silenced." - Vincent Van Gogh

There are times in our lives when we are faced with opportunities. We can choose to do something or choose not to do something. Sometimes those choices are easy. Do I ride this skateboard down this steep street or not? The obvious answer here is, of course, you do! At least that is what my younger self decided. But I would not do that today because I "know" too much or bad things that could happen to me. I would not discourage a younger version of myself to do it either because there are lessons there that can only be learned by taking the opportunity. Do I try and make this relationship work? Do I take this job or that one?

The other side of this decision-making dilemma is, can I? Can you do this or that? When you are posed with this question in your own head, who are you going to listen to? Can is a matter of capability. Can I ride my skateboard? I could when I was much younger, and I probably can now. However, if I were to do that now the pain is going to be far more than it would have been when I was younger. Can I work on this relationship? Can I do this job? The voice in your head is going to say yes or no. Which one will you listen to? Which one helps you to grow, and which one causes you to shrink?

We can be our own worst enemy when it comes to decision-making. We can also be our biggest cheerleader, fan, or support system. Which will you choose because it is a choice? Will the choice hold you back or propel you forward? Will it cause you inner turmoil or excitement? You can if you want! You will do it if you want! The choice is yours whether you like it or not. You are the architect of your future, the planner of your destiny.

Today, I will make choices that help guide me down the path that I want to go. The path is mine to make as I move forward because I can do a lot of things, whether I have tried them before or not.

BALANCE   MAY 5

"Balance, peace, and joy are the fruit of a successful life. It starts with recognizing your talents and finding ways to serve others by using them."
– Thomas Kinkade

Balance is difficult to find and maintain at times. If you have ever been on a balance beam you can understand what it is like to have your balance one moment and lose it the next simply because we shifted our weight. The beam has not moved but something within us has. Life is very much like that. We are in balance and things are going smoothly then we lose balance and we have gotten off track. Too often in life, we do not realize that we are off track until we have been off for a while. That makes it more challenging to get back on track. What is it that throws you off track, your job, your relationships, your personal habits? All of these can throw us out of balance, and we are no longer at peace. Like when you were on the balance beam, and you are in balance things are good. You feel great and have confidence. When you are out of balance you feel anxious, fearful, or even desperate. Find a way to get back into balance and learn what it will take for you to stay close to that balance point.

Today, I will take the steps I need to get in balance in my life and stay as close to balanced as I can.

BASKING IN THE MOMENT   MAY 6

"I'm thankful for every moment." – Al Green

When you have momentous victories in your life, do you take the time to sit in the moment and appreciate the victory? I am not talking about being an arrogant jerk and throwing yourself a party but taking the time to understand the breadth and depth of what you just went through? Sometimes we need to take the time to stop and appreciate the moment, to truly reflect on the success. Understand the hard work or the stroke of luck that afford you the opportunity to get what you got. Throughout your life, you will have those opportunities to breathe in the enormity of a job well done. Take the time to look around and remember where you are and note the smells, tastes, and emotions associated with that victory. Maybe you go and celebrate with loved ones with a special meal, a special bottle of wine or bourbon. Making good memories is the key. Basking in the moment is more than just celebrating a win but creating a memory that will serve you well in the future. Make sure that you do this for yourself and for those around you. Show your appreciation for those that helped you achieve your goal or big win. You want to remember these times and making a special memory will help you recreate that in the future as well.

Today, I will find a way to bask in the moments to help create memories that will last a lifetime.

NEXT! May 7

"Life is about not knowing, having to change, taking the moment and making the best of it, without knowing what's going to happen next."
– Gilda Radner

Life is full of "nexts". We just sold a job and turned in the paperwork and now we are ready for the next one. We just ran mile two and we are moving on to mile three. We successfully or unsuccessfully finished a challenge, and we are ready for the next one. Like the quote states above, we have no clue what is going to happen next. We have done our work and we know what we are hoping for or what we expect but that is not always the way things will turn out. Are you excited about the next client, or opportunity? I enjoy not knowing what is going to happen next so that I get a chance to learn something new.

I was consulting with a client, and I had some expectations based on previous consults I had done. About five minutes into the conversation, I learned that I was being asked about things that I had not been asked before and I was learning about a potential new product that could help our world, especially during the COVID-19 laced situation. Whatever your view on next has been maybe it is time to look at it differently? Maybe it is time to look at this as a fresh start. You could learn something new, or you could help someone learn something new.

Today, I will find a way to enjoy the next thing that comes my way not knowing what it may bring.

AWARENESS   MAY 8

"Let us not look back in anger, nor forward in fear, but around in awareness." – James Thurber

Do you do more than just notice things and have an awareness in you that is able to see and feel things around you? Awareness is consciousness. When you have the ability to be aware it can give you clarity, especially in certain situations. When you are aware you are living in the present and not in the past or the future. You are able to listen to your senses and the things around you and be a part of the experience. You are listening. When you are listening, you are in a good place. You are able to put other things out of your head so that you can hear what is being said and what is going on around you. Then you are truly aware.

Today, I will find ways to improve my awareness, not just conscious of my surroundings but truly aware of what is going on.

Blindness   May 9

"We're blind to our blindness. We have very little idea of how little we know. We're not designed to know how little we know." – Daniel Kahneman

Being born without sight or losing your sight would be a challenging thing to deal with. However, we can create our own blindness over time if we are not careful. We can put up walls or defenses that do not allow us to see things as they really are. That is when we become prideful and arrogant so that we cannot see with clear sight. We become blind to our own blindness. I liken this to the Pharisees in Jesus' time. They were part of a very knowledgeable group that studied the scriptures and made sure that they were well educated. However, they wanted a king to raise them up in power, to be over people like the Romans. They were so blinded by their own desires they were willing to kill someone because he challenged their belief system and desires. We can do the same thing when we do not want to listen to someone that has a different thought or an opinion that does not align with ours. We can close off our ears and eyes physically and emotionally and not hear or see what they are saying causing us to be blind. It is hard to strip away all that you know and listen to a person that is blind. Can you do that? Can you hear what they have to say? Some of these things are meaningless to you or for you. Some of them are important for you to see and hear.

Today, I will find a way to remove the obstacles that prevent me from being able to hear and see what others are saying.

Chances   May 10

"Take chances, make mistakes. That's how you grow. Pain nourishes your courage. You have to fail in order to practice being brave." – Mary Tyler Moore

In sales, you take chances. You make mistakes and you figure it out. What about your day-to-day life, are you taking the chances with that too? Sometimes we take chances where we do not need to, and we do not take chances where we need to.

One late Friday afternoon, I was on a sales call with a couple trying to help them relace both of their HVAC systems. I had plans in the next couple of hours and I needed to finish the sales call, but I wanted to help them. I created a proposal that I believed was a safe choice for them and me. As I was doing the presentation, I knew that there were more options. I stopped and said that there were two other options that I had not mentioned, and I showed them what they were. When I started explaining what the top-of-the-line system did and how it worked, the wife said, "I want that one." It was the top-of-the-line system, but she understood how it worked because I took the time to share it with them. I took a chance and it paid off. What does it take for you to take chances, step out on faith and make the decision to move forward?

Today, I will find ways to take chances that will help me move forward.

CHOICES   MAY 11

"You write your life story by the choices you make. You never know if they have been a mistake. Those moments of decision are so difficult." – Helen Mirren

We are faced with a series of choices every day, multiple times a day. Some need a crystal ball in order for us to understand what path is the right one. Others are noticeably clear due to past decisions, moral or ethical beliefs. The reality of that is that no matter what we chose we are making the right choice. Sometimes we need to learn from things and sometimes we need to move past things. We can look back at decisions we made in our life and think we made bad choices, and though that may be true, you learned from that choice. Most people when asked if they could go back in time to change something in their life would say no. That is because that seemingly poor decision, and others, were what made them the person that they are today. I have made some decisions that in hindsight may not have been the best choice for me. However, at the time I did not know all the facts or information that would have given me better insight into what would happen as a result of that decision. I would not change that decision at the time that I made it because I learned from that choice and many more. One Sunday I drove back to college by myself. I was learning how to be more spiritual and decided to take some time to pray during the drive. I rolled up the windows and turned off the radio. I did not intentionally close my eyes, but it was a hot day, and it was about three in the afternoon when my food coma usually was beginning. As I prayed, I fell asleep at the wheel and my car started to drift across the two-lane road into oncoming traffic. Luckily, no one was seriously injured. Though the situation was not good at the time, it taught me to be well-rested before taking even a three-hour drive again.

Today, I will see the decisions that I make today in my life as opportunities to learn for the future.

COMMITMENT   MAY 12

"The difference between involvement and commitment is like ham and eggs. The chicken is involved; the pig is committed." – Martina Navratilova

When you are committed to something, you are all in. You cannot commit to something when it's convenient or if you plan to abandon the project when it gets too hard. It just means that you were never really committed to it in the first place. If you have ever been on a sales call and you are so-so about trying to win the customer over, do you think you are really committed? Starting a business is scary. When I started my business, I knew what I wanted to do and where I wanted that to lead, but

I was not sure how I would get there. It made me anxious thinking about how I would get where I wanted to go but I knew I could get there if I just did what I knew I could do. Do the work and success will follow!

I have confidence in my work ethic and abilities. I have been doing it for years and had my share of success and failure, but my success outweighed the failures. Starting the business with just me needed to be a commitment on my part I was not just involved. I took the chance and started the business. Are you going to commit or just be involved? Being involved is not a bad thing but for you to really find the joy and excitement of a job well done, you must be committed.

Today, I will look at how to commit to the things I need to commit to and only be involved where I need to be involved.

DIRECTION   MAY 13

"If you don't know where you are going, any road will get you there."
– Lewis Carroll

We have probably all stepped into the kitchen at some point and thought, "now why did I come in here?" If you go out for a jog or a walk without a purpose or a route, then why are you going out? For some fresh air? Nothing wrong with that but is that why you got dressed up to go for the walk/run? In life, we can do similar types of things when we just go with the flow and do not create a plan to direct us to our destination or goal. Direction is important so that we can chart our progress. Don't wander aimlessly along the road toward something, plan your route.

Early in my career, I felt like this. I had not planned with the end in mind. I wandered in my career for a while figuring out what I did not like and what I liked. It took me a few years to figure out that I liked commission-based sales and the ability to control my income based on how hard I worked. This is not for everyone and that is ok. I liked it so much that when I was offered a sales manager position with a company, they wanted to pay me a salary plus bonuses, and I said no. I wanted to be paid 100% on commission. The owner was not sure about that until we came up with a mutually agreeable plan. When you find what you love to do you will do whatever it takes to do that.

Today, I will look for the direction that I want to set for me and my future.

WAIT FOR IT!   MAY 14

"This night is going to be Legen…wait for it…dary!" – Barney Stinson

Waiting for anything can be a challenge, even if it's something exciting. The birth of a child, the wedding day, the bonus check, the promotion, the raise, the new client are all things that we might anticipate, and hold hope for their arrival. Sometimes we cannot understand why we have to wait. The timing is not right, or we are not ready for that thing to happen. This is the challenge. Have you ever been in a situation where you went into it thinking that this will be great when this happens? Yet, when you get into the situation you realize that something is off, not right. Do you have a positive mindset that maybe the timing is not right, and it will come around, but it needs, or I need some more time? When I thought I was ready to take on more responsibility at my college job working at a pizza place on campus, I was given the opportunity to "manage" the lunch shift as the boss was going to be gone and his second was also not available. I was young and thought I had a good idea of how to make the workflow happen. I failed. The lunch rush was not something I was used to anticipating and as a result a number of the lunches were coming out later than they should have. I did not have the experience to handle the situation properly. My boss was very gracious and did not get upset with me but used it as an opportunity to teach me, and I learned from it.

Fast forward to my first opportunity to run a company. I had years of experience at this time and had been in leadership positions before, but this was going to be different because I was going to be responsible for everything, but I also had help. I was offered a position to move to the Midwest and manage all the sales in the Midwest, but we could not come to terms because they wanted me to do two regions for one region's pay, so I declined that opportunity. Then I had another opportunity to move to a smaller location that needed some help and turn around leadership. I was not ready, nor did I have the experience to turn around a company, so I declined that opportunity. Then I was given the opportunity to run a company that had been doing well and was pretty healthy but needed new leadership because the old manager was getting promoted to a larger company. I learned about timing and being patient for the right situation to come along. All of this took about a year to work itself out. I learned a lot of things in the time that I got to lead that company. We had some successes and some failures, but we learned from all of them. Sometimes when you wait for it, it can be legendary!

Today, I will learn to wait for situations to be more in line with my situation and my growth.

COMPASSION   MAY 15

"True compassion means not only feeling another's pain but also being moved to help relieve it." – Daniel Goleman

It can be easy to feel empathy when you watch a video of someone falling or getting hurt. But when was the last time you felt compassion that moved you to take action? Compassion is not always found in everyone. Sometimes you need to work at having feelings because you have trained yourself to not have feelings and to harden yourself to empathy or compassion.

When I was younger, I learned how to push my emotions aside and as a result, I was not able to have a lot of empathy or compassion for others. When I went through the deaths of loved ones and the pain of hardship, I was able to feel the feelings that came with those experiences. As I got older, I continued to learn how to feel the feelings and gain empathy and compassion for others as I watched others suffer through their losses and hardships. Use the opportunities to learn how to have empathy and compassion. Having compassion is what helps separate the good salespeople from the not-so-good salespeople. When you have empathy and compassion for people that you are working with, whether a co-worker or a client, you will be more effective at what you do, that is both in your personal life and work life.

Today, I will seek out ways to be more compassionate in all aspects of my life.

COMPETITION   MAY 16

"Obviously, it is good to have competitiveness in the team and that urge to want to beat the driver next to you, but at the same time, I think we are gonna respect each other." – Lance Stroll

Being in sales, you will naturally have a competitive spirit as one of your strengths. This can also be a weakness of yours. Being competitive can help you push through things that would normally give most people pause. You will have thought of most of the ways that you will overcome all the things that will get in your way or prevent you from succeeding. Being competitive can provide you with blinders and that may not be a good thing. Have you ever been so caught up in winning that you cannot see the obvious things around you? Like other things in your life, you need to learn how to handle the competitiveness within you. There are certain things that you get to control in your life, and how you handle yourself and your actions are some of the most important. Being competitive is helpful and can help you to succeed, just do not let it overrun you.

Today, I will look at how I can be competitive and use it in a positive way.

## Desperation											May 17

"There's nothing like desperation to sharpen your sense of focus." –Thomas Newman

Desperation can be a good motivator and can help you to focus on the task at hand. Desperation can also make you paranoid and anxious. I was a manager and one of my employees was in a tough spot. He was used to making a lot more money than when he was working with our company. He had bills to pay, and it was weighing on his mind constantly. Every time I saw him in the office, he was on edge and talking about how much he needed to make and the number of calls he needed to run. He made it clear that he was the best at closing and that his personal life was not affecting his ability to sell. As you can guess, it was having a glaring effect on his ability to sell because he was desperate and put himself under immense pressure.

We have probably all been there, felt that pressure, and did not realize that we were the ones that were applying the pressure to ourselves. Sometimes you need to take a step back and understand where the desperation is coming from so that you can do something about it. If you can get some perspective and correct the situation then you have made a move in the right direction. If you cannot fix the desperation, then you need to change your situation.

Today, I will find a way to clear the path of the desperation that is hindering me.

## Compliments											May 18

"If you live off people's compliments, you'll die from their criticism."
– Cornelius Lindsey.

Compliments are a tricky thing and so is the criticism that can come in its place. Some of us need to know that we are doing a good job. That validation can mean more than we realize. Others do not need this information because they believe no matter what they are doing their best all the time. We all have been in a situation when we have done a great job and a not-so-great job, deserving a compliment or a criticism, depending on the situation. However, we can get caught up in the need for the compliment. If we do not get the compliment and get the criticism, it can crush us. Even if we just do not get the compliment, it can have negative effects on us, especially if we have been doing things well for a while and we do not get any compliments. If you are on the giving end of either of these, you may need to understand the power of your words and what they can do to others. Find ways to compliment people and not criticize if possible. If you need to correct someone, find a way to do it privately and not in front of others. Compliments and criticism are things that need to be done and when done properly can help people.

Today, I will look for ways to compliment more and criticize less.

CONFRONTATION   MAY 19

"I'm opinionated, and I'm comfortable with confrontation. I'm very happy to say if I believe the opposite of what you think." - Jodie Whittaker

How do you handle confrontation? I used to get very uncomfortable when I was confronted in most situations. Part of it was because I do not like to be confronted and some of it was because of the person confronting me and how they confronted me. Hopefully, you are comfortable in your own skin and can let people know when you do not agree with them and not feel like you are arguing with someone with raised voices and raised tempers. There is nothing wrong with confronting people and sharing your difference of opinion.

I have a friend that enjoys raising people's ire, especially online. He will post something that is inflammatory and argue with anyone that wants to argue, but then he will only argue with someone if it fits his agenda. Confrontation is a part of life, and you can try to avoid it but that will not always work out well for you and can stunt your emotional growth. If you can learn how to handle confrontation, then you can learn how to grow through the challenge.

I have learned to handle confrontation and when I need to, I have learned to confront people and situations with little anxiety or stress. Take a deep breath, defuse the situation so that you can hear what you need to hear and address only the things that need to be addressed and try to remove any personal feelings that may prevent you from hearing what you need to help you gain the understanding and knowledge you need. If you are one of the people that like to confront people, look at how you confront people. Is it harsh or over the top in terms of aggressiveness? Is there a better or more effective way to get the job done? If you are overly aggressive, do you think you are getting your message across, or are you simply intimidating people?

Today, I will look for ways to deal with the confrontations that come up in my day, determine whether I am being too confrontational or not, and adjust where I can.

CONFIDANTES   MAY 20

"We tell our triumphs to the crowds, but our own hearts are the sole confidants of our sorrows." – Edward G. Bulwer-Lytton

Having a confidante or being a confidante to someone is a valued position. You give or receive secrets. You build a relationship with someone, and you have a deep trust that goes beyond the average friendship. You are able to show restraint and not share what you have learned about someone, even if it is innocuous or mundane to you it means a lot to that person that entrusted it with you. Likewise, when you trust someone with a secret of yours you want to know that it will not go anywhere beyond the confines of your conversation with that person. If you do not have someone to share these types of things with then you might have to look at your ability to share secrets with others. Trust is a two-way street and if you are not trustworthy then who will share their confidences with you?

Today, I will look at the people that I trust and see who my confidantes are. If I do not have one, I will find out what it will take for me to get one. I will also look at how I can be that for others. When the time is right, I can be a strong confidante to others.

Energy   May 21

"Life begets life. Energy creates energy. It is by spending oneself that one becomes rich." – Sarah Bernhardt

Where does your energy come from? Does it come from the good things that happen to you during the day? Maybe it comes about by a song that inspires you. Sometimes you notice a lack of food has drained your energy but that is still different than what I am talking about here. Your energy can be felt by others throughout the day and people can feed off that energy, whether good or bad. In sales, your energy can help you or can be your downfall. When you are meeting with a client and you have no energy, the customer can see that and picks up on that energy. It can negatively affect them to the point where they do not want to work with you. You can be full of energy and the customer picks up on that and it overwhelms them. How aware are you of your energy especially when you are with others? Find your energy and work with it. Make it what you want it to be. It can be cheerful or peaceful or any number of things but whatever it is, it is yours!

Today, I will see my energy as what it is, mine. I get to share that with others, and it can have any number of outcomes. The question remains, will it be to help others?

Contributing   May 22

"It takes a caring community to raise a child that will be a whole person and a contributing citizen." – Jessye Norman

When you hear the word contribute, what comes to mind? Does it pain you to think about it and make you cringe, or does it give you a sense of excitement and joy? For a number of years, I did not look at this idea as something positive. "Contribute" had such a negative connotation for me. I was speaking to a friend and when I had told him a little bit about my life, he said you need to talk about that more. How you want to contribute to people and things and companies and causes.

My high school coach sat down with each of us after our season ended to discuss our future, like college ball. I told him and the other coaches that I wanted to play football in college, and he said that you will never play football at a large college. I was crushed and thought, he does not know what he is talking about. I chose to walk on to the University of Illinois football team, which means I did not receive a scholarship from them, so I had to try out for the team. The team had a few tight ends at the time, and they gained a couple more top players in the country that year and in the next couple of years to come. I just wanted to contribute in any way I could. I played college football, got two varsity letters, and played in the Peach Bowl. Sometimes, just being able to contribute can help. Do you need to be in the spotlight, or can you be an individual contributor and be okay with that? Are you willing to help, no matter the recognition or the outcome? We may not always win when we contribute but will you be part of the team to help others?

Today, I will find ways to contribute to others, whether in the workplace, at home, even to a stranger.

Control Issues   May 23

"You don't have to make life happen. In fact, you can't. Let go and let it happen." – Melody Beattie

We are often faced with people and situations we want to control. Maybe not on the surface, but subconsciously we want to take control so that we can have a hand in the outcome. Essentially, we are trying to make life happen. Why do we want to control everything in life? Are we afraid of what might happen if we let things play out? Are we afraid of the possibility that the outcome will force us to have some unpleasant thing to deal with or is it that we are afraid that we just do not know what the outcome will be and that alone scares us? We want to control the outcome so that we will feel better about knowing what will happen next. I am saddened at the thought that I used to want to control things like that. I was afraid of the outcome, the result, or the very thing that I might have to learn as a result of the outcome. When I was able to learn how to let things go and let life happen and unfold the way that it is supposed to, then I was a happier, and mentally healthier person. I am not in charge, and I do not have to be to control my happiness or another person's happiness. I am not in control of their happiness, even as a parent with my children. The bigger question is, what do we get to do with all that time we spend trying to control life, situations, or people?

Today, I will stop trying to control situations or people around me and focus on what I can control, which is me.

Devotion   May 24

"I would like to tell the young men and women before me not to lose hope and courage. Success can only come to you by courageous devotion to the task lying in front of you." – C. V. Raman

Devotion, by definition, is the love, loyalty, or enthusiasm for a person, activity, or cause. We have all felt devoted to a person, whether a parent, a friend or a lover. Likewise, we have probably felt devoted to a sports team or athlete that we enjoyed watching. Hopefully, we have felt that way about our work as well. We show our devotion in different ways but mostly by the time that we give to that person, activity, or cause. We work late, we spend hours with friends and family, we watch every event that we can to support our favorite player or team. When you are not devoted to something or someone, then you do not want to spend time with them or spend time working on that relationship. I liken this to the salesperson that does not want to role play or learn about their competition. If you are not devoted to sales and learning how to get better, then why do you do it? Being in any career path takes a certain level of devotion. You must spend time perfecting your craft, whether it is sales, sports, parenting, accounting, marketing, etc. If you are in a relationship with someone you have to spend time getting to know that person to develop that relationship. Devotion is about doing something that is important to you. What are you devoted to and what do you want to be devoted to? Hopefully, you can answer both parts with the same answer.

Today, I will look at how my devotion shows itself in my life. If need be, I will change the ways that I show my devotion, not to be more visible, but to show how devoted I am to the things that are important to me.

The Pessimist, The Optimist, And The Realist   May 25

"The pessimist complains about the wind; the optimist expects it to change; the realist adjusts the sails." – William Arthur Ward

There are often three distinct views of people. One is skeptical and may not be able to see how things are going to be different. One is overly positive that things will change and expects things to change without their involvement. And one sees the situation for what it is and does something to make it change. Which one are you? Does it depend on the situation?

If you are a pessimist, optimist, or realist, you are probably that way most of the time. How do we change if we are a pessimist or an optimist? The first question you should ask is, are you ready to change? Then you can start work on the view that you have of a situation or the world. Instead of looking at the problem and complaining about it or expecting the situation to change on its own, maybe you could find ways to offer solutions.

Which one are you currently and which one do you want to be? How do you make the change?

Today, I will find a way to be more like a realist, seeing the situation for what it is and making changes where necessary.

Fulfillment   May 26

"The difference between happiness and fulfillment is the difference between liking something and loving something. Happiness comes from what we do. Fulfillment comes from why we do it." – David Mead and Peter Ducker

I have been in sales for over thirty years, and I have found it fulfilling most of the time. In the last several years, I was interested in doing more and being a part of the bigger picture, contributing to others successfully realizing their dreams and goals. The things that fulfill me have changed with my life experiences. We learn as we go along, and we find the things that we really enjoyed before are no longer things that we find joy in. It is not that we do not like them, we just do not like them as much as other things. We may like vanilla ice cream but once you have tasted rocky road you find more to like about it. Vanilla is good and will work in certain situations, but rocky road brings a different level of tastes and that brings joy.

To me, a career in sales has been fun and has helped me feel fulfilled over the years. Now I find something more gratifying about helping someone else find that fulfillment that they desire. Maybe you have been working in a similar position for years and now it does not seem as gratifying or fulfilling. I think some people consider this a midlife crisis. People feel unhappy and start to find a thing that will bring them happiness or fulfillment. The reality is that a new car or beach house is usually not the thing that has been missing in their life, but they cannot put their finger on the thing that is leaving the empty feeling. You do not have to go out and change your life completely, but you must make some changes to find that fulfillment. Finding little things to change can help you find the thing that is missing to help bring you fulfillment and not just happiness.

Today, I will look at the things in my life that make me happy and see if they fulfill me as well. Then decide if I need to make some changes so that my happiness can lead to finding that fulfillment.

LEARNING FROM LOSS   MAY 27

"Loss is part of life. If you don't have loss, you don't grow." – Dominick Cruz

Death and loss are shared experiences. I have experienced loss on several different levels over the years. From grandparents that were in their eighties and nineties, to a stepfather that was a mentor to me, to my younger brother, and most recently my father, each one had a different effect and impact on me. My grandparents were at an age when their death was somewhat natural though it was not easy watching them pass and feeling the empty space that the lost relationship did leave. I learned how to say goodbye and start the rest of my life without them. When my stepfather passed it was harder because it was somewhat untimely, he was in his seventies. He died from complications that occurred after a car accident. It had more of an impact as he was a mentor to me. I learned that I need to not only have one person that I look to for direction in life and business, but that maybe it was time for me to become a mentor to others. The next person that I lost was my younger brother and that was the hardest so far because we were close friends as well as brothers. My brother struggled with mental health issues and died as a result of those struggles. Life has some hardships, and we all need to ask for some help sometimes to get through the hardships. Most recent was my father who died from complications due to a recent surgery he had. He was older and though the timing seemed somewhat normal for his age it still left a hole. With his passing, I was reminded that life is fragile and losing a loved one is never easy. In all these situations I learned that sometimes you do not always know all that a person has gone through in their life until they are gone. Some are secrets that were never told or supposed to be told and some were just things that I did not know, or maybe did not want to know. When people are gone from your life, you have a space that you held for that person. We all hold space for everyone that has meaning in our lives. Some have more space than others, but it is still space. I am not sure if that space ever gets replaced. Although sometimes, I feel like that space is on a rotation, like a conveyor belt of sorts, and when it comes back towards the front it can bring smiles and some tears.

Today, I will look at the loss that has taken place in my life and the lessons that I can and have learned from it.

NETWORKING   MAY 28

Networking has been cited as the number one unwritten rule of success in business. Who you know really impacts what you know." – Sallie Krawcheck

What does networking look like for you? Do you find it frustrating because it involves being around a lot of people and conversations about things you do not like? Is it energizing to see a room filled with people all wrapped up in conversations that appear to be meaningful and deep? I have found it to be both for me at different times. Although I have an extrovert type of personality, I can find networking events to be overwhelming. I want to go sit in the corner of the room and let the noise of the room provide a type of white noise effect as I drift into a numbing type of people watching. At times, I am not interested in having a bunch of conversations that just scratch the surface of who I am and who they are. But I am interested in finding a connection with people and learning how I can contribute to what they are trying to achieve. Do I know someone that can help them and could be a good person to connect them with so that they can help each other out? Can I hold space for this person in front of me because they are trying to start up their company? They do not want to be here, but they are really trying to get out of their own head so that maybe they can meet someone that can help them.

Networking can open doors for you that you were not aware of. It can open your mind to new ideas and thoughts that you were not able to find on your own. I have found that when I attend a networking event with the goal of helping people rather than getting a bunch of connections/business cards, I feel more fulfilled and get more than I thought I could from the event.

Today, I will find a way to help others especially when trying to connect with them through networking or other means of connecting.

LOVE WHAT YOU DO   MAY 29

"Great dancers are not great because of their technique; they are great because of their passion." – Martha Graham

You know what passion is or feels like! It could be for someone or something that you do. I remember playing sports and feeling passionate about playing, whether it was football, basketball, track, baseball, or volleyball. I enjoyed playing sports. When I started working, I found a similar passion. I enjoyed sales because, initially, it was like sports to me. Early in my career, my passion was the competition and the struggle to figure out how to be successful at sales. That passion eventually shifted to helping people, though being "the one" that helped people still drove me, it was more about helping others. Over the past several years, my passion has shifted again to helping people and letting the sale happen as a result of helping others. I am finding my passion for helping people through what I do brings much more joy and fulfillment to my life than I ever thought it would. People have told me when I start telling them what I do and how I get to do it, they see the passion in me. My eyes light up, I get excited, my conversation steps up in energy. When you are passionate about what you do people can see it, hear it, and feel it. What are you passionate about and do you get to do that as a part of your career? They say that when you get to do what you are passionate about, you will never "work" a day in your life. Sometimes we have to work to support the thing that we are passionate about because we have not figured out how to monetize our passion. Sometimes we figure out much later in life and our careers what our passions are and it becomes difficult to make the switch.

Am I passionate about my job? What can I do today that will get me closer to having a career that is my passion versus just punching a timecard?

Coping   May 30

"A lot of time, people enter the most depressing situations, and they are the funniest people on earth, because they have to be. It's a coping mechanism." – Daniel Kaluuya

How do you deal with the stress? What are your coping mechanisms? Do you withdraw from friends and family, or do you engage in binge eating or stop eating for days at a time? Do you sleep or drink too much? My go-to has been to ramp up the sarcasm and get harsher with it. We learn how to cope with stressful situations when we are young. We can tend to carry through life the things we learned at a young age if we do not learn how to work through the stress in our lives. Stress can be self-induced. We have external things that put pressure on us, like work, school, or even relationships. How we manage those pressures depends on the level of stress that we feel. Some people seem to live a stress-free life while others seem to constantly be living in a pressure cooker. Learning how we can handle the stress in our lives can make all the difference in the world.

When I first became a manager, I found out that the job and the people that I managed could create some stress in my life if I allowed it. There were constant situations that required my attention and I needed to learn how to deal with the situations. The previous manager was a micromanager, and all the decisions were made by the manager, and no one else in the company was given the opportunity to make the decisions. I had to let the team members make decisions and only provide input if there was a need. When the other employees started taking on the responsibilities of making those decisions, I had less pressure. Sometimes the best way to cope with things is to meet them head-on and deal with them rather than push them to the side with other coping mechanisms.

What can I do today to remove the coping mechanisms that I have created in my life? I will start with the things that cause stress, the root problem before putting a band-aid them with the coping mechanisms.

Your Past   May 31

"Don't ignore the past, but deal with it, at your own pace. Once you deal with it, you are free of it; and you are free to embrace your life and be a happy loving person because if you don't, the past will come back to haunt you and keep coming back to haunt you." – Boris Kodjoe

I thought I had a normal childhood growing up. Though my parents got divorced before I was eight, I lived with my two brothers and my dad. We worked with my dad during the summers in his landscape company, I only knew that as normal. The lack of true emotion that ran through our house and my life was not realized until much later in life. The emotion that we got to see was mostly anger and fear-based manipulation that presented itself as love simply because that was probably taught to my father by his father and others in his life. There was not a lot of happiness or celebratory joy based on things that went well. There was not a lot of love shown or talked about. I learned to avoid talking about my emotions while I was growing up. I learned how to put them away and, as a result, I did not know how to deal with the sadness of my relationships that ended, the death of a loved one, or the eminent failures that happened in my life. I kept pushing through the feelings and shoving them to the back burner to "deal" with them at another time or not at all.

As I got into my twenties and thirties, I got to see that my childhood was less than normal, but I still did not ask people to help me understand how to deal with my past, and I was not ready to deal with it either. I used to tell people that they needed to keep moving forward in their lives because if they stopped and looked back a whole lot of stuff would catch up with them. Little did I know that when you deal with your past, you find a release from the pain and pressure that comes when you do not. Your past is what helps form the person that you become. It does not define you! Learning how to effectively talk about your past and get help, even if you need it from a professional, can help you to live a life worth living. The things lost in my childhood are no longer a burden. I have learned from them, blame no one for my shortcomings, and have been able to look towards my past as a healthy reminder of what helped me become who I am and why I do the things I do today.

Today, I will look at my past with reverence as it helped form me, but I will no longer let it define who am I am.

JUNE

Serial Perfectionist   June 1

"I'm a perfectionist. I can't help it. I get really upset with myself if I fail in the least." – Justin Timberlake

Being a serial perfectionist can take its toll on any person. You constantly want things to be perfect, but you know that they cannot be. Nothing is perfect. It is a control issue, at least with me it has been. It is the one thing that I can control, and I want it to be right, so I do not fail. I push and push for this idealistic image knowing full well that I cannot achieve it. It gets in my head and like a ravenous dog, it cannot let go. I can spend too much time working on a PowerPoint presentation because the letters just do not line up perfectly or the graphics are not just right. I know I do this and still struggle to allow it to run its course without me intervening. I have learned how to let some of that go, but it is still a challenge. Things can be good enough without my interfering. I ask myself what will the extra, whatever, add to this project, this report, this blog post, this video? If I cannot answer with something that is a value add then I am done. I cannot say everything that can or needs to be said about the subject at hand in a blog, a video, a report. I can do what I can do and then I have to move on. There are more things that need my attention. This may sound trivial as if I am fine with being mediocre. I am not. I cannot keep working on this one thing while I have many more things to do. In sales, we can be like this too. Always second-guessing what we could have said to get the client to work with us. If only I would have said this, I could have… Sometimes we need to let go and know that the thing we said or the thing we wrote in the email was enough and exactly what needed to be said at the time. We may get the chance to come back later and tell the rest of the story if it is necessary and needed.

Today, I will look at how I can let things be good enough for now and not get caught in the paralysis of perfectionism.

New Chapter   June 2

"I think every artist's next work will reflect a new chapter in their autobiography. Each album tells a story about where they were at during a particular period and how they have evolved." – G-Eazy

Sometimes we face challenges in our lives that put us in a position to evaluate where we are and where we are going in life. I am a fairly healthy person that works outs occasionally, eats healthy, and does things to take care of my body. Being a former college athlete, it is still important to me to take care of myself. I am in good shape and though I may be carrying a couple of pounds more than is ideal for me, I am not in bad health. I recently had to deal with a major health issue. I came down with COVID-19 pneumonia. I was in the hospital for a week. My life got put on hold. Friends and family were worried about whether or not I was going to be there for them tomorrow let alone the next holiday or family gathering. This all sounds dramatic, and I am not trying to make it that but that is the level that I was dealing with.

When I returned home and started to live life again as the new normal, I found myself asking, is this a new chapter or just a new verse? We mark time by events in our lives, births, deaths, other meaningful events play a role in this marking of time. This is one of those events for me. I will forever mark time by this event as it had an impact on myself and those I love. Trying to be in tune with all of this and gather what I can from it. I am finding that I can and need to be more mindful of things that I do and the ripple effect of these things that I do reach much further than I think. In all this, I am reminded of how much each of us matters, is loved, and is cared for, regardless of what we think is truly going on or how bad things might appear. You matter! Look at what you have around you today and appreciate the fact that you have even the simplest thing, a breath.

Are you facing a new chapter in your life or is it simply a new verse? Either way, know that you have the power to make it as great as you want.

ISOLATION   JUNE 3

"No one can live without relationships. You may withdraw into the mountains, become a monk, a sannyasi, wander off into the desert by yourself, but you are related. You cannot escape from that absolute fact. You cannot exist in isolation." – Jiddu Krishnamurti

Have you ever been truly isolated? Left in a room alone for hours on end with nothing really to do but maybe stare at the walls and contemplate life or just sit in your head for a time? Isolation is a very interesting thing and I found it to be rather disturbing after a couple of days. I was isolated due to quarantine, for seven days, as in left in a room and not able to leave that room. I had medical people that would come in and do what they needed to and leave within minutes, probably no more than five minutes at a time and this happened about every three or four hours. I got to be alone the rest of the time. I had a tv in the room but after the first few hours that become nothing more than a time suck that did not seem to help much at all. I was able to think about things for a couple of days but then I was lost in thought about nothing. I found it hard to focus on things I wanted to focus on. Friends, family, and work were all things that I would try to bring up but seemed at a loss to dwell on them for any amount of time. Some of the lack of ability to focus could have been on the illness but I felt like some of it was the result of the isolation and the loneliness associated with that. How often do you put yourself in some sort of isolation? Do you place yourself in time out to get away and recharge or regroup and if so, that is probably a good thing to do? Hopefully, you will not have the opportunity to learn what it is like to be placed in isolation, away from the world for more than a couple of hours or a couple of days. The lack of human interaction was something that was probably the hardest to deal with. I found it difficult to have any meaningful conversation while in isolation. I found it difficult to connect socially and that was very difficult to wrap my head around. It took leaving the isolation to realize it and to put a finger on it.

Today, I will look at the time I spend alone and make sure that I am getting the human interaction that I need to maintain a healthy perspective on my life and those around me.

INTENTIONAL GRATITUDE — JUNE 4

"I don't have to chase extraordinary moments to find happiness - it's right in front of me if I'm paying attention and practicing gratitude." – Brené Brown

Sometimes we can get caught up in what we are doing that we forget to look around and see what is happening right before our very eyes. We lose sight of the wonderful things that are presenting themselves every day. In sales, we can get caught up in the daily routine of going to the client meeting, doing the presentation, making the sale, turning in the paperwork, and then going home to start our evening routine before bed. We can forget to take a deep breath as we step out of the office and appreciate the fresh clean air that is before us. We can lose sight of the beauty of the trees or the flowers along the road that we are traveling.

Do you take the time to notice these little things? Do you stop and take a breath, see the flowers blooming on the roadside, and appreciate all the memories that are spawned as a result of seeing those things? I have found myself on a golf course with a client and admiring the rolling mountains in the background. I have been able to see the person smiling and it reminds me that I have people in my life that make me smile and it brings the joy of those memories to mind. I have been able to find gratitude for the little things that I have in my life because dwelling on the things that are negative can destroy all that joy in a short amount of time.

Today, I will take time to be intentionally grateful for the little things I see and hear. I will make the effort to find the good around me so I can feel the joy that this world can bring.

Diligence   June 5

"What the world really needs is more love and less paperwork." – Pearl Bailey

Every day we are faced with tasks. Things that stand in our way of getting something else done. In sales, when you sell something, that is when the work begins. You usually have paperwork to fill out and turn in so that the process of delivering the product or service that you just sold can get into the customer's hands. I know people who hate paperwork so much that they put it off until the last possible minute. There are a couple of things that you can gain by doing your paperwork as soon as possible. When I was in HVAC residential sales, as soon as I made the sale I would go to my vehicle and fill out the appropriate paperwork before I left the customer's house, if possible. I used to wait until I got home, spent time with my family, and waited until everyone went to bed before I finished my paperwork. That meant that I was usually up later than I wanted to be and should have been. When I did the paperwork before I left the customer's house, by the end of the day, I got to go home and do whatever I wanted to do and not worry about the paperwork. There are other things like this that we all get to deal with. Whether it is filling out paperwork, filing the report, updating the spreadsheets, doing the PowerPoint presentation, etc. when we do it now, or as soon as possible, it takes the burden off our shoulders, and we can work a lot more effectively throughout the day. If you do not do that task, then you are constantly thinking about how you need to do that one thing.

Today, I will do the things that I can as soon as possible, so they do not hang over me like a cloud all day.

Ideals   June 6

"Ideals are like the stars: we never reach them, but like the mariners of the sea, we chart our course by them." – Carl Schurz

We can get frustrated when we set our hearts on our ideals and do not achieve them. Ideals are supposed to be like goals that we can shoot for. Like shooting for the stars and hitting the moon, we can set an idealistic goal, and if we hit something that was along the way, out of our realm of possibility before, does that mean we have grown? Hopefully, you can see that.

Too often we get caught up in the mindset that we did not hit the ideal/goal, but that is the idea behind a goal/ideal is to set our sights on something that we did not think was possible to achieve? When I was beginning in sales, I had never been on straight commission. I always had a base salary plus bonuses or commissions. When I was given the opportunity to take a job that was one hundred percent commission, I was intimidated, and as a friend of mine and I were talking about the potential income that I could make. I was looking at making the leap in income that would have nearly doubled what I was making at the time. He tried to keep my mind in the real world and said what if you only make twenty-five or fifty percent more than what you are making now, are you ok with that? Of course, I said yes, but I was fully intent on doubling my income. That first year I did just what my friend had said and only saw a twenty-five percent increase in my income. That was still an increase and a decent one at that. I would have never seen that opportunity if I were to stay at the other job. I was able to increase my income and spent the next sixteen years of my career in HVAC after that. Sometimes we need goals/ideals to get us out of our own way or even a rut. When we set our ideals or goals, we can push ourselves to do more than we thought we were capable of doing. We get to see what we can achieve if we set our hearts and our minds on things far greater than just us.

Today, I will set my ideals/goals with the intent of improving myself beyond where I am today.

Mistakes   June 7

"Experience is simply the name we give our mistakes." – Oscar Wilde

How do you view your mistakes? Do you get angry that you made a mistake, again or even for the first time? Hopefully, you can see the bright side of making mistakes. You should gain something when you make a mistake, and that something is wisdom or experience. You should be able to look back and say how can I do that differently, so I do not make that same error? Sometimes that is hard to see what we can gain from a situation especially when it is so raw or fresh in our minds.

I tend to be an overthinker, so making mistakes can sometimes put me in a tailspin because I do not understand how I could have made that mistake in the first place. I thought about this situation six ways from Sunday and I missed that. But when you are able to separate yourself from the situation and look at it with a purity of heart, you can see what happened and how you can correct it. Mistakes are not a big deal unless it is harmful to your health or someone else's. You can do things differently and you get the chance when you make a mistake. Step back, look at the bigger picture and see how you get to do it differently, better next time.

Today, I will see the mistakes that I make as simply an opportunity to grow and change.

Dealing with the Source   June 8

"We are too busy mopping the floor to turn off the faucet." – Unknown

I have been the victim of my own circumstances. I can get caught up in trying to fix the problem, but I am looking at the wrong end of the horse, so to speak. We tend to look at the problem at hand and deal with it instead of looking at the source of the problem and dealing with that. Typically, in sales, we are tasked with finding a solution to a problem. If we ask the right questions, we can actually find out the source of the problem and then find a solution for that. If we do not ask the proper questions, we will only put a band-aid on the situation. I have been in thousands of homes throughout my career in HVAC. Meeting with people and listening to the difficulties they are having with heating or cooling their home. I got to the point where I could ask a few questions and look around the home and could come up with the source of the problem that was not found by others because they simply wanted to just replace the equipment and that would "fix" the problem. Sometimes the problem is right in front of our faces, like turning off the faucet to stop the water from getting on the floor. Sometimes we need to look a little deeper and ask a few more questions. We can start with something simple like, why is there water on the floor? This can lead to, is what is the source of the water on the floor, i.e., is there a faucet on, a toilet that overflowed, etc. If nothing is on or overflowing, then we have to dig deeper. Did someone spill a glass of water? Do not just assume that the water just appeared, and we will get rid of it by mopping it up.

Today, I will look for the source or the root of the problem that I am trying to solve. I will ask the proper questions and not be satisfied until I find the source.

LEARNING татTO LET GO   JUNE 9

"It doesn't take a lot of strength to hang on. It takes a lot of strength to let go." – J. C. Watts

Letting go is not as easy as it sounds. If you are holding on to a plane that is flying at ten thousand feet and you have a parachute, then yeah you might be ok. If you are holding on to a past relationship in hopes that you might still get back together and the other person has moved on and is in another relationship, then yes you probably should let go and move on. If you are holding out hope that a client is going to work with you and yet you cannot get in touch with them, they are not returning phone calls or emails, then maybe it is time to move on. Sometimes you need someone in your ear to let you know it is safe to let go. When you find the strength to let go it can be liberating. It can feel like the weight of the world has just been removed from your shoulders. Sometimes we hang on so tight that we forget that there are other things waiting for us to get to, things that are far better for us and maybe more prosperous.

I went to work for what I thought was the perfect company for me. We had a similar why statement, they were under the leadership of a man that genuinely believes in making employees a priority, they make a really good product and are one of the best in the world at it. I wanted it to work so bad that I made myself believe that this was the right place for me to potentially retire. People around me could see I was not happy and that I was trying really hard to convince myself that it was right, I learned this after I left the company. But it was the right company to help set me up for my next venture and to help me during what would be an incredibly challenging couple of years in my personal life. That was good for me to be at that company during that time. When I was let go by the company I was not upset because I knew it was not right for me, I was disappointed because I wanted to go on my terms, but I was afraid to let go. They helped me let go, and I am thankful! When I was able to let go, I was able to see the clear path of my next step. It became so clear that I could not deny what I was going to do and how it was going to come together. Now I cannot imagine doing anything different than what I am doing and the things I get to do are so fulfilling. When I was able to let go, I got more than I could ask or imagine in return. What are you holding on to that may be holding you or someone else back? Is there a relationship, a job, or some other obstacle that you are holding on to that may be holding you back from becoming who you want to be? What can you do to let go of those things to move in the right direction? This is not about a pipe dream but about the things or people that may be holding you back.

Today, I will find the strength to let go of what I need so that I can be open to new things that I need.

Toxic People   June 10

"As important as it is to learn how to deal with different kinds of people, truly toxic people will never be worth your time and energy - and they take a lot of each. Toxic people create unnecessary complexity, strife, and worst of all, stress." – Travis Bradberry

I have had people in my life that are toxic, and it took me a while to figure it out. I wanted to help and fix them, this is never a good idea and rarely works out for either person (at least in my experience). I had a long-time friend that lived on the other side of the country, and I had not seen this person or spent time with them in years. We went to school together for a few years and we got very close. Then they moved away, and our ideals changed, our passions changed, and our surroundings were different. We grew apart but we thought we were still the same person that we were back in school. We saw each other about twenty years later and things seemed to be back to normal as we picked up our friendship where we left off. I would not see them again for another fifteen years and this is when I got to see how different we really were. I got to see the toxicity they had in their life and were projecting, unknowingly, in their daily life. I was amazed and dumbfounded. How could this person be that way, think, and say those things? That last visit spoke volumes to me, and I realized that I could not be around them or even talk to them on the phone because I would spend the majority of the time on the phone listening to them complain about all that was wrong in their life and how they were really the victim. I tried to help a number of times but to no avail. In those last conversations, I felt like the blinders had been removed so I saw their true colors. I finally understood that there was nothing I could do and being a friend to them was only hurting me. I cut off communication with them and they got angry with me. They started to blame the other people in my life for cutting them off as well. They could not understand why I would not want to talk with them, especially since we had been friends for so long. I had to let them know it was not others that made the decision, but it was me. I eventually heard from them about 2 years later asking if we might be able to keep in touch. It was the same type of text that I had seen before, but I kept it brief on my end, knowing that I was not interested in engaging in the conversation. Toxic people tend to be bitter or angry about something or a number of things in their life.

Sometimes we are the toxic person, and we need to see that and change that, or people will not want to be around us. You are the only one that can change you. Can you see the toxic people in your life? Usually, they are someone that can bring your mood from happy to sad or angry in a split second. Sometimes you have a client that acts like this, and you have to decide, do I want to do business with them, or should I walk away? Sometimes it is better to just walk away and keep your mental health in check.

Today, I will start to remove the toxic people from my life. If I am the toxic one, then I will look for ways to change my bitterness and anger.

INADEQUACY   JUNE 11

"Women put ourselves through so much. Really, everybody does; it's not a gendered thing. I think all of us are always gonna be tortured by some sense of inadequacy, no matter what. I don't know if there's a way to tell people to not do this to themselves." – Keala Settle

Where does the feeling of inadequacy come from? For some it could come from as far back as their childhood, stemming from a lack of support or encouragement. It can also be from years of failing at a particular task. When we are not up for the task, we would rather be anywhere else. You could be making a presentation on something that you just do not feel comfortable presenting because you cannot grasp the concept and you do not believe the words coming out of your mouth. It could be the spreadsheet that you have been asked to work on again and again and you just do not like doing it because it is hard for you. It could be the written summary of the meeting, or a written document and written words are not your strong suit. You cannot write a well-worded document no matter how many times you have tried. I have felt that too! I have felt like a phony in front of a client because I did not practice what I preached, or I could not give them the best solution and so I tried to fake my way through the presentation only to lose the deal and feel worse. Instead, I should have told them to go with another vendor because my solution will not meet their needs. I have felt like the email or report that I was trying to summarize was all wrong and I was just putting down words to fill a page not doing the email or reporting any kind of justice. When I looked at the word document, I decided that I could do better, but I needed to learn how to be better. I started writing emails in multiple sessions to get better. I wrote what came to mind as if I were saying the words to them directly face to face. I just wrote everything out, then I would go back and change some of the words and remove the angry or bitter tones or things that just did not feel or sound right. I then would look at it one more time to make sure that I was clearly saying the things that needed to be said. As for my presentations, I had to practice and study my competition. I had to better myself and when I did, the lack of responses went away. I was able to say without hesitancy, I have the best solution for you, or I know that I have a product or service that will do this, that, and the other, but I am not able to meet that need of yours. I was able to remove the inadequate feelings with honest answers. Doubt and uncertainty will always make you feel inadequate. The only way I have found to overcome that is with knowledge and truth.

Today, I will find the strength to overcome the inadequate feelings that I have by gaining knowledge. When I do not have the answers, I will say that I do not have the answer, but I can get it.

Over-Promise and Under-Deliver — June 12

"They didn't want it good, they wanted it Wednesday." – Robert A. Heinlein

This is a common mistake among salespeople. They want the client to sign with them so bad that they make statements that are going to be a lie. They will promise to have things done by a certain date and it will not happen because the salesperson is not taking a realistic view of the timelines involved in delivering the product or service. They end up underdelivering on their statements. This is not the proper way to work with clients because, especially in the digital world we live in today, people write reviews, and it does not take long before you hurt the reputation you and your company had. I have found that when I am upfront with the client about the timelines and what we are able to deliver that they are good with the information that I am giving them. I have lost a number of deals because we could not commit to the dates the client needed. Air Conditioning is very important in the South. It is not something that people take lightly especially when the temperatures outside reach above the mid-eighties for more than a couple of days. If you cannot replace a system soon then people will go elsewhere and the value, you provide no longer becomes a factor. The challenge with this is that people do not understand what they give up just to have it done sooner. I learned that people can make do with window units until the system could get installed, which was another value that we brought to the table. If you cannot deliver the goods in the time that you are promising then why are you bringing it up? Learn how to bring more value to the situation or find another way that you can compete. What if you set the expectation differently and were able to look like the hero because the product came in sooner than expected or the client got more than they thought they were going to get?

Today, I will learn how to adequately under-promise and over-deliver.

Nature   June 13

"He who does not become familiar with nature through love will never know her." – Karl Wilhelm Friedrich Schlegel

Some people love to live outdoors and take in the smells and the views and be a part of nature all the time. They are at home when they are living among nature. Others do not do very well in nature. Someone once said their idea of camping was staying in a hotel near the woods. I enjoy seeing the mountains, going to the ocean, I even enjoy a good hike (nothing super difficult because I am not interested in the hike), I like to see and be around the beauty of nature. I like the views on a golf course near the mountains. I like watching the sunset on the water or seeing the sunrise on the mountains. If you enjoy this type of view or just being in nature, do not wait to go on vacation to see those things. Find a place near you that you can escape to and enjoy the quiet time. Listening to the birds or just breathing in the fresh air on the mountain. The colors of the trees or the flowers in the spring and the fall. The sand between your toes or under your feet as you walk along the water. Get out into nature and experience the sights and sounds and appreciate them for what they are, a gift.

Today, I will look for opportunities to enjoy the nature that is around me and appreciate all that it has to offer.

Proactive vs. Reactive   June 14

"You need to be proactive, carve out time in your schedule, and take responsibility for being the healthiest person you can be - no one else is going to do it for you." – Mehmet Oz

Are you more proactive or reactive? There are different points in our lives that we can lean more on one side or the other. Being reactive can get frustrating because you can feel like you are always chasing your tail, always trying to put out fires. When you are proactive you can feel like you have got things under control. In sales, you can get the same type of feelings. If you are always reacting to the clients and not anticipating what they will say or do, then you are always behind and chasing your tail. It is frustrating!

I know a number of salespeople who, when we discuss role-playing, cringe or get uptight. They freeze up and do not know what to say or they fumble all over things that they have known for years and have said a lot of times. They do this because they are reactive and not proactive. If you are proactive you want to spend time going over what the client might say or do so that when you are in a sales opportunity you will have the confidence to know what to say at the appropriate time. Not to be right but to help your customer see the value and that you just might have the best solution to their issue or concern. I love to role play because I learn something new every time. I hear something that I can use, and I start right then. I like to be one of the first to role play because if I go early, I can get my turn out of the way, and then I can sit back and watch others and learn from them. Plus, no one wants to go first when role-playing. I find it easier to learn when I am role playing too. I am in my natural habitat, as I am speaking to the client and thinking about how I can help them. Role-playing should be a natural thing for a salesperson. Much like batting practice to a baseball player, or running routes to a receiver, it is muscle memory for you to role-play. When you practice you become better and more proactive because like a good comedian, you have practiced your lines over and over until the words naturally come to you at the appropriate time. When you do not practice, you are reacting to the client and you may have the right answers, but you may not be closing the deals either.

Today, I will look for ways that I can be more proactive, taking time to practice and learn how I can better help my clients and myself.

Luck   June 15

"Luck is what happens when preparation meets opportunity." – Lucius Annaeus Seneca

Do you believe in luck or are you a believer in preparation and opportunity? Either way, you must be doing something to find this luck. I guess there is dumb luck where you did nothing to make the situation turn out the way it did, and you just happened to be there when the vending machine gave you two items for the price of one. Most times we must do some work on our end to make things go our way. We must make the calls, stop by the customer's place of business, have the conversations, and so on. I have had a number of things happen that may have appeared like luck, but I worked very hard to set things up to make things fall into place. Was I manipulating the players or the events? No, I was doing the things that I needed to do to prepare for the situation if and when it arrived. When it arrived, I was ready and stepped in. Do you prepare for things that have not happened and could happen?

You can set the stage in your mind, asking the questions in the right way, responding to their questions, asking for the close, and them signing the paperwork. Now we do not use PMI like we used to but when we role-play, we can get the same type of PMI that helps us see the positive actions happening and our successful execution of the situation. When you win a client over because you have been role-playing the situation over and over, are you manipulating the situation? Maybe you are seeing the same situation that has been played in your role-playing in a similar fashion and now you know what to say to execute it properly. Preparation meets opportunity!

Today, I will look at how I can prepare for the opportunities that will lie ahead for me. I will find ways to be lucky.

QUESTIONS   JUNE 16

"When people ask me, 'Are you happy?' I respond with, 'You've asked the wrong question.' There is a deep kind of satisfaction you get from building a company. This kind of satisfaction transcends happy, sad, hard, or easy. I seek satisfaction. I want to be positively disruptive." – David Ulevitch

How do you ask the right questions? Do you know when to ask open-ended or close-ended questions, and do you know the difference? If you have been in sales for any length of time you know the difference between open and closed questions. The first allows the responder to answer infinitely, the latter with finite words, usually one or two. Beyond the types of questions do you know how to ask the proper questions? Do you know how to get to the root of a concern for the client? Can you ask questions in such a way that does not feel like a parent interrogating a child after a night out with your friends? Can you make it conversational, or does it sound like you are reading from a predetermined list of questions? Are you listening to understand or to be understood? When we listen to the client explain what they are going through or dealing with consistently, then we can hear things that need to be clarified or discussed further.

I was on a call with a client, and he said I can see where this product could be useful in most situations. Since I was observing I was able to hear the next question, or what it should have been. What do you think the follow-up to that should have been? I was thinking it should have been, so what types of situations do you think this product would not work well? Why ask that? I want to know what he thinks are the shortcomings of the product might be. Maybe this is a chance to further show the benefits that he does not currently see, and that will turn him into a buyer. The question was never asked nor answered.

Are you able to hear the questions that need to be asked? Some people have that ability because they have been in sales for a while and have been in these scenarios before. Some are so concerned about getting through the script they are not even listening to the responses from the client. The more you practice, the more you will learn how to ask the right questions at the right time.

Today, I will make a list of all the questions that I can ask during a client visit, whether it be a discovery meeting or a product/service demonstration.

PREPARATION   JUNE 17

"I do find that there's a fine balance between preparation and seeing what happens naturally." – Timothee Chalamet

Preparation is not easy, especially when you do not like the preparation. Cooking can take a lot of prep work, playing sports has a lot of prep work, and our careers can be a lot of prep work too. We do a lot of preparation for the short number of tests that we have in our lives. When I played football, I learned that games were broken down into six or seven-second bursts of energy. There are usually sixty or seventy of these in a game. That is a very short testing period yet when I played it felt like an eternity. All the time we put into studying for school and it all comes down to a couple of one-hour tests to determine if you were able to retain the right information. In life we get the opportunity to have a career, that can vary from an office job to a c-suite job, to an outside salesperson, to a clerk at a bank. All of these have moments of downtime and moments of fast-paced, we need it done immediately moments too. We tend to not like the slower times when we are learning or having to prepare for our one shining moment to show everyone that we learned and can do our job well. How you prepare can make all the difference in the world. When we look for the chance to grow ourselves, we are preparing for the next step. We are prepping for the next big challenge. When I did not like to practice selling, handling objections, or the building value, I walked on the side of seeing what happens naturally, and sometimes that worked out for me. It showed me that I have some talent for this sales thing, and

I could probably wing it more often. The problem was when I got into a competitive situation and my peers had been practicing the ways to improve. I was losing more deals because I did not properly prepare. I got to a point where I had to learn, and I wanted to learn to get better. I was not content with losing.

Today, I will find ways to prepare myself for the things in life that are important to me, whether it is my job, my relationships, or just being a better human. I will prepare for the things that life brings to me.

Personal Pride   June 18

"I take a lot of personal pride and motivation to be able to make a difference in areas that may fall through the cracks in R&D across the industry." – Vivek Ramaswamy

What do you take pride in? Do you do work that can be seen by others? Do you make something, or install something, or do you sell something that is visible to others and has an impact on them? Whether your work is visible or invisible do you take pride in doing it the right way? When I was growing up, I got the opportunity to work for my father in his landscaping company. We would go out every day and change the way people saw their yards for their new homes. At my young age, it did not dawn on me to make things look a certain way, but it was taught to me to make things look right, do the job right so that they looked beautiful. That was the thing that I got to learn when I was young, make it look the best that you can by doing it right. I remember that feeling of personal pride when we would leave the job and the landscape had changed, dramatically! It was a different house than when we arrived that morning. It now had grass and bushes and trees that added color to the homes. I loved that about landscaping, I could see the immediate change. I took pride in that work much like my father and my brothers did. Now I am in sales, and I do not always get to see the immediate change, in the person, the company, the people's lives, that I have impacted. Maybe that is why you should always follow up with your clients to see the impact afterward. Leading salespeople, I do get to see the impact more because of the way they react to the leadership I provide, the ways that they improve because of the guidance I have shown them. All things that are visible allow me to take pride in the ways that I can have an impact. What are you doing, and do you take a personal interest in the work that you are performing? Do you have pride, a healthy sense of gratitude, and accomplishment, in the work that you are doing? If not, then what can you do to change that? Can you have a career that you can take pride in? It may take some work, and you may have to change jobs or careers, but I believe that we all can take pride in the work that we do.

Today, I will find ways to appreciate the work that I do and find my own personal pride for the things that I have done or helped provide.

POWERLESS   JUNE 19

"Words - so innocent and powerless as they are, as standing in a dictionary, how potent for good and evil they become in the hands of one who knows how to combine them." – Nathaniel Hawthorne

Have you been unable to act, move, or form a retort that would stand up against the powerfulness of what you just heard or saw? We have moments in our lives when we can feel powerless. But have you ever let yourself feel powerless? Given yourself over to the idea that you do not have any power against this thing in your life? It may be something that has beaten you, time and time again and you feel like there is nothing you can do to overcome this thing. Some people have addictions and have felt like this.

Some people have a defeatist attitude and cannot seem to see their own strength to overcome. Some of us have had failures, losses, and we struggle to feel powerless no matter what the situation. I grew up thinking that there was little that could stand in my way if I do not allow it. I felt like I had the power to control the things in my life. Being powerless does not mean weakness as many of us may believe. Allowing yourself to be powerless takes a lot of strength. Do you believe in a higher power? Maybe it is God or the universe or any number of things that you choose as a label. Do you allow yourself to submit to the higher power? If you do then you are allowing yourself to be powerless. When you do this, you are allowing your higher power the ability to help guide you. You are turning over the steering wheel and letting someone else drive. I remember a time when I was not happy with my job. I knew the time with that company was coming to an end. When my boss sent me an appointment time for nine the next morning with nothing more than my name, I knew the end was near. The thoughts were rushing through my head, but I knew what this meant. I tried to rationalize it, but I could not. When the time came for the phone call the next morning, I felt truly powerless. When my boss spoke the words that I knew were coming, I said nothing more than, "I understand." I was powerless to say or do anything more. I did not feel anger or guilt or even sadness. After I got off the phone, I realized that I felt a huge sense of relief. A burden had been lifted because I knew that I did not belong there. Things happen around me and to me which causes me to take action, and how I react is in my hands. Being powerless is not a bad thing, it means that you are removing your own power from the situation.

Today, I will look at the situations in my life and see if I need to be powerless or powerful.

Fear of Death   June 20

"Even death is not to be feared by one who has lived wisely." – Buddha

A lot of people fear death. They are afraid because no one knows what happens when the heart stops beating. If you believe in the afterlife, then you think you know what happens. If you believe in reincarnation, then you think you know what happens. But no one really knows, even those who have died for a few minutes and came back cannot explain what happens because they did not leave and experience the fullness of death. Anything that I tell you, and anyone else tells you, is pure speculation. So, why do you fear death? Is it because you want to believe that the life you are living is worthy? The life you are living here is making a difference and therefore you cannot leave this world yet. I have felt that way. I have lost people in my life at a young age and older age and each of them had a different impact on my life. A friend died around the age of thirteen, another friend in his thirties, and others have died in their eighties and nineties. So why have we lost people that were making a difference at any stage of their life? Is that the criteria for living or dying?

When you live your life to the fullest, meaning that every day you get up and do the best that you can with what you are given, then you have done all that you can do. There is nothing to fear. Does that mean that you make an impact every day? Maybe. Does that mean that you fall short some days and have failures? Maybe. Does that mean that some days you see good, and you see bad, and you are stuck between the two choices? Maybe. None of these days that were described were reasons that you should live or die. When you learn that you get to be here and the reason may be clear or not so clear, you still get to be here. That is not something to be afraid of. I have learned that I am here for an undisclosed amount of time. None of us have an expiration date on our birth certificates. You get to live without fear of death. Now is the time to go and live. If you feel like you need to change some things in your life, then make the changes. If you feel like you are living your best life, then keep on doing that.

Today, I will remove the stigma of death and the fear that I have about it. I will find the life without fear of death I am supposed to live.

SELFLESSNESS   JUNE 21

It is amazing what you can accomplish if you do not care who gets the credit." – Harry S. Truman

Do you go about your life seeing what you can get out of everyone else, or do you find ways to use your talents and abilities to help others excel or progress? Often, we are more concerned about our next promotion, our credit for doing the right thing, our self-promotion versus lifting other people up. Do you look for ways that you can help others grow or are you just about making yourself look better? Learning the value and joy of helping others to grow and mature is incredible, especially when done with no ulterior motives. This can be a hard lesson to learn when most of what you hear is, "What's in it for me?" Being selfless means loving others more than yourself. The other side of this is codependency, where you are reliant on helping others in their bad habitats or character traits. Being able to find the balance is a good thing and can be refreshingly rewarding.

Today, I will look for ways to lift others up with a pure heart and see the selfishness that I can put aside for others.

TIME   JUNE 22

"Time stays long enough for anyone who will use it." – Leonardo da Vinci

Have you ever noticed that when you *need* time it is hard to find? Yet, when you do not need time, it is always there. What activities do you do that you lose track of time while doing them? I have walked out of a sales appointment and thought how did I spend that many hours at that person's home? I have been involved in sporting events that I lost all track of time. Thankfully, it was a timed event, so it ended. I have also been a part of things where all I could do is watch the clock and wonder when is this going to end? Planning for time is very important, but it is only planning how we will use that time. Time marches on no matter how we feel about it, worry about it or try to control it. It can be easy to just let time takes its course and sometimes we need to allow time to pass over us. Times of mourning and grief, times of reflection, times of thoughtfulness, and times of meditation or prayer are all good times to let time run its course.

Today, I will be mindful of my time and what I do with the precious time that I have. What are you going to do with the time you have today? What do you want to do with the time that you have today?

STRENGTH FROM DISTRESS JUNE 23

"The real man smiles in trouble, gathers strength from distress, and grows brave by reflection." – Thomas Paine

How do you gather strength from distress? Are you calm in the storms of life? This is a character trait that you can build in your life. Sometimes you must experience the storms and go through them to realize that you can handle them better. Are you able to not get caught up in the storm and see the stillness outside of it? You must be able to still yourself before you can still others around you. When you are in a chaotic situation you have a choice to be calm and collected while the storm rages on around you so that you can clearly see the resolution. When you are able to stay in the moment and not get caught up in the emotions of the situation you gain strength. Strength can build from you staying the course every time you work through those situations. Strength builds character. "Perseverance must finish its work so that you may be mature and complete." – James 1:4

Today, I will look for opportunities to learn from the distresses in my life, not making stressful situations but learning from the ones that pop up during the day.

Open to Experiences JUNE 24

"The good part about getting older is you stop trying to prove anything to anyone, including yourself. All you are in the pursuit of is collecting experiences - beautiful, fragile little soap bubbles that you store in your heart, and every once in a while, you pull one out and gaze at the delicate pictures it shows you." - Twinkle Khanna

I am not sure the thing that taught me to be open to experiences and take chances, but it seems to always have been a part of my life. I have not bungee-jumped or gone skydiving, but I have experienced a lot of things in my life. When it comes to experiences are you willing to step out and take a chance? Do you weigh the consequences, understand them the best you can (given the situation), and step forward and say, I will give it a try? I have been able to see things and do things that still amaze me, because of their beauty, or majesty, or because I did not think I would be able to do those things. My list of "accomplishments" is not awesome by most accounts, but I do raise people's eyes when I mention a few of the things I have been able to see and do. That makes me think, and know, that I have done a few things that are different, but I have done a fraction of the things that others have been able to do. When my kids were very young, they had their favorite ten foods, and they did not want to deviate from that shortlist of things they liked. I made a rule that they needed to try something at least once before they decided they did not like it, because it may be something that they really like. If they did not like it after they had tried it, that was ok, but they had to try. They still talk about that "rule" today and how much they tried and liked as a result. I have learned that as I have gotten older, I tend to say, "why not?" to things. I am looking for the experiences now and with good reason. It is not a matter of taking huge risks that do not make sense or have not been thought through with advisors. But it is saying yes to the things that come your way when we are used to just saying no to something new and different.

Today, I will find the experience that I have wanted or needed and plan to start living for those experiences.

My Path   June 25

"My path has not been determined. I shall have more experiences and pass many more milestones." – Agnetha Faltskog

You have decided to go for a hike in a new place. You arrive and get out of your vehicle. You take a deep breath of the cool morning air. It feels great as it fills your lungs, and you feel the oxygen rejuvenate your body as you pull in the air. You put your earbuds in and start playing your inspirational music, book, or podcast to shut out the world. You walk over to the opening of the path you have chosen and see the pathway that will inspire you on your journey. You do not know where it will go and there are variations along the way. Not one path but several that you get to choose from while you go about your walk. You have no idea what lies ahead except the newness of the hike and the strength that you will feel when you have finished.

Our days can be like this. We wake up and though it is the same place, it is a new day. A day that we get to make choices. It is up to us. We all have choices every day. Sometimes we see the same people and say the same things to them when we see them. Sometimes we have an extra spring in our step, and we are feeling a little spicy and decide to mix it up a bit and use different words to describe how we are doing today. Today, we get to decide if we will follow the same path or choose a different one. If you are in sales, you will meet different people today, some may be the same. You can start the conversations with the same old tried and true greetings or you can have some fun and mix it up. You get to decide! Your path is not chosen for you even if you work at the same cubicle, with the same spreadsheets, doing the same keystrokes day in and day out. You still get to decide how your day will go. If you are open to new possibilities, your life can change even though your surroundings do not. Our path is not predetermined! Go and make your day different and choose how you want it to be.

Today, I will determine how my day will go. I will flow with the circumstantial changes that come my way and decide my path.

SURRENDER   JUNE 26

"Never give up, which is the lesson I learned from boxing. As soon as you learn to never give up, you have to learn the power and wisdom of unconditional surrender, and that one doesn't cancel out the other; they just exist as contradictions. The wisdom of it comes as you get older."
– Kris Kristofferson

Learning to surrender is a difficult concept. We have many opportunities in our lives to surrender. We can surrender to the thoughts that are in our head telling us we are not good enough, or the opposite, that we are awesome and can do anything without harm or consequence. Learning how to surrender to the positives in our lives can change the way we think, act, or even alter our overall position in life. It took me a while to understand how to listen to the proper things going on around me. As stated in the quote above, once you have learned how to never give up, you must learn the power and wisdom of unconditional surrender. Surrender does not always mean defeat.

I worked most of my career in the corporate world. Most of the companies I worked for were top in their industry and a few times I got to work for the little guy, struggling to make payroll keeping their head above water. I never thought about owning my own company because I liked the idea of someone else being responsible for the payroll, the expenses, the insurance, etc. I got the opportunity to surrender my thoughts on this idea when I was fired from my corporate job. I had been asked by a number of my customers, when are you going to start your own business? I brushed it off and thought very little about it. When I let my customers know I no longer worked for the big corporation they said, we want to work with you, and so will others. I took the weekend to think about it and concluded that it was time to surrender. People now tell me they get to see the passion in my eyes when I talk about what I get to do and how it inspires me to contribute to and inspire others.

Today, I will look for ways to listen to those around me and understand that I can surrender, and it will probably be better off for me in the long term.

BUILDING A FOUNDATION — JUNE 27

"You can't build a great building on a weak foundation. You must have a solid foundation if you're going to have a strong superstructure." – Gordon B. Hinckley

We are currently living in a world of instant gratification. We want things now and do not want to wait. We have things around us to support this type of thinking. We have smartphones that will tell us anything in mere seconds. We have microwaves to heat up or food in mere minutes. We have vehicles that can transport us from one location to another in no time. We have all the movies and tv shows at our fingertips and we do not have to wait a week for the next episode or for a movie to get out of the theaters before we can watch it at home. We are duped into believing that this instant thing is how our lives are supposed to go. We want to have a relationship, friendship, or romantic, that immediately meets all the criteria. We want our jobs to give us gratification and the six-figure income without putting in the time to gain the expertise. We must build a foundation for all things in our lives to be built upon. Hard work gives us an appreciation for the things that we can and will acquire in our lives. Curiosity gives us the desire to constantly learn and not rest on what we already have in front of us. Learning gives us the ability to grow. Whether that is mentally or emotionally, we must continue to grow.

Humility gives us the opportunity to see that maybe we do need to learn more or be more than we are so that we can do more for ourselves and for others. When you build the foundation, you are setting yourself up for success. You have a better chance of surviving the storms that life throws at you, and more than likely, they will come your way. Better to prepare for the storm that never comes, than to not prepare and be destroyed time and time again by the ones that do come.

Today, I will look for ways that I can build the foundation in my life no matter how old or how young I may be.

Rough Road   June 28

"For me, I had a close family. There were others like me who were going through a lot of rough times, so we always came together. It was understood that we would overcome hate, as long as you surround yourself with love and what's real." – Luol Deng

Have you ever gone to a place and the road that had to travel got a little rough? Does that stop you from going to that place? You may have to decide if the event you are going to is worth the "trouble" of going down this road. Sometimes it might be worth it to turn around but most of the time it is a temporary setback, and you keep on moving towards your destination. Life can be like that as well and we can get thrown off track because things get a little rough. We have a manager that is not friendly to us, a colleague that has created a rocky path for us, a relationship that hits a hard time and you have to decide, do I keep going or do I turn around? I was working for a manager that did not want to hire me, but because corporate said he needed to hire someone for this position, I had the job. I was not aware that he did not want me around until we got a few months into the job. I was leading a meeting and the top salesperson did not like what I said we were going to do and so he turned to my manager and said, "Are we going to do that?" My manager said no you do not have to do that, and I knew at that point I was there for show. I went into my manager's office after the meeting and asked why did he disagree with me and side with the salesperson? He gave no answer and said I need you to focus on these other projects. I did the best I could for the next several months and when we got close to the end of the year, my manager decided to change my role so that he could make his bonus for the year. That was a hard situation to be in. I had to find other ways to build bridges with others in the company if I was going to stay with that company. I was able to get another role that was a promotion. That was a rough road, and I could have turned around and left the company when those things happened. I chose to stay and find another way out that was beneficial to me and my family.

Today, I will decide to either go through the rough road ahead, or if it is not worth it, I will decide to turn around and find another way.

INTIMACY   JUNE 29

"Communication is a continual balancing act, juggling the conflicting needs for intimacy and independence. To survive in the world, we have to act in concert with others, but to survive as ourselves, rather than simply as cogs in a wheel, we have to act alone." – Deborah Tannen

Too often when we hear the word intimacy, we immediately think about the sexual side of it. I was talking to my daughter about her college classes, and she said one of her favorite classes was called intimacy. I had to hold my tongue and listen to her as she explained further what the class was about. She said they talked about how to communicate on a deeper level. I was relieved and started to ask more questions. Why did she like it? What are some things that she was changing as a result of the class, etc.? What a great concept to teach a class such as this at the college or even the high school level. How can we communicate with more intimacy? When we are with friends or family, we can strive for this type of relationship. We want to be closer to people and so we learn to be more intimate, asking the right questions and sharing tough or embarrassing stories.

What about with your customers? What are you doing to share with them, communicate with them? Now you should not go sharing about your childhood trauma with clients, but you should share with them about things that are relevant and can help them to see that you are a real person and not just someone trying to sell them something. Being intimate is about being authentic and sometimes vulnerable. We have to be ourselves and have a certain level of independence, but we also need the intimacy, the closeness of friends and family. There are people that do not crave this type of relationship, but the majority of people are like this. Find the balance, find the best way to be the truest version of yourself while with friends, family, and your clients.

Today, I will look for ways to better communicate on a deeper level, understanding that it may take some time to learn to be and get comfortable with being more intimate.

OVERSHARING   JUNE 30

"In real life, I try to be honest but not overshare. There are people that turn every conversation into a therapy session, and you want to start charging them." – Hugh Dancy

Have you ever been in a conversation and found yourself asking "Have I shared too much?" I have been on both the giving and receiving end of that conversation. We cannot seem to help ourselves and we spill over with information, details, or other bits that add no value to the conversation. It is like we just want to say all that we can before the clock tells us our time is up. In sales, we call it throwing up on the customer. We want to tell all about the product or service that we offer with little or no regard for what the customer needs. Then ask the customer, what do you think, as if looking at the target and trying to find the holes made by our shotgun approach. Chances are really good that we miss completely because the target got turned sideways, making it even more difficult to hit. I have been there and done that. It is embarrassing, to say the least, and very difficult to recover. If you do not ask the right questions, in the beginning, you will force yourself to answer all the unasked questions in the end.

Today, I will look at the ways that I communicate and make sure that I am not oversharing but asking the appropriate questions to give the appropriate answers.

July

DISAPPOINTMENT   JULY 1

"The size of your success is measured by the strength of your desire; the size of your dream; and how you handle disappointment along the way."
– Robert Kiyosaki

I'm sure we have all felt the sting of disappointment. You believed someone would be better, yet they failed to meet the expectations that you had. If you did not have those expectations, do you think you would have been disappointed? We will never know because you had those expectations. I have been to places that I thought would be great, beautiful, or take my breath away and it did none of those things. Maybe you were told about this great restaurant and the food was tasteless, the staff was less than friendly, and your overall experience was not what you had hoped for. You wanted to go to the amusement park, the movies, or the theater and it left you looking for more. I have felt that in all of those and more situations. This movie will be great, and it was not something that could even hold my attention. The amusement park has all these great rides, etc. and there was not a thrill to be found. I have been with customers that I connected with, and we had a good conversation yet could not close the deal. What do you do? How do you move on? Was it your fault, could you have done something different to make this go better? Sometimes we can do better and more but that is not always the case. It truly can be completely out of your control. If you do all that you can, ask the right questions, and set the proper expectations, then you can reduce your amount of disappointment. How you handle the disappointment is part of your success, as the quote above says. If you get stuck in it, that is on you and no one else. Wallowing in hurt or disappointment does not make you stronger or better. Find out what you could do differently, apologize where necessary and then pick up your mat and walk!

Today, I will find ways to better resolve my disappointment, whether by understanding my expectations better or understanding the situation or people that I am working with.

OWNERSHIP   JULY 2

"A wise man makes his own decisions; an ignorant man follows the public opinion." – Grantland Rice

Do you take responsibility for your own actions, thoughts, and what you say? Do you own the actions, thoughts, and words of others? We can get caught up in blaming others for what we say or for our actions. They made me do this or they made me say that cause of what they did or what they said. At what point do we own our actions and words? If someone pushes you, do you push back, whether it is physically or verbally? Are you the one that pushes first? We have to take ownership of our decisions. We can go a step further when we own our thoughts. All of this is possible and necessary for us to truly be free. When we own someone else's words and actions, then we are trying to control something we cannot control, even our children. We can teach them and help them to develop their own words and thoughts, but we do not own them. Likewise, we own our own words and actions, and we cannot put them on others. If we find that we are not acting the way we want or saying the things we want around certain people, then it is time that we draw our own safe boundaries. If that does not work and we find we are still struggling with the ways we act and speak around others, then maybe it is time to move away from those situations/people. It may mean that you spend less time with them, or you stop hanging out with them. You have to take ownership of your words and actions and let others have ownership of their words and actions.

Today, I will own what are my actions and words, let others own their actions and words, and learn how to spot the difference.

SECRETS   JULY 3

"Nothing makes us so lonely as our secrets." – Paul Tournier

We all have secrets, things that maybe we did or happened to us that we are not proud of and are not ready to share. We may never be ready to share some of them because of their nature. Secrets can make you feel a certain way. You can have excitement because it is about a birth, a relationship, or a career change. It could be something very sad, like the loss of a job, a death, or something that you felt you had to do at a time in your life, that now brings you shame or embarrassment. Secrets can put us in a very lonely place because no one will understand the reason I did this or that. They cannot relate to the feelings that I had at the time, and I am the only one among the billions of people on this earth that ever had to go through or deal with such a thing. Did you catch that last sentence? Did you hear the audacity in that statement? We are the only ones that could feel a certain way or think a certain thing or do something so hideous. We are *not* alone. We are not the only ones to think, feel, say, or do something so…embarrassing or tragic. We all make mistakes to varying degrees. How we handle them and when we are ready, talk about them that helps us overcome the fears that we have about them. When we make poor choices, we have to face the consequences at some point, otherwise, we will live in the loneliness of our secrets.

Today, I will look at how I handle my secrets. I will figure out what needs to be revealed and if I am ready to reveal them to someone that I trust and will not hold them against me.

DREAMS VS. REALITY JULY 4

"Do not dwell in the past, do not dream of the future, concentrate the mind on the present moment." – Buddha

Have you ever woken from a deep sleep while you were in the midst of a dream? Maybe it was a dream that did not make sense or was mixing the past with the present. Today was one of those days for me. It was hard for me to separate the dream from reality. My mind was mixing the things that I thought were important in my past with what I am making important in my present. But the things from the past were exaggerated. I was doing things related to the past but they were beyond movie extreme and yet I was able to do them. Climbing walls, doing tasks in certain buildings, driving vehicles to chase something, and then having the vehicle change mid chase so it would fit the situation, i.e., a car to a motorcycle because now I was having to drive on railroad tracks versus a street. I missed an important meeting in the present because of the tasks I was doing from the past life. I lost track of what day it was and that upset me even more. You may have heard or experienced someone having a similar type of dream. But they wake up mad with a loved one because of what they did in the dream. Can you separate the two, the dream from the reality? Was there something for you to gain from this dream?

I do not remember dreams very often, so when I have something like this happen, I ask if there is significance to it. Maybe the thing in the dream that I am making out to be important today is like the thing from the past? The level of importance is relative to the timeframe. In other words, what I view as important now may not seem important in the future. How do you put things in perspective in your life? How do you figure out if something is important or insignificant? Maybe you dream about client meetings and what you said versus what you could have said. What can you learn from that or is it just a dream? Do you just let the dream go, or is it something to learn from?

Today, I will look at how most things in my life can help me whether a dream or reality. I will see if there is something that is speaking to me from my dreams or in real life.

Sobriety July 5

"Take on the day with the sober understanding that your fears are lying in wait." – Unknown

The other day I was asked what sobriety meant to me. I have friends who are in recovery, and I think I know what it means as it pertains to them, but I have not struggled with drug or alcohol addiction. I stumbled for the words to define what I thought it might mean to me, but I could not give a clear answer at the time. It was late and I was not in the right frame of mind for a deep conversation, and we both knew it.

Sobriety by definition is, 1) the state of being sober. 2) the quality of being staid or solemn.

To be sober means to be serious or to take things seriously. The bible uses it when talking about how people should view the enemy, the devil, with soberness or sobriety. When we do not take things seriously, we can be like someone that is an addict, afraid to confront the very things that lie before us. I understand sobriety to mean that we get to have real relationships, real conversations, real connections with other people and we get to have truth back in our lives. We are no longer running away from what scares us but facing it, knowing it has no power over us because we are in control. If we take things seriously, we can do these things, and get the help from others that we need to succeed in our daily lives. Sobriety is about being serious and that seriousness can be about a number of things in life but mainly about facing what scares us.

Today, I will look for ways to deal with my fears seriously and soberly.

TODAY   JULY 6

"Did I offer peace today? Did I bring a smile to someone's face? Did I say words of healing? Did I let go of my anger and resentment? Did I forgive? Did I love? These are the real questions. I must trust that the little bit of love that I sow now will bear many fruits, here in this world and the life to come." – Henri Nouwen

What are you going to do today, or what did you do today? Any of the questions from the list above is a great one to ask alone, yet together make a great start or end to any day. In sales, we hear what have you done for me today? When you only look at today you can get frustrated or hurt by your lack of performance. I had days when I could not give anything away, but I put a smile on someone's face, I passed along love to a loved one, friend, or even a stranger. Do you believe that you can pass along something as small as a smile, an act of love/kindness, even say words of healing without ever knowing the impact it made on a person or a community? What happens to you when someone does any one of those things for you? Do you keep it to yourself, or do you pass it along and/or tell people about it? When you are with someone, even the smallest gesture can be noticed and received. Do not forget that you have something unbelievably valuable to pass along today. It may be a powerful message or just a smile and some kind words. What will you do with today?

Today, I will make the effort to do something, even if it seems small, it can be unbelievably valuable to those who receive it.

FORGIVENESS   JULY 7

"To forgive is to set a prisoner free and discover that the prisoner was you." – Lewis B. Smedes

Forgiveness can be a challenge, especially when we have been hurt and wronged. Letting go of what they did to hurt you whether on purpose or by accident. You have to be ready to forgive someone before you can actually do it. If you are not ready that is okay, but you may want to eventually deal with it so that it does not hurt you for an extended period of time. Forgiving takes strength and character. Forgiveness is for us to move forward and not so the other person can see how they have wronged us and be a better person. They may not have the capacity to do that. I have learned to forgive more completely in the last few years. I learned how to forgive years ago but something still did not feel right about the relationship afterward. I found myself not feeling whole, especially when I was around that person. The angst, the hurt feelings, the betrayal, were right there all over again. When I learned how to completely forgive someone it helped me to learn two things. First, I did not have to feel bad feelings when I was around them and second, I did not need to be around them. Now the second one is easier for a lot of us to understand. They hurt me, I no longer need to be around them, period! But the mere mention of their name or memory of them brings up the hurt feelings or the shame or the guilt. When you forgive someone completely, you can hear their name and see their face and not have those ill feelings. You can choose not to be around that person to protect yourself from further pain

How do you forgive someone completely? There are several ways that you can do this, but you have to find what works best for you to feel complete. Maybe you need to write it down or verbalize it. There are some things that work better than others, but I needed to say it and even write about it. When I was able to get it out, I was able to deal with it completely. Then I was able to move on in my life. Remember, forgiveness is for you to heal. Not forgiving someone can hold you back emotionally. It can also cause you to lose focus or distract you from the task at hand, your job, or your relationships.

Today, I will see if there is anyone that I need to forgive and if so, and am ready, will start moving towards that so that I may begin to move past the hurt feelings that may have been holding me back.

TEAM   JULY 8

"Remember upon the conduct of each depends the fate of all."
– Alexander the Great

Being part of a team is a wonderful thing. When you work alone you have to find people to work with that can help you achieve your goals. Some people do not want to work with a team and in fact, want to work alone because they do not feel like they can rely on others or that they can do all the work themselves. When you work as a team, you learn to rely on others to do their job. When I played most sports, I was part of a team. I needed the others on the team to be a unit and work together to accomplish a goal. I can do sales, but I am not very good at marketing, human resources, or accounting. Though I can do all those things, they are not my strength, and I would be much better off letting others do them. Although I have my own company, I still need help running my business. I need help with marketing, my website, and keeping my financials in order. If I do not do my part, then the whole team/company will fail. If someone on the team does not do their part, we can all fail.

Being part of a team can be a great thing and something to be proud of, or it can be something that hurts the innermost part of your being. Are you a good teammate, and do you do your part well? Are you on the right team, with the right teammates that help everyone do their best so that the team succeeds? Sometimes we are on the wrong team, and we cannot get along enough for the team to do their best. Pieces may do well but not everyone is able to thrive and that hurts everyone.

Today, I will find ways to do my part so that the team will succeed. If I have been doing all that I can, and the team is not successful then maybe it is time to find another team to work with.

Right Place — July 9

"Who could have imagined that life would have taken such marvelous twists and turns or that I would often be so fortunate to be in the right place at the right time?" - Julie Andrews

Did you ever wonder, "how did I get here?" All the things that you have seen, heard, and experienced has led you to this place at this moment. You are in the right place, for you, right now. Could we have made different choices along the way? Yes, but we would not be the person we are right now. That is not a bad thing. We could think, if I made this choice, I would have this job, or this relationship, or this amount of money. We tend to think our lives could be better than they are. What if we took that job and we ended up making less money? And because we took that job, we ended up making other decisions that changed the way we treat people. Would we still have the friends we have? I am not trying to be negative here but what if we made worse choices along the way? It can all start with one choice. We missed the boat, the bus, the train, or the plane, and here we are in the wrong place at the wrong time. The reality is, you are exactly where you need to be right now.

I have been through a number of things in my life, let alone the past couple of years. Looking back, it would be easy for me to say, I would change this or that decision, or action. But if I changed anything from my past, I would be taking away part of me, a part of who I have become. I am not saying all the decisions I have made in the past have been right, but the things I have learned and continue to learn along the way have helped form the person I am today. I get to be the person I am because of the experiences I have had. I am thankful to be in the right place, for me, right now.

Be thankful that you have had the experiences you have had so that you could be the person you are today. If you want to take another path, make a different kind of decision and see where it leads you.

DECISIONS   JULY 10

"It's not hard to make decisions when you know what your values are."
- Roy E. Disney

Are your decisions off the cuff, spur of the moment, or are they thoroughly thought through? Do you spend time considering the consequences of your decisions? Sometimes we make quick decisions because the situation dictates that we do so. Those types of decisions are made based on past experiences because we are reacting or using muscle memory. Other decisions require more contemplation, considering all avenues and consequences of the decision. Who will be impacted by this decision and how will they be impacted? Sometimes we think that the only "big" decisions in our lives are about our relationships and our careers. Yet, every day we make some decisions that can impact us far more than those two areas. What we decide to eat or if we decide to drink alcohol can impact us and those around us. When we decide to stay up late to play video games, read a book, go out with our friends, or just watch videos, it can impact us and those around us. We make decisions all the time and we do not always consider the outcome or the consequences. Most choices have little or no consequences to us or the people around us because we know what would happen based on prior experiences. One of my first experiences of being a manager hit me like a ton of bricks. The decisions I made would impact the people that worked with me and the company, not just me. I was responsible for seventeen employees and their families. That caused me to pause. Now I was looking at the impact those decisions would have. Some people wanted to test my decision-making ability, daring me to make the hard decisions, and I made them with pain in my heart. Someone wanted to test my leadership versus their perceived power or impact within the company. They felt like they were more valuable than they were at the time and thought I was going to see their side as more important than the best interest of the company. Unfortunately, they chose poorly that day. When they came back the next day, they were remorseful about the decision that they made but I knew that they made that decision that day and they would do it again soon if I allowed them to go back on their decision. Their decision was going to impact me and the business for a short period of time. I decided after seeking council, that the short-term pain was worth it for the future of the company. Much like being a parent, it was not easy to watch my children make some of the decisions that they have made but sometimes I have to allow them to make their own decisions and understand the consequences that come along with those decisions. What I did learn from that leadership position and from being a parent is that, if you make tough decisions, people will respect you later for having to make those decisions. When you make decisions based on the values that you have, it does make them easier.

Today, I will understand the depth of the decisions that I get to make. Whether the decision is something as simple as what I eat, when I sleep or starting a new career, I know there is an impact from each of them.

BOUNDARIES   JULY 11

"Being a nice person is about courtesy: you're friendly, polite, agreeable, and accommodating. When people believe they have to be nice in order to give, they fail to set boundaries, rarely say no, and become pushovers, letting others walk all over them." - Adam Grant

When I was younger, I did not understand how to set boundaries and the importance of that act. I wanted to please people and did a lot of things that made me think that I was doing the right thing by allowing others to do what they wanted and not doing what I wanted. I thought I was being humble, and servant-like in my denying of self. What people did not tell me is the importance of self-care. I was trying to take care of others and ruining myself emotionally. I was pushing myself to do things and it wrecked me emotionally, physically, and even mentally. I would go to extremes to please people, even to the point of hurting myself, so that the other person would get what they wanted. Being humble and having a servant-like heart does not mean that people are allowed to walk all over you and take advantage of you. Though people seem to want to do that when in a position of power. Learning to set boundaries was difficult but freeing. I could say no and that was it, no shame, guilt, or pit in my stomach. I may have struggled with insecurity and doubt when I first did that but that was on me not them. Standing up and saying no should not be a traumatic thing for anyone, though for some it is extremely difficult because they have not been taught how to set boundaries. They were probably always taught that they were a lesser person or worse, treated as property. We must learn how to say no, or yes because it is best for us. We must take care of ourselves first before we are capable of caring for others. Setting boundaries is taking care of yourself, making sure that you are safe.

Today, I will set boundaries where I need to so that I can feel safe and cared for personally.

ARE YOU READY? JULY 12

"You can't knock on opportunity's door and not be ready." – Bruno Mars

Have you had a time in your life when you thought you wanted to change, but it simply was not happening? When we are not ready for change, we may not see the signs or hear the words that will help bring any of those things into our lives. If you are looking for love, are you giving love and ready to receive all that it has to offer? The joy the heartache, the peace, the happiness, and the fulfillment. If you are looking for a career change, are you open to the options that may be presented even if you never considered the possibilities? We need you to move here and take on this responsibility. We need you to be in this position, not that one.

I was working for a large corporation and one that I really liked because of the values of the company. I liked a lot of the people that I worked with as well. I realized that it was the wrong place for me eventually. I needed to be at that company for a time. I was learning about self-care, about how to do what I really wanted to do with my career, and about my financial security. It took me a while to see that and when I started talking to those close to me, who knew me, I was able to hear what they said and what was beginning to open up around me and for me. When it was time, I was able to listen and act upon the things that were being presented to me. I moved on to something better suited for me and my overall well-being. Can you listen to your inner voice, your friends and family, your mentors, and your peers?

Today, I will open myself up to the possibilities that may be going on around me and prepare myself for the things that I want and need in my life. I will be ready to listen to the things that I need to hear and do.

Mentors   JULY 13

"For every one of us that succeeds, it's because there's somebody there to show you the way out." – Oprah Winfrey

Mentors are all around us. Whether in our personal or professional lives, we probably have one or two people that we work with or have worked with to help us and we help them. Some of us try the solo route and maybe we are savvy enough to go through a time in our lives when we can make it alone. We have read the books, listened to podcasts or lectures on how to improve our lives in business or personally. I have found that the times I have not had a mentor seemed to be more challenging because I was having to do all the heavy thinking myself. I have found that I do a lot better when I have people that I know, like, and trust in my corner, or in my ear. Maybe it's someone to call and get advice or someone that calls me and asks for advice. I learn from those experiences as well because then I think about situations that I need to change as well. These kinds of relationships are invaluable. They can be like a diamond in the rough.

Do you have someone that your respect and admire in business? Someone that you can spend time with and learn from and they may not even be in the same business as you, but you trust the way they think about business, and they inspire you. We all need someone that we can go to about tough business decisions. Someone that has been down that road before you and is able to see with much better clarity the things we need to see, or maybe you have great sound ideas that you need to have validated by someone that will give you honest feedback. Find someone or maybe a round table of people that you can get with to bounce ideas with that can sharpen your ideas and help to cultivate others. When you have a mentor, it can help you move your professional life and even your personal life in the direction that you want or need.

Today, I will find a mentor or a number of peers that I can get input from both professionally and personally.

Reprogramming   JULY 14

"Reprogramming the unconscious beliefs that block fuller awareness of creative/intuitive capabilities depends upon a key characteristic of the mind, namely that it responds to what is vividly imagined as though it were real experience." – Willis Harman

Do you ever feel like you need to reprogram yourself, that your way of thinking and your actions are just a little off, and a reset would be helpful to get you back on track? We all make adjustments in our lives almost daily. We see something that is not in alignment with who we are or who we want to be, and we adjust. Reprogramming does not have to mean a major reset. A revamping of our entire belief system or way of doing things. We can just start by simply believing our imagination can come true. We can believe in making a difference in the world, so we start making a difference in the way we spend our money or give our time to charity. Years ago, I belonged to a church group that had a charitable arm that did a lot of really good things for those in need. Not just money but food, clothing, and relationships. I liked being a part of that group and the feeling of being able to give back to my community. I moved and ended up in a place where I got away from giving back to the community and the local charities. I was going through some challenges personally and professionally. I needed to reprogram my mind and, in turn, my efforts. A few years ago, I changed jobs and it allowed me to have my weekends free. I started to look around at how I could give back to my community. I found a way through a local charity to help on Saturdays. I now spend most Saturdays working for a local charity that I believe is making a difference in people's lives. We can do this with our job, our relationships, even our personal growth. If we want things to be different, we can reprogram our minds to be different and do things differently.

Today, I will find ways to reprogram my mind so that I can do things that align with where my heart wants me to act.

QUESTIONS VERSUS ANSWERS   JULY 15

"Judge a man by his questions rather than his answers." – Voltaire

People are judgmental. We tend to look at the wrong things when we are judging people. We want to ask people questions and then determine the character of the person. When was the last time you looked at the questions that a person asked? Are they insightful, probing questions, or are they surface questions that are more self-serving? When you ask questions are you trying to learn or show someone how you are smarter than them? We have a chance to learn every day from those around us, and that means everyone, no matter their education level. We can learn from the purity of a child's heart when they ask the simple question, why? They are trying to understand how things work and why we do things the way we do. They are asking in innocence, and we too can learn from that type of heart. When was the last time you asked something simply because it did not make sense to you, and you truly wanted to know why? Can we take the same type of mindset when we are in a meeting with a client or a company meeting to learn rather than show how smart we are? I have been learning how to not always have an answer. I do not always have to contribute to the discussion, especially if it is not going to add anything other than self-proclamation. I have to stop, listen and learn. What kind of questions do you ask and how can you improve them? Can you ask questions that will draw out my information from the speaker and make them look like the hero? Questions about their insights and their thought process that can bring clarity to the room? Can you ask the client things about their business that will help you understand better how they do business so that you can help them better? What can you learn from the situation, from the speaker, or from the group?

Today, I will look at how I can ask deeper questions, not for my gain, so that I can learn more from those around me.

MAKING A DIFFERENCE   JULY 16

"It's easy to make a buck. It's a lot tougher to make a difference." – Tom Brokaw

Are you interested in making money? Most of the rest of the world is. Are you interested in making an impact? I hope so because we need more people that want to use their talents to help others who do not. That is how you make a difference.

When I was younger, I was not concerned about making an impact on the world around me. I was worried about not being like everyone else. I was worried about making money so I could travel, have a certain lifestyle, drive a certain type of car, and own a certain kind of house. I did not want to be a statistic, though I was doing everything so that I would be the very thing I did not want to be. I wanted to stand out for selfish reasons and not necessarily to make a difference. I started learning about impact and the ways that people in history had influenced others and what that looked like. That appealed to me. Although it took me many years, I started to give of my time and my money to things that needed time and money. I am mechanically minded and have an aptitude towards that type of stuff so I could help make or build things. I had been in sales, and I was making enough money to share with others, so I started to find ways to do that, though not in a flamboyant way. It was and still is, important to me to give back to people without public recognition because I do not want the focus on me but rather on the project or the people that deserve it. What can you do that will make an impact on the world around you or far away from you? Can you give freely of your money? Can you give freely of your time? Do you have a special talent that can be taught to others that do not have the ability to pay you?

Today, I will look for ways that I can give back and make a difference in my little slice of the world or globally.

## HAPPINESS							JULY 17

"Some cause happiness wherever they go; others, whenever they go."
– Oscar Wilde

We have all met that person that can light up a room. They have the smile, the glow, the charisma to bring joy to a room just by entering it. Maybe you have been that person, or maybe you have just seen that person, or even know that person. What is it about them that makes them light up a room? What is happening inside that person to bring them such joy that it exudes from them into a room full of people? We can all be this type of a person if we choose to be. This is not limited to a select few that have the confidence, charm, and electric personality. I know there are times when I feel confident and full of joy when I go to a gathering. I can feel the overflow of love as I see friends or loved ones when I enter a room. My smile is genuine, my walk is filled with confidence, my head is held high, and I know no fear as I walk into this room. This is not the cockiness or the arrogance that I am feeling but rather the joy and peace that has filled my life. When you are filled with happiness nothing can stop that but you. People can say things, events can happen, but you decide when you will let that happiness go from you. Remember you can bring happiness when you show up or when you go. Hopefully, you are not the latter person that brings happiness when you leave.

Will you bring happiness when you show up or when you leave? Make that choice!

MAKE TIME FOR YOU   JULY 18

"Health and wellness does mean different things to different people."
– Denise Morrison

I grew up playing sports and continued playing until I was well into my mid-thirties. I was in pretty good shape during most of that time too. I got sick but a few times I was knocked down a few times when I was not paying attention to what was going on with my body. I got shingles when I was nineteen years old in college, playing football as a walk-on, and had about fifteen to sixteen hours of classes that semester. Stress may have had something to do with that situation. The shingles virus is usually rare for someone nineteen years old and is more common in people over sixty. I also had my first gout flare-up when I was about thirty, which is rare as well. It usually starts around forty to sixty years of age. In both of those situations, I had to make time to get healthy. I was pretty hardheaded too and it took several more years before I truly listened to my body and what it was trying to tell me. I learned later in life that my health and well-being are my top priority. It took multiple gout attacks to wake me up to this reality. A gout attack is when your body has a buildup of uric acid, which can crystalize and settle in your joints like your big toe or fingers, etc., and is very painful. It felt like someone was taking a sharp object and stabbing the joint being affected by gout.

I had a very bad gout attack in my left hand, and I had gotten to the point where I had taken steroids to help overcome it. Within a day or two of finishing the steroid treatment and feeling somewhat better, I had another flare-up in my right elbow. The treatments were no longer effective and in fact, my body was telling me to stop and fix the problem. I had to look at my diet and lifestyle and determine how to get a hold of this because I knew that I did not want to live like this. I also did not want to live the rest of my life on some sort of drug if I did not have to. The good news is that I learned about what my body needs and with the help of a holistic doctor was able to start to heal my body from a proper diet for me. When I am healthy then I can do so much more than when I am not healthy. If you are not taking care of your health, then you will be forced to take the time to recover from your illness. I used to wake up in the morning and the first question I would ask myself was, "what hurts today?" I would proceed to do a mental body scan to see what pain I was in for today. I no longer ask that question in the morning. I get to ask more important questions.

Today, I will listen to what my body is trying to tell me and make time to get and be healthy.

Rituals   July 19

A ritual or tradition can be as simple as something you do every night, like read a story to a small child, or something you do weekly, such as go out for Chinese food." – Elizabeth Berg

In sports, there are a lot of rituals athletes participate in. Some of these are born of necessity others are born of a need to ward off the bad that may happen or superstition. Some people in sales will do the same type of thing because they think that when I do this ritual, I get this positive result. When we create rituals, we can become more effective because we are creating positive habits from those rituals. Speaking a certain way, doing certain activities in a certain order, all give us the ability to do what we do better.

When I was in HVAC sales, I would look up the place where I was going and when I got into the neighborhood, I would start to look at the HVAC equipment at each of the houses as I drove past them. Testing myself on which brand it was but also recognizing the dominant older brand to get an understanding of what I might be seeing at the client's house. After the meeting with the homeowner, I would call one of my buddies that I worked with to see if I missed anything or to get some input on what I could have done better. These were all part of the ritual or rituals that I would do when I was in that job. It made me better at what I did because I developed a regular habitat. It was my routine. I have other rituals now because I am doing something different, career-wise. However, when I drive into a neighborhood, I cannot help but look at the HVAC units to see if I can identify the brands that I see at the houses I pass. What rituals are you doing to help you improve your craft? What are some things that you can start doing that will turn into positive habits?

Today, I will look at the rituals I am doing and determine if I want or need to create new ones that will improve my habits.

Unlearn What You Have Learned   July 20

"Always with you, what cannot be done. Hear you nothing that I say? You must unlearn what you have learned." – Yoda

"Alright, I'll give it a try." – Luke Skywalker

"No! Try not. Do or do not. There is no try." – Yoda

Growing up we are all taught some things that just do not settle well with us, and it is not until we are faced with a situation later in life that we have to decide to stay with it or unlearn what we have learned. One of the hardest things for me when working with people is when they say, "we have always done it this way." They know it is wrong and it is not producing the results, but they stick with it because it was the way they were taught and the way it always has been so why change it now? We have all been there. Thankfully, we all have the chance to change, and we probably did change. Sometimes we have things that are deeper than making cookies a certain way or driving a certain road just because. Some of us are faced with deeper character things, like how to raise our children and what we should teach them about our prejudices.

I grew up with my father and my two brothers. Not a lot of female influence in the house, so we learned about emotions from the street, well from our friends. We learned about touchy-feely stuff from others because it was all about being tough and working hard in our house. My dad's dad died during my second year of college, but we got to spend enough time with him to know what type of a person he was. Again, not a lot of touchy-feely stuff with him either. So, it was not a surprise that my father was that way with us boys.

I was blessed with daughters, so I got to learn about touchy-feely stuff. I got the chance to unlearn what I had learned. When something new comes along that does not match with what you know or have learned over the years, are you resistant to it or are you willing to learn? Are you willing to do things differently though it goes against everything you know? Is it too embarrassing to go in a different direction because you cannot be wrong for so many years? Hopefully, when presented with a new way of doing things you will not shy away from it or push it off but will instead, look at it and study it and find a way to incorporate it into your life for the positive.

Today, I will not push away new ideas just because they are different from the way I have always done things. It may be time to unlearn a few things that I have learned.

REFLECTION   JULY 21

"Without reflection, we go blindly on our way, creating more unintended consequences, and failing to achieve anything useful." – Margaret J. Wheatley

Do you take time to reflect on your current situation, your life, your job, or even your relationships? I am sure all of us take the time to do so, but what do you do after you have reflected? Do you take steps to improve on what you are doing? I have heard that every day you are taking steps, either forward or backward never sideways. You take a step forward and one back, or two forward and none back. But you never stay in the same place each day. This can be difficult to handle, especially when you know that you have had a bad day. We can equate that to steps backward. That is not necessarily true though. Just because you have a bad day does not mean you are taking steps backward. You may be learning a lot during those bad days and making steps towards your growth spiritually, mentally, or even physically. I have learned to take time in the morning to reflect on all the things that are going on in my life. I cannot give attention to everything, but I survey all that is going on and decide what is important and what is just noise trying to distract me or steal my attention. I let it go. I get to go through my day focusing on the important things and some of the not so important that may become important if I do not deal with them. I can overthink things but when I do, I have found that I am trying to control something like the outcome of a decision or situation. Overthinking is dwelling on how bad you feel and thinking about all the things you have no control over. Reflection is mindful consideration.

Today, I will find ways to reflect on what is important so that I can find ways to improve.

SELF-DOUBT   JULY 22

"And by the way, everything in life is writable about if you have the outgoing guts to do it, and the imagination to improvise. The worst enemy to creativity is self-doubt." – Sylvia Plath

We have an inner voice, and it can be our greatest cheerleader or our worst critic. Some of us have done things to remove that inner voice, and that may have proven beneficial at the time, but it also has some downside. Having the ability to talk yourself out of a dangerous situation is a good thing. "Walk away from the edge, you could get hurt!" However, not taking chances leaves us a very dull life. "You are not good enough to take that job, you will fail more than you will succeed." If we doubt everything that we do to the point that it does not allow us to function, then we are getting nowhere. We are stifling our creativity. When we choose to take some risks, we can find out what we are capable of doing or achieving.

I was finishing up my final season of high school football. We came into the season with a large number of returning starters and a junior class that was really good as well. Several others and I were starters on both offense and defense and had great hope for the season. We ended up not winning a single game that year. I walked away and started doubting my abilities, though I succeeded in athletics for years. I made plans to attend U of I in the fall and there was no other option for me, in my mind. I decided not to play high school basketball that year because I was feeling sorry for myself and thinking I am not good enough, though I was a starter most years and always was a contributor to the basketball team. I finished up the year, decided to attend the U of I, and I was going to try and play football. I learned a valuable lesson that year. Someone's opinion of you should not determine your abilities or limit your desire to follow your dreams. That situation caused me great self-doubt because someone in my life shared their lack of vision for me. But I decided to take a chance and not listen to the doubters, both external and internal. I got to meet some great people along the way, played football with some amazing athletes who would go to the NFL and shine. I made some friends along the way that have forever shaped my life. I made some life choices that, despite my self-doubt, changed my life in amazing ways.

Today, I will stop listening to the self-doubt and start looking at the ways I can grow beyond what I think I cannot, or what others think I cannot do.

WILLPOWER VS. SURRENDER　　　　　　　　　　　JULY 23

"Willpower should be understood to be the strength of the mind, which makes it capable of meeting success or failure with equanimity. It is not synonymous with certain success. Why should one's attempts always be attended by success? Success breeds arrogance and man's spiritual

progress is thus arrested. Failure, on the other hand, is beneficial, inasmuch as it opens his eyes to his limitations and prepares him to surrender himself. Self-surrender is synonymous with eternal happiness."
– Ramana Maharshi

We often think that we must *make* things happen. We must push and prod and manipulate people to get them to do the things we need them to do. I have pushed too many people away by my actions and words. When we learn to surrender, we can be happier and less frustrated. If we try to manipulate people to be different so they can fit in our model of what they should look like, act like, or even talk like, then what are we doing but creating a robot? We will create a resentful relationship that probably will not last. None of us should be puppets nor should we be puppeteers. Either option is a lonely place to be. Surrendering to the things that present themselves can be difficult especially when they do not align with our way of thinking or timing. When I learned to surrender, I found that people are just doing the best they can with what they have or know. I can try to help but that is all I should do. I cannot (and should not) force my beliefs on someone else. When I surrender to the way a person acts and talks and generally behaves, I can then make the decision whether I want to be in that person's company or even have conversations with that person. This is especially hard when that person is a relative or a longtime friend. We do not want to upset the apple cart but at the same time, we are struggling to be around this person and their words and actions. They may be abusive emotionally or physically, they may be emotionally unavailable, they may be toxic in other ways that make it near impossible for you to be around them. This is not the time to make them change, because they may not be able to change, or want to change. Just because we want something to be different in others does not make it so. It can be the same when we meet with clients. How many clients have you won with sheer willpower? How did that situation work out in the long run for you and for them? Did they cancel the minute you left, or did they last a month before they changed their mind and went in another direction?

Today, I will stop trying to force my thoughts and beliefs on others. I will surrender to the things that are available to me and learn to live in peace rather than constant conflict.

PARENTING   JULY 24

"Don't worry that children never listen to you; worry that they are always watching you." – Robert Fulghum

Parenting usually can be challenging. We find ourselves in situations we did not expect to be in our have to deal with. Reading books can help but nothing usually is able to prepare us for some of these situations. We get to see firsthand how to handle a newer version of ourselves. Parenting can be easier if we allow ourselves an ounce of grace, then we can extend that to our children. It has to start with us because often times we feel like parenting is a reflection on us, and to a certain extent, it is. We seem to have a certain way that we want our kids to grow up, act, believe in certain things, etc. We put so much pressure on our kids and to what end? So that they will be a model child and be more than we were? Most of us want our children to have more and be more than us. This need to push our children came from our parents and the society that we are living in. There are parents who let their kids be kids. There are parents that allow their kids to ask all kinds of questions and act in ways that others find disrespectful. When we act like the people that we want our children to be then our kids will see that. Sometimes we set such a bad example that our kids have little choice but to follow or do the exact opposite.

Being a parent, I got the chance to either be like my parents or set a new standard. We all get the chance to be the parents we wanted or needed when we were kids. Let that sink in, much like it needed to sink in for me. My parents were not horrible parents. They did the best they could with the tools that they had, and I got the chance to do the same.

They said things and did things that hurt my feelings and remain with me to this day. Good and bad. That is part of life's experiences and that is part of what makes us the people that we are today. If we choose to be parents, we get to choose to be like our parents or like the ones that we wanted or needed. Whatever you choose to do as a parent, know that you are not just being heard, you are being seen, even if you do not think they can see that or understand that. They see and hear more than you will ever know.

Today, I will learn to be the parent that I wanted and needed to be for my children. No matter what age they are currently, we always get the chance to change.

Do You Know Better? July 25

"Do the best you can until you know better. Then when you know better, do better." – Maya Angelou

Too often, we can get frustrated because we cannot find the right words or the right actions. We want to do better than what we are doing but cannot seem to make the right steps to get there. Being an athlete most of my life, I was able to get away with bad eating habits. I thought I could eat whatever I wanted, and it did not affect me. I was wrong and it caught up to me by the time I was thirty. I did not know any better, but I had to learn or live in constant pain. It was not until I reached my fifties that I decided to do something drastic and not just treat the symptoms. I went to a holistic doctor to find the root of the problem. I had to eliminate everything I was eating and start to build back up from the basics, with just fruits and vegetables. I was able to get my body back into proper health by rebuilding my foundation. I know more now about healthy eating and the effects it has on me and my body. I know better, so I do better. What about you? Are you trying to be more effective in your conversations with family and friends? Do you know how to ask the right questions so that you can learn more rather than staying with what you know?

Today, I will find a way to learn more so I can do better. I will not be complacent or content with where I am currently. I want to be better!

How Are You Doing?   July 26

"Nobody cares how much you know until they know how much you care."
– Theodore Roosevelt

I was talking to someone the other day and the above-mentioned quote came up indirectly. They mentioned that I was one of the only people that asked how they were doing, and that meant a lot to them. It almost brought me to tears because I care deeply for this person and their well-being. I want them to know that I care so I ask, how are you doing? We can do this with friends and family, and it can become almost rote when we do it. We get the typical response of I am fine, or good. But does that satisfy you? Do you check it off your list of things to do when I see my friends and family? When I ask someone, I want to know how they are doing. If I do not want to know or engage in that part of the conversation, I will not ask. Does this type of behavior extend to our clients as well? If you care about people, it will show. Clients are people too and they have feelings, they have good days and bad days. Do you care enough to engage with them on that level? Are you having a hard time connecting with people in general? Are you struggling to have that Jerry McGuire moment with your clients, where you can connect with them emotionally? Some people will tell you that it is not important. If you want to be successful in life as well as business, you need to care about people and their well-being. Go beyond the surface stuff and find out how people are really doing. You cannot fake this because it will be obvious. If you do not care, do not ask. When I am coaching people, I like to say that I cannot make you care about people, I can only show you how important it is.

Today, I will ask myself how am I doing? If it is important to me, I will ask others how they are doing?

Forgiveness vs. Permission — July 27

"It is often easier to ask for forgiveness than to ask for permission."
– Grace Hopper

Have you ever done something with the thought that it will be easier to ask for forgiveness for what I have done than to ask for permission? I have used this phrase before when I wanted to make the customer happy and get the sale done now instead of waiting to talk to my boss for approval. Someone wanted to work with me, and my company and I had to give something to get something. This is hard for some people to understand. Some people try and take advantage of you and ask for the moon when negotiating. But you can walk away and say no. I think people tend to forget that. How have you done this with your personal decisions? Do you make the purchase knowing you will have to ask forgiveness later? Did you agree to help a friend when you forgot that you had plans with the family?

I was working with someone that was a "friend" of the owner of the business. I made a mistake in the words that I used when I offered them some financing, and this person was very financially savvy and took advantage of what I said. I said to the person that what I said was a mistake. The price I offered was not correct, the customer was not having it and said you made the offer and that is what I will pay. I could have walked away but I decided I would honor the mistake and ask forgiveness from my boss. I went back to my boss and said, "I made a mistake, please take it from my commissions." My boss understood the situation and offered to pay me full commissions despite the mistake.

Whether we make a mistake or we offer something that we know is going to cost us or the company a little more in order to win the deal, we must ask forgiveness. Do not assume it will be granted. We have to learn when the right time is to make the deal and when is the right time to walk away.

When is it right to ask for permission and when is it right to ask for forgiveness? Wisdom and time will be your guide.

FOCUS ON THE RIGHT THINGS   JULY 28

"It is wonderful how much time good people spend fighting the devil. If they would only expend the same amount of energy loving their fellow men, the devil would die in his own tracks of ennui." – Helen Keller

Sometimes we can fall into the trap and fight certain battles thinking we are doing the right thing, only to find out later that the battle should have been focused on something different and better. When I was in college, I became involved in a church group that helped me to learn about God. I became passionate and zealous about helping people. So much was my desire to help people that I focused on the wrong thing, which was telling people how wrong they were living their lives. I later learned that what I needed to focus on was loving people, and through love, people could see for themselves the difference a follower of Christ's life could be.

Although I thought I was loving people by helping them change their lives the approach was lacking the proper direction. I could have shared about how my life was different in love instead of bitterness, hatred, or self-loathing. I got a chance to be different because someone loved me, I could make changes in my life because of love. It took me a while to see this for myself. If people around me were saying this then I was not hearing it. I learned that I was beating myself up for my past and was taking it out on others, which was worse. When we are in sales we can suffer the same affliction, not seeing the real issue in front of us. We focus on getting the sale and not caring about the client in front of us. We can force a sale and get it and think nothing more about it. Was it the right solution for them or did I just want to get my commission? When you focus on the right thing, life, work, everything gets easier not harder. I found that when I do my job properly and focus on the right things, the money takes care of itself. I am happier and more fulfilled. I sleep better, smile more, care more, and I love more deeply. Helen Keller was right, when I focus on love, the devil does not affect me. He takes his shots and I have my struggles, but he is not my focus.

What will I choose to focus on today? Will it be love and how I can pass that on to others? I hope so.

STUCK   JULY 29

"Whenever I get stuck on something, I'm like, 'What would I do if I wasn't afraid? What would I write if I wasn't afraid? What would I say in this situation if I wasn't afraid?'" – Phoebe Waller-Bridge

Sometimes we can get stuck in life or on a project at work and we cannot seem to find the solution. Sometimes it is fear that holds us in place and other times it is something much bigger saying hold on. I need you to see something. I want you to hear this. Look over here. Do you believe that there is something bigger than you that can stop you in your tracks so that you can see or hear something different than what you currently know? Maybe it is a character issue that can now have a resolution? Maybe it is a relationship that you are meant to be in? Maybe it is a career choice that was not even on your radar? Maybe it is the gentleness and calm that you need to see and hear that is getting your attention?

I was speaking to a friend of mine the other day and telling him about a direction I was considering with my business. I have been operating under the understanding that I should have a broad spectrum and serve any type of sales client. I was feeling uncomfortable, in my business, and I could not figure out why. I mentioned it to my friend, and he said maybe you should focus on what you know and the industry that you came from for the past seventeen years. It made sense and I needed to hear it because I was stuck trying to help too many people in too many different areas. It became clear when I was speaking to someone I just met on the phone. I was getting input on how he was doing his business and how that compared to mine, and I mentioned how I was thinking about creating this niche for my business. He said that it was perfect, and he was excited for me that I had a niche for my business. He said he wished he had one and was working on it for his business which he had been doing for years. I knew at that point that I needed to finalize that decision and focus my attention on my niche clients.

Are you feeling stuck today and not sure which direction you should go? Ask your friends, your family, a person you met for the first time, ask God and the universe. Help is out there waiting to be asked for!

FIX THE UNFIXABLE   JULY 30

"A-tone-ment - it's a chance to fix the unfixable and to start all over again. It begins when you forgive yourself for all you've done wrong and forgive others for all they've done to you. Your mistakes aren't mistakes anymore, they're just things that make you stronger." – Glenn Beck

I grew up with my father and two brothers. As a child, life felt very out of control. Dad was trying the best he could with the tools and knowledge that he had. Fast forward to adulthood. I am now in a position where I get to make choices and they have an impact on not just me but others around me. I learned what it means to have control and take control of situations and people and I like to fix things. So, I start looking for things that need fixing. I look to relationships that need fixing and I do all kinds of stuff to make them right, but they do not work. I find someone that is emotionally unavailable and try to help change them because I can fix things. I try and help someone that has had a loveless childhood and pour out what I think are loving ways because I can fix things. I try and be a good friend to someone by always being there and supporting them because I can fix things. All this was doing was preventing me from fixing myself. I was the one with the loveless childhood and the emotionally unavailable one because I did not have the proper tools or support. Like I said earlier, my father did the best he could with the tools that he had. He did not know how to break the cycle or pattern that he was taught. He did a little better than his dad. I think I am doing a little better than my dad. I got the opportunity later in life to break the cycle or pattern. I have learned and am still learning that I get to fix me and only me. If I try and "fix" others, then I get frustrated, they get frustrated, and it makes for an awful relationship. Are you trying to fix people around you? Are you frustrated when people do not see the error of their ways and how you are trying to provide the answers and the help that they need to make it right? There is this condition called, "you spot it, you got it." It is easy to see the flaws in others especially when you have the same flaws.

Today, I will stop trying to fix the unfixable in others around me and focus on how I can fix myself.

ASKING FOR HELP   JULY 31

"Anytime you see a turtle up on top of a fence post, you know he had some help." – Unknown

Do you ever stop, look around, and wonder, "how did I get here?" We can get caught up in the day-to-day, making progress going along the path and suddenly, we are in a far different place. It can be a physical location. It can be an emotional state. It can be a maturity level. We all need help and if we do not ask, we will not get it. Sometimes we get insecure about asking for help, thinking we are not enough or will look weak for asking for help. Sometimes we are too stubborn to ask for help. When we ask for help, we open ourselves up to new possibilities. We can get help discovering whole new ideas and paths. Early in my career, I had a hard time asking for help. I grew up having to figure things out because I was not taught how to ask for help. That is not a cop-out or blaming it on others, we were always taught to just figure it out. Some things we were taught because it was dangerous or not intuitive like cooking or driving a dump truck at a young age. This concept continued to escape me when I would start a new job. I would ask for some help in the beginning but then, I figured I should know some of this and try to figure it out on my own. It proved to be a really bad idea because I would start my new job and it seemed like I was slow to pick things up. It would take me longer than it should have to start making a difference at my job. I was given my first chance to be a trainer in my early thirties and I asked for help. I was asking for help from my colleagues who came before me and my former boss and my current boss. I got to go to a train the trainer class. I enjoyed that job from the beginning. I liked helping others succeed and helping them develop as better sales/service people. I got to travel throughout the U.S. and Canada. I got to be a part of the Project Management team for the new field software we were having to develop and roll out because of Y2K. Asking for help allowed me to see things and do things that I never would have seen or done if I did not ask.

What do I need help with today? What can I do to get the help I need to be like the turtle on the fence post?

August

Who Needs to be Taught?   August 1

"It's no good trying to teach people who need to be taught." – Aleister Crowley

I had a friend tell me about a situation that he was dealing with at work. He was going to have to go back to the office and tell this person again, how they had made a mistake. I asked him how many times he had a similar conversation with this person. He said that this would be the fourth time in about a year. I asked him who was going to benefit from the conversation. He said what do you mean? I said are you doing this for their benefit or yours? I then asked if he felt like the person was ready to change or if he was just frustrated with the person not changing the way he wanted. I looked at the conversation differently. He was looking at the situation as this person was not listening and changing the way he wanted them to or as quickly as he wanted them to change. So, who needs to be taught?

We can feel the need to teach people something that they do not want to learn. People are going to change when they are ready to change, including you! Sometimes we are forced to change but most of the time we change when we are ready to change. Maybe we are tired of the same results or getting hit in the head by the cabinet we left open. Have you had a conversation with your child, spouse, or coworker about the same thing more than twice? Do you think that maybe you are the problem and not them? Maybe your lack of accepting where this person is right now, is as good as they can be for now, is the problem. If the problem is a safety concern for you or others around, you then that is a different discussion. If the discussion is about something that they do that bothers you, then maybe you are the problem. Maybe they are not that mature, yet. Maybe they do not move as quickly as you do or make decisions as quickly. There are several reasons that we can get flustered but that does not make any one of them right. You cannot make a rock change simply by telling it to move.

Today, I will look at the situations and the people that I am trying to teach and ask myself, do they want to learn, or am I trying to teach this because I need to learn? Sometimes we change because we want to, and other times change is thrust upon us. Either way, we have changed.

CONNECTIONS   AUGUST 2

"Everybody talks about the weather, but nobody does anything about it."
– Charles Dudley Warner

How do you connect with people? Can you find common ground with others? We all have a person in our lives who talks about the weather. My dad was that person for me. He was a landscaper for most of his life, so the weather was important to him. It was also something safe, it kept him from talking about feelings or deeper types of stuff. I lived in Georgia, and he was in Illinois, and he knew my weather and would point out when his temperatures were higher than mine in the summer. He knew about both of my brothers as well, they lived in different states. When I was in HVAC, he made a point to discuss it even more. This was my father's way of connecting with me. He was not a very emotional person, in fact, I rarely if ever remember seeing my father cry. He felt the connection through talking about the weather and how that was impacting me and eventually my business. The weather can be a good ice breaker for people and get the conversation started. Then moving into things with more depth and importance, especially to them.

What does it take for you to connect with someone? Sometimes it begins with something simple like the weather. Other times we need to dig deeper. Opening up to others allows us to connect with them. When you learn to be vulnerable it allows others to be vulnerable as well. It can help you to connect with others when you show the real side of yourself. I was checking up on a friend recently as they had just lost a life-long best friend. They said you might regret asking, then proceeded to share the "other" things that were going on in their life. It was hard life stuff that steals our happiness and can leave us feeling depressed or angry. I did not regret asking. In fact, I think I was sent to ask by God or the universe to ask the question and have a conversation. I thanked them for sharing and then shared something that had encouraged me when I was going through some similar type of stuff. We connected a little deeper that day.

Today, I will find ways to connect with people that are more meaningful and heartfelt, even if it starts with the weather.

LOVE IS... AUGUST 3

"Love is not a because, it's a no matter what." – Jodi Picoult

It is hard to love someone "no matter what." It is also hard to be loved when you want to please people and you do not know how to receive love. We can love our spouse, significant other, children, parents, etc. with a because type of attitude. Because you did this, I will love you. Can you love someone with no expectations of a return? This type of love is hard, never receiving can hurt and get destructive for you. It is called unconditional love. There are different ways that we get tested on these two ideas. A family member needs money, we have some money, but it will make things a little tighter for you to give that up. When you do it with no expectations then you are doing it with unconditional love. You are not expecting a return or even a thank you, which seems really hard but that is what unconditional means, right? When you give of your time to do something for others, make them a meal and take it to them because they are sick, or they just lost a loved one. You are loving unconditionally.

I was at a networking event one day and I was listening to a couple of people tell us what they did and activities that were important to them. I thought with one person, I could connect them with a couple of people that had similar interests and maybe they could collaborate on a project or two in the future. After I connected them, the one that I met at the networking event said, I owe you and I will do whatever I can to find someone to connect with you. I was perplexed by this and thought, that is not why I connected you with those people. They were trying to make what had just happened a conditional gesture, not allowing it to be a no matter what. We can stop people's love for us by trying to return the "favor" or the act of kindness they have provided in love or kindness. When you let people love you, you are loved. If you keep repaying everyone for the love that they have given freely then you are pushing their love away. You can do something for those that love you, but can you let it be without condition? You can also do things and show love for strangers. Have you given your money or time to a homeless person? Can you give money to a beggar without passing judgment? There are many ways to show your unconditional love for those you know and those you do not know.

Today, I will find ways to show my unconditional love for others.

How do You Measure Yourself? August 4

"Judge Smails: Ty, what did you shoot today?

Ty: Oh, Judge, I don't keep score.

Judge Smails: Then how do you measure yourself with other golfers?

Ty: By height." – Caddyshack

In life, we can get all caught up in trying to compare ourselves to other people. Growing up we are taught how to be competitive and if we are not careful, we can become competitive about everything we do. How fast we eat, drink, drive, even our work can become competitive. We constantly are comparing ourselves to others and for what? That kind of mindset can carry over inside our own minds and we compete against ourselves. I am not saying that you should not look for ways to improve yourself, but when it becomes obsessive and it controls you, that is a problem.

When I was growing up, I cannot remember what triggered the

thought but, in my mind, there was never enough food. I am not saying there was not enough food or that ever went hungry but that is the belief that was formed in my young mind. As I reflect on those times, I think because we were always so busy working in the summer months that we had limited time to eat, therefore it became competitive. So even the "relaxing" sit-down meals became this competitive eating contest. This behavior carried over into my adult life and I will still find myself eating fast for no reason. When I see myself falling into that habit, I consciously will slow down, put my fork, or spoon down after each bite is taken. It is healthier and I actually savor the food. Learning how to not compare yourself to others or always be competitive is a good thing. Teaching yourself that you are good enough at times is important. Beating yourself up because you are not as good as so and so, can cause a lot of other bad behaviors. Why do we need to be better than someone else? Can we be better than we were yesterday and that be enough? Sometimes competition is a good thing, and it helps us to push past our laziness or lack of drive. Finding the balance of when to push ourselves and when we need to be happy with where we are currently is something we call can work on.

Today, I will see the competitive ways in which I act and ask, is this good for me or tearing me or others down? I will seek to find the competitive balance in my life so I can be better than I was yesterday not necessarily better than someone else.

GARBAGE IN, GARBAGE OUT   AUGUST 5

"I get one hour, really twenty-five minutes in a sermon on a weekend, to combat all the hours of the week that people are told you are what you have through billboards, commercials, and sitcoms, and so forth." - Max Lucado

What are you listening to during your day, your week? We can listen to things that do not have a positive message or are not uplifting to us or others. Do you listen to podcasts that stir your heart to become a better person? Do you read self-help or business books that promote growth in your life and others? Do you watch movies that challenge you to be a better person or better leader? I love going to the movies and seeing a good action-packed movie. I like listening to a thrilling novel with mystery and a good detective to solve the problem. I also add the books that will challenge me and help me be a better version of myself. I also like the movies based on real-life that teach me something. I like engaging in conversation that is meaningful and helps people grow and change for the better. We can be just like computers if we are not careful. Garbage in, garbage out.

Today, I will look at what I am "consuming" and how it affects me and those around me. Understanding that I have a choice in what I watch, listen to and read.

Responsibility   August 6

"Find joy in everything you choose to do. Every job, relationship, home… it's your responsibility to love it, or change it." – Chuck Palahniuk

Responsibility is a word that some love and some do not. It means being held accountable for your actions. It can cause some of us to shutter. It can cause some of us to swell up with confidence and say I got this. Not everyone wants to be responsible all the time. There have been times in my life when I wanted to step up and take responsibility, to show what I could. Sometimes it went well and others not so much. Then there have been times when I did not want anything to do with being responsible. I was in my early thirties when an opportunity came up for me in my career. It meant moving to another state where we only knew a couple of people in the area.

My wife and I discussed the options and considered all the

possibilities that were available to us at the time. Then she said, it is up to you. She did not intentionally put all that on me but that is what I felt like at the time. All the other things we discussed were out the window and this final decision was up to me. Do you take the red pill or the blue one? Life decisions can be hard, and this was one of them. I made the decision to take the job and make the move. That move led to many more opportunities and decisions just like that one and ones that were even tougher over the years. It was and still is a part of the growth that I got to experience. It has helped shape who I am and continues to help me make decisions like that today. What are you taking responsibility for and how is it shaping you?

Today, I will take responsibility for the decisions that I must make. It could be the start of something very powerful in your life.

WORRY   AUGUST 7

"I just stay in my own lane and not worry about what anyone else is doing and settling my own pace." – Roddy Ricch

When I think of the word *worry*, I cannot help but think about the biblical verses in Matthew and Luke. "Can anyone of you by worrying add a single hour to your life?" Every time I worry about something my mind gets caught up in stuff it does not need to, so I think about these verses. I have yet to add any time to my day or my life by worrying. In fact, I lose whatever time I spent worrying, and then I am more upset with myself. If only it were as simple as catching yourself in the act and you say stop it! But it can be. Like any other thing that our mind gets us into, we can stop the activity.

We cannot expect change to happen without practice. Learning how to stay in our own lane and not worrying about what others are doing takes work. Once we learn how to do that it becomes very freeing. I used to worry about making sales. When you are living on one hundred percent commission, it can be scary! I had to learn how to trust in myself and work like I knew I could, to make the sales. When I stopped worrying about making the sales and I made the sales, I was able to relax and make the sale. That may sound oversimplified, but it helped me realize that I could not help myself when I worried. I could only help myself when I was focused on doing my job. I do not worry about money. It deserves my attention, and I pay the bills and I work to make money to do all that but, I do not worry about money. I believe that when I do my job the money will take care of itself. That is what being on a straight commission plan has taught me. Learn how to stay in your lane and not worry about things. Having concern is different than worrying, and we need to concern ourselves with certain things.

Today, I will learn how to focus on what needs my attention without worry. I will take steps to learn how not to worry about things.

ENOUGH IS ENOUGH!   AUGUST 8

"He who knows that enough is enough will always have enough." – Lao Tzu

There comes a time in our lives when we realize we have all that we need. Some will argue this point with me because there will never be enough for them. Maybe they grew up in a household or a time where they had to struggle to put food on the table or clothes on their backs. My grandparents lived through the depression in the 1920s and they understood what it meant to live without certain things. They made do with what they had and appreciated what they did have. My grandmother grew up on a farm with many brothers and sisters. Everyone worked, helped with the daily chores, and had to find time for their schooling as well. When my grandparents dated, they could go out to see a movie and get a soda for only a dime. That was a lot of money to them back then and it was considered a special treat. Later in life, my grandmother worked at a department store. She worked the cosmetics counter and become one of the best salespeople selling over a million dollars a year in cosmetics. She knew what the value of money and things were and had plenty. She was not rich by any means, but she had what she needed and was able to give to others as well.

What is enough for you? Will you know it when you see it or have it? When we get focused on getting the most toys, money, etc. we lose focus on our fellow man. When we have enough, we find ways to give to others.

Do you have enough to take care of your basic needs? Are you fed, have clothing and shelter? Then you may have enough, and you can look for ways to give to others that do not have enough.

BAD DAYS   AUGUST 9

"There are good days and there are bad days, and this is one of them."
– Lawrence Welk

We all have good days and bad days. The bigger question is, what are you going to do with them? When you are having a good day, you never want it to end. When you are having a bad day, you may want to crawl back in bed and start over. The days can run together and give you a string of good or bad days. That can be hard. When I have a string of bad days it can seem like I am doing something wrong to cause this to happen. Maybe I am the cause but maybe I am not. Maybe things are happening around me that just suck.

Years ago, we had two dogs. One we had for over twelve years and the other about one year, but the latter was a rescue and was already about eleven when we got her. The two of them died within about a week of each other. That was a string of bad days. They were hard!

I have had several days in a row when I felt like I was in a funk and could not shake whatever was going on. I felt like a dark cloud was hovering over me and it would not go away. Depressing, negative thoughts that will not go away. I am not good enough. I am no good at this task. I am not a good parent. I am not good at relationships. I am not good at sales. I am not a good manager. I am not a good employee. The hits would keep on coming. I lost sight of the good things that were going on around me. When I am in the midst of a bad day, it is hard to remind myself of the good happening around me. Harder still is the understanding that I am growing during this time and the things that are happening are helping me to learn a lesson. Probably more valuable than I know. What do you do when you are having a bad day? Do you have a positive talk with yourself? Do you call on friends or family? Do you perpetuate the situation by diving deeper into negativism? If you do the latter, you may need to get some help to overcome your way of thinking. We all can change the way we think. Some can do it more easily than others, but we can change. Start by recognizing the negative thoughts, call them out, just like you would a good friend. Let them know that they are not allowed to be here. Move to more positive thoughts or statements. I can do this. I may not be the best at it, but I can do this. If you cannot do it, get some help. Call a friend or colleague and ask for help. Sometimes we think we have to do things all by ourselves. We all have bad days. So, what did you learn from yours?

Today, I will learn how to make the bad days better, by recognizing them for what they are sooner and not dwelling on them.

ARE YOU BROKEN?   AUGUST 10

"Broken people save broken people." – The Guilty

Have you ever felt broken? Maybe you were crushed by a relationship that went sour. Your dream job was just ripped from your hands. A loved one was taken from you by death's hand. Maybe you made some bad choices, and the consequences were nothing like you imagined.

While watching the movie, *The Guilty*, I heard the line above, near the end of the movie. It gave me pause. I had to rewind it and listen again. It took the main character a little while to figure out that he was broken. He was put into a situation that he did not like because he thought he could and should be doing more. He made some bad choices and ended up in a position that he did not like. He was a 911 dispatcher while under investigation and he was not happy about having to be in this position because he wanted to be out on the streets helping solve crimes. He received a phone call and things start to go off the rails. Throughout most of the movie, you are given little clues as to who he is and why his life is falling apart. But it was not until the end that you find out most of the truth. He was broken! He did not see it, though others could.

When we are broken, we can often think we are unworthy. We are not suitable for anything, let alone helping others. When I have been in this mindset, I was not fun to be around. I can look back now and see how I was harsh, critical, and selfish. I felt like my life was not what it should be, and I was in no position to help others. But what I found is that when I was broken, I could help other broken people, much like the character in the movie. I did not see that until later. When I saw my issues, I became more relatable. When you are not in the situation or have never been in the situation, you may not be able to relate to what someone is going through. If you have been broken by your poor choices, you learn from those choices. When you lose a loved one, you understand the pain and emptiness that loss leaves behind. When you are broken, you can help save other broken people.

Today, I will see the truth behind my brokenness, I can help others! I can also get help from others that have been broken, but I must take action in either case.

HARMONY AUGUST 11

"It's easy to play any musical instrument: all you have to do is touch the right key at the right time and the instrument will play itself." – Johann Sebastian Bach

When I was in college, I developed my love for singing. I found some friends that shared the same passion for singing and we formed an acapella group. We had anywhere from five to seven people, depending on what was happening with others. Learning to sing was fun but not always easy as we had to work together to make sure that we were on key together. Unlike playing the piano, where you need to press the right key, each person had to remain in tune with the rest of the people for it to sound right. It takes hours of work to make that happen properly. Playing an instrument is the same. It takes hours of work to figure out how to play the proper notes at the proper time for the harmonies to be right, and the song to be complete. Life is like that too. It takes time for us to find the right notes, (things to say, think, and act) to get our lives in harmony. When we find the balance in our lives, things happen around us and in us like a world-class orchestra playing one of the most complex sonatas with ease. It is amazing to live in harmony, but it takes work to not only get there but stay there for any length of time. Finding the right balance in life takes time and should not be forced or rushed. Keep working at it and be persistent.

Today, I will find ways to be more harmonious in my life, with the way I think, the things I say, and the way I act.

FRUSTRATIONS AUGUST 12

"Being alone with fear can rapidly turn into panic. Being alone with frustration can rapidly turn into anger. Being alone with disappointment can rapidly turn into discouragement and, even worse, despair." – Dr. Mark Goulston

Life can be frustrating, especially when things do not go the way we plan. We push a little harder or give up and try another direction or activity. I was talking to someone recently and they were talking to me about their frustration with having to deal with a certain situation. They felt like they were the only ones who could handle it due to the circumstances. When you are new to management, parenting, or another type of responsibility, you can think that you are the only one that can solve the problems that arise. Not that you cannot seek out others that can help but when it comes to making the decision and executing the plan, I am solely responsible. That is a tall order and very tough to manage. Being in those positions myself, I have learned that you can only do so much. Yes, the decision making is up to you, but it does not mean that you are the only one to execute the plans. Getting help keeps us from getting frustrated and, as Dr. Goulston says, can lead to anger.

This has been a control issue for me, and it is why I would get frustrated in the past. When I am trying to control the outcomes of people's actions, or decisions, it can be a burden that I put on myself. It is unfair of me to do that, to myself! Just because I want things to go perfectly does not mean they will. I remember realizing that I can only do so much to teach my children the right things to do. Then at some point, they will make their own decisions, their own mistakes, learn their lessons from life. I wanted to do the best I could with the time that I had. When the time came for them to make their decisions/mistakes, I would do my best to be there for them if they wanted me or needed me. Leading people is similar to this in that, we only get so much time to teach them, and then they are responsible to make the right moves. The right moves may not be the way that you would have initially done it. It could be a better way and gets the same or better results. Do not allow your frustration to dictate situations because it will make you angry.

Today, I will find ways to not try and control situations or people and start reducing the frustrations in my life as a result of those decisions.

What Are You Aiming for? — August 13

"We aim above the mark to hit the mark." – Ralph Waldo Emerson

You have probably heard about aiming for things like the stars and being content with reaching the moon. Sometimes we must shoot for something so far out there so that we can go further than we have ever gone before. We put a target of $2.5m in sales when we have only hit $1.7m in the past. When we hit $2.1m we are disappointed we missed the target but happy because we went well beyond what we have done in the past. In sales, we are constantly setting goals so that we can get motivated to do the extra stuff during the week to meet or surpass our goals. There is an old saying that if you aim for nothing you will hit it every time.

Goals are important, and so is aiming. Wayne Gretzky is known for saying, "you miss one hundred percent of the shots you never take." Aiming is not enough, you have to shoot. Setting goals and doing the work to get to the goals is all part of what we do. Find a way to make a goal, take aim, and take your shot!

Today, I will look at the goals that I have made, and do the work daily, weekly, and monthly to make that goal.

Which Path — August 14

"When you come to a fork in the road, take it." – Yogi Berra

Do you find that you get frustrated some days because things just are not going the way you think they should be? We grow more determined to do what we want, and we fail to see what may be happening. Sometimes it may be that we are not supposed to be headed down that path. We can get caught up in wanting something to be right for us and yet it could turn out to be the worst thing for us. God, fate or the universe has a different plan for us at this time and we are not wanting to see that. As I sat this morning and thought about good days and bad ones, the thought occurred to me, maybe the bad days are days when we were not following the path we are supposed to be on. Now, I do not believe that we are all predestined or that we have a course for our lives fully mapped out. I do believe that we learn and grow, and things become evidence of what is right for us and what is not right for us.

Yogi Berra was known for his comments or quotes and this one is no exception. Sometimes we come to a decision-making point, and we must choose left or right. Sometimes it is clear and others not so much. When it is clear and we come to the decision-making fork, we move forward with ease and confidence. Other times we make a choice, and it can become clear when things do not go very well. But we can learn from it and make a better choice next time. Do you find yourself happy with the life choices that you are making? Do you find that you are frustrated by the way things seem to be going?

I have been in sales for most of my career. There were a couple of other avenues I tried to pursue, and it was made clear to me that they were not right for me. I tried my hand as a telemarketer, customer service rep, inside sales rep, and operations manager, all of which left me frustrated and wanting something very different. None of those fit my personality or what I was supposed to be doing. Every time I came back to outside sales, it made all the difference in the world, or at least in my world. Which path are you on and is it the right path for you? A difficult time does not mean you are on the wrong path, but it may. Learn to listen to God, or the universe, so that you can learn what you need to learn and get on the path that is right for you.

Today, I will be honest with myself about my path and where I am headed. If it is the right path, I will confirm it. If it is the wrong path, I will confirm it and find ways to change my path.

Teamwork   August 15

"Gettin' good players is easy. Gettin' 'em to play together is the hard part."
– Casey Stengel

Have you ever been part of a team that just could not work together? Maybe you had some great players, maybe some great coaches, but it just was not working. Teamwork is not something that just comes together easily. We have seen it when you have a group of great athletes come together and they just cannot win because they do not play well together. Too many want to be a leader and not enough want to be followers. Too many cooks in the kitchen spoil the soup.

My senior year in high school, we had a great group of players returning from the previous year, and about half of us were returning starters. We had a great group of juniors that were going to be a great addition to the team as well. There were high expectations for the team because of this. We experienced some injuries as all teams do from time to time. We never won a game that year. We were winless and it was very hard for me and others to comprehend how that happened, but it did. Was it the team, was it the coaches, or was it something greater than all of us? It is hard to see all the things that could have contributed to it but one thing I know is we did not have the teamwork to win.

Can you see when your team is not working and make adjustments? What does it take to right the ship? We can see things if we are interested in the team's success and not just ours. When we go into a team situation, we have to look out for each other. There have been plenty of movies made, books written, and lives lived to help us. In the movie, *Remember The Titans*, the team was able to come together under some very adverse situations, both internally and externally. They were able to overcome those obstacles and work together as a team. It started with the coaches, players, and worked its way throughout the rest of the community. Some stayed on the team and others left, but they came together as a team to make it work. What can you do to work better as a part of a team?

Today, I will find ways to work as a team member and not as an individual. Though we are working on individual things we are all part of a bigger team.

CREATIVITY   AUGUST 16

"It's not just about creativity. It's about the person you're becoming while you're creating." - Charlie Peacock

Are you a naturally creative person? Where do you go to be creative? Your red chair? Different people find places that help them to be more creative.

For me, sitting quietly in a room early in the morning is a great place. Sometimes I will go for a walk and get lost in my thoughts or just enjoy the scenery. Sometimes, I just need to cook. Sometimes you will need to get out of your office or your house and find the creative side of you. Write down the ideas or say them into a recording device to save them for later. We can all be creative if we allow ourselves the opportunity. We do not need to write a book or draw/paint a picture. Some are great with cameras, others are great with music, and others are amateurs but would like to get better at some point. Go ahead and give it a shot. Let your creation out. There are all kinds of methods to creation. Who will you become or what will you do today?

Today, I will give myself time and space to create a little or a lot.

RECEIVING   AUGUST 17

"When you are not willing to fully receive, you are training the universe not to give to you! It's simple: if you aren't willing to receive your share, it will go to someone else who is." - T. Harv Eker

How do you react when you are given a compliment, a gift, or even a simple hug? You might argue that it depends on the person. But overall, do you receive things well? When a coworker compliments you for a job well done do you let it sink in or do you brush it off? When someone shares their affection for you can you receive it and embrace it without some sort of deflection?

For someone that grew up in a household that did not show much affection and did not get many compliments, this was a lesson to learn. I continue to learn how to receive. When someone says nice things about me or gives me a direct compliment, I thank them and let it sink in. I remember when I was at my brother's funeral and strangers, to me, would come up and hug me and express their heartfelt condolences. It was not a time to be cold and rigid or to reject their expression of love for my brother. It was a time to receive the love of others. It was awkward at first, but I soon accepted what they were giving, without fear, judgment, and prejudice.

Today, I will receive what I can receive and sit in the feeling of love and fulfillment of what is being said or done on my behalf.

WHO ARE YOU? AUGUST 18

"Well, who are you? (Who are you? Who, who, who, who?)

I really want to know. (Who are you? Who, who, who, who?)

Tell me who are you? (Who are you? Who, who, who, who?)

Because I really want to know. (Who are you? Who, who, who, who?)"

– The Who

How do you answer the question in public settings? How do you answer that when you are alone in a quiet space? Is the answer the same or different? I know the answer can be different depending on the audience, the environment, and even the circumstances leading up to the question. But do you know, and can you tell others, who you really are? Something that is not just name, rank, and serial number?

I had the chance to meet someone that I admired from a business standpoint. Like meeting a hero for the first time, I was nervous and struggled to find the words to explain who I was. It was like I was dumbstruck and forgot everything about me. We can play the words through our head sometimes that we are not enough. We can tell ourselves that we are more than we really are. The lyrics above describe a couple of scenes with different people doing things that they would be embarrassed to do when others were around. Is that who we really are? Can you describe a person with emotion, depth, and character? This is like playing the why game with a child. Like the song, keep asking yourself, who are you? Take the time to develop the answer and come to grips with the real answer. I am a lover, a fighter, a peacemaker, a troublemaker, an emotional wreck, a polished professional. I can be whomever I want to be. But at the core of my being, I am…

Today, I will ask, who am I? Because I really want to know.

Time to Reset Yourself   August 19

"I usually head up to the mountains or out into the desert. Somewhere nobody is. There I can dig deep and find the core that got me where I am today. It's sort of like my reset button." – Nathan Parsons

Do you ever feel like you just needed to hit the reset button so everything could go back to normal? I wish I could do that sometimes. But I have found that it is possible is to clear my mindset and move on. Sometimes, I can do that just by going for a walk. I can do that in my red chair sometimes too. I have to lock out all the distractions. My phone gets put away maybe even turned off. No computer, no tablet. I have a journal to write things in so that I can write out some clarifying thoughts. Understand some truths by putting them down on paper. Once I can put all that in place, I get to start working on clearing out the junk conversations my mind has programmed lately. It is almost like watching tv and it is stuck on the infomercial channel and you cannot change it. Remove the negative thoughts, the negative influences, and start with a clean slate. You are good enough, you are smart enough, you are beautiful, you are funny. You are enough! Sometimes, that is all that it takes. It can be that simple and it can be more challenging. But you have to start somewhere. Clean the blackboard of your heart and mind, not just with the chalk-dust-filled eraser, but with a clean damp rag. Remove all the previous stuff so you can have a clean slate to work with. When you reset yourself, you are not changing the way the world acts, you are changing the way you view the world and the way you act in the world. So, what are you waiting for? Go ahead and start. Then you can hit the reset button in your heart and mind.

Today, I will find a way to make time and reset my heart and mind. I will clear out the world and start my day with a clean slate.

MESSAGES AND MESSENGERS   AUGUST 20

"The return we reap from generous actions is not always evident."
– Francesco Guicciardini

We can find ourselves in a place in our lives where we are questioning everything. One of those questions may be, why is that person in my life? Or why did our paths cross? Maybe we did something kind for someone else and this is a sort of payback. Maybe this is God's way of showing us we are doing the right thing and we need to stay on this path. One night I was out with the woman I had been dating for about a year, and we were driving in Atlanta, I think we were on Peachtree Ind Blvd. We came to a stoplight and the man in the car next to us motioned for us to roll down our window. I thought he needed directions or some other kind of help, so I put the window down. He said, "You make a beautiful couple, you ought to stay together." The light turned green and away he went. We looked at each other for a moment and were left speechless. Later that evening, we went to a grocery store, and one of the men working at the store made a similar comment. When we returned to our vehicle, we looked at each other and tried to explain away the kind words.

We both were trying to figure out if this relationship was a good one, one that would last. We were one foot in and one foot out in our hearts. We had both asked for help, guidance, and understanding about our relationship. The answer was provided. We had just encountered two different people that made clear statements to us about how our relationship appeared to them, I felt overwhelmed by love at that point. If you are asking for help to understand something in your life and you get affirmations from not just one stranger but two, in the same evening, it may be time to realize your questions/prayers have been answered. Both individuals were genuine in their statements. Have you ever been on the receiving end of this random act of kindness? Have you ever been prompted to say something like this to someone you did not know? Know that you may give or receive something like this in your life and you should not be surprised when it happens. Do you know why that person is in your life, long or short term? Maybe you needed to hear what they had to say. Maybe you need to feel the overwhelming love that was missing from your life. Whatever the reason, know that a person or persons came to you with a purpose, maybe they did not know why or maybe they did.

Today, I will appreciate the reasons people come into my life. It may be temporary or for a lifetime, but they are there for a reason.

LET IT OUT   AUGUST 21

"Strength comes in so many forms. Not just the physical strength, but to understand the emotional strength. To have emotional vulnerability, to show that's not a weakness." – Cory Barlog

In life, we can come to a certain point where we just need to let it out. Let our hair down. Shout at the top of our lungs. Have a good cry. Sometimes we just need a good emotional meltdown/release. The pressure cooker is full and now it is time to release the pressure that has been building. Too often, we do not know how to properly release the pressure and we get burned by the steam that was just released. We were never taught *how*. Men are famous for not reading the instructions and just "figuring it out." When we just figure out how to release our emotions, we can hurt others and get hurt as we lash about like the steam being released from a pressure cooker. When we learn how to let it all out, we can be like the pressure cooker that needs to be released. When it has a release, the pressure gets reduced, and it is safe to open. There is a way to safely let out our emotions.

I learned how to stuff my emotions when I was a young boy. I grew up without a positive emotional example. What that means is a positive role model or mentor showing me how to work through and handle the emotions that we all will feel and go through in our lives. I learned not to talk about the bad stuff, things that hurt emotionally. It paved a way that I had to unlearn years later. If you have ever seen a brick patio that is now uneven and maybe a brick is missing, that was me, emotionally. The bricks may be good, but they needed to be removed, the foundation reset and then laid again with the proper level and then secured and firmed up with sand. We all have things that add to the emotional pressures that we feel in life. How you choose to deal with them and when you choose to deal with them can either add to or release the pressure in our hearts and minds.

Today, I will find the ways that I am keeping my emotions inside and learn to let them out, safely and productively.

Go With the Flow   August 22

"Do not struggle. Go with the flow of things, and you will find yourself at one with the mysterious unity of the universe." – Zhuangzi

Life is like a river. It continues to move forward, whether we want it to or not. We may get stuck along the bank or on some large rocks, it may slow us down as we go down the river of life. We may try to fight against the current, hoping to stay in a place, or trying to rescue someone else. There are some that seem to just float peacefully down the river. Not paddling, just relaxing. What we do not see is what it took for them to get to that place of peace. Sometimes, we need to just sit back and relax. Just go with the flow of life. Have you ever done that? I do not mean when you are on a vacation or on a lazy weekend. During the workweek, have you allowed yourself to relax in the day? You may have some appointments, meetings, etc. but you do not force anything. You let it flow in and out of your day. That can seem counterproductive to some, but to others, it is a means to an end.

We have to learn how to go with the flow sometimes to find the peace that we want and need in our lives. Today is that day. Take a deep breath, meditate for ten minutes to clear your mind, and set the tone for the day. Now go with the flow of the day. Things will get done. You will get through the day. When you are ready to end your day, come back and meditate again and see how peaceful your day has become.

Today, I will go with the flow of the day. See where the river of life takes me and how peaceful it can be.

KNOW YOUR STRENGTHS   AUGUST 23

"A computer once beat me at chess, but it was no match for me at kickboxing." – Emo Philips

When did you find out you were good at ___? I realized, when I was younger, that I was good at sports. I could play almost any sport and I was decent enough at it to play, maybe not excel but I could play. I found out I was good at speaking and persuasion in college, which led me to sales. I took a class on persuasion and one of the assignments was to get the class to act on our call to action. I spoke about having the class over to my place for lunch and everyone in the class, but one person, showed up. The teacher showed up and brought her boyfriend as well. After some gentle persuasion, she changed my grade from a B to an A. I did not realize until I was much older, that playing collegiate football at a division one level was a big deal. I just played. I walked on and I lettered. For me, that was normal because it was my life.

My strengths have grown over time, and I have gained some and lost some as well. What have you learned about your strengths? What are they? Do you take time to evaluate and develop them? Knowing your strengths can help you avoid frustration and feelings of defeat or shame. If you are not a very good chess player, you may want to work on it or choose not to play. If you are finding sales frustrating and you are not very good at it, then maybe it is time to evaluate your strengths again. Ask friends, family, or colleagues. Listen to what they have to say. Listen to the inner voice that is telling you what you like and dislike. Your strengths may be something that you have not considered in a while, and it may be time to follow that path.

Today, I will find out what strengths I have and discover others that I did not realize were there. I will find ways to develop them or move on from them depending on the fulfillment it brings to me.

WHY IS THIS HAPPENING TO ME? AUGUST 24

"I wouldn't change anything. I think that it's important to let things happen and stay 'happened'. I think that's all part of the learning curve, part of fate. I'm just glad that it happened." – Mike Peters

Have you ever asked yourself, "why is this happening to me?" We can fall victim to the mindset that we do not deserve the garbage in our lives. How do you learn lessons in your life? How do you see what needs to be corrected? Most of us are not perfect and need to change something at some point in our lives. How do you know? What is the trigger for you to know when it is time to change something in your life? Sometimes there are subtle things that remind us, sometimes there are big things that happen. We can stub a toe or break a leg. We can run into an old friend or have a nasty breakup with someone. I have had all kinds of reminders in my life. Some good and some painful. Some situations I was ready for, others were big surprises.

I had a job that I enjoyed and felt very qualified for. I was enjoying the progress that was being made, not only for me but for the company as a whole, as a result of the things that I was involved with at the company. The new president of the company had different ideas. He decided to eliminate the department that I was in, and I was offered a different position, a demotion back to a previous position that I held with the company. I had the opportunity to move to one of three locations in the U.S. and go back in the field. I was excited that we got to move but very disappointed that I was going back to a previous job. I did not do as well in that new job and within six months I was let go and looking for another job. Because I was young, I was asking myself, "why this was happening?" I realized, years later, that when a new manager, president, etc. comes into power, they may not hold the same values and visions that you do. There is nothing wrong with that but, if you cannot make the transition then it is probably time to move on. I should have moved on earlier. I needed to learn about humility and building value in what I was doing in the position that I was in. I was a company trainer and the new president wanted to eliminate the non-revenue producing position and push the responsibility back onto the regional managers to train their team and new hires.

Are there signs that you need to change? What are they? Can you see them with a gentle nudge, or do you need someone to shake up your world to get your attention?

Your Story   August 25

"When you are telling your story, hold your own ink pen. Don't let anybody else tell your story." – Tracy Martin

If you could write the end of your story, what would it look like? Do you become the hero? Do you ride off into the sunset alone or with your partner by your side? Do you get old and have this amazing impact on your world and leave a legacy behind that lives on for decades? Why do we always want a storybook ending? Why do we want to live this life that everyone talks about later? Can you live out your life dreams now?

When we live our best life now and stay in the moment and not focus on the future, we get to experience a life worth living. If we do what we think we are supposed to do in this life, we will be remembered by those that matter. We will leave a legacy that goes beyond our wildest dreams. We will become a hero for someone to emulate. So, what does your story look like? Can you start now, or do you have to wait until things get a little better, or just right? Do you need a bigger audience to witness what you do? You will get the audience that you need when you do the things you are supposed to do. The number of people that follow you, like you, or watch your videos is a fleeting thing and most will forget you once the next person comes along. It is human nature to follow the bouncing ball. Your story starts now. Your ending is one that can wait and will wait until you are finished writing your current chapter. Little steps make big changes. What can you do today to start living like you are supposed to be living?

Today, I will focus on the present and not worry about the future or how my story will end. The story will end when it is supposed to, and it will end with greatness because it will be a life well-lived.

Equality   August 26

"Weeds are flowers too, once you get to know them." – A. A. Milne

Equality has been a struggle for the world since the beginning of time. When you treat people as less than yourself or your peer, there is an imbalance. People are different and should be noted as such. The conflict comes when you look down on people because they are not as educated, not as artistic, not as talented, or do not have as much money as you. What gives you the authority to tell them how they ought to live so it fits your narrative on how people ought to be? What if someone thinks differently than you do? If they have different values, different religious beliefs, or choose to wear certain clothing that you would never wear, does that make it ok to pick on them, talk down to them or make you feel more or less human?

I used to have a different view than I do now. I grew up learning about inequality and feeling a certain way when I was around people that had more or less than we did. People that were naturally smarter or not as smart. I was taught to believe a lot of these things by a lot of people not just my circle of influence. I have learned that it does not matter what my job is or what another person's job is or what they choose to have or not have. People have different talents, gifts, and things that they can tolerate. Some people love to create food, buildings, manage others, follow others, create documents, file documents, or manage the chaos of self and others. We are not equal, we are not all the same, and treating everyone as if they should be the same person with the same values and the same religious beliefs would be very shortsighted. Understanding that people are different and have different needs and wants is what the world is all about. Learning to let people live their lives the way they want is ok too, as long as it does not harm others. If we were all the same, the world would be a very sad place. Diversity is what makes the world a better place.

Today, I will learn to live and let live without the view that everyone should have the opportunity to live as they choose without my condemnation or judgment.

INSPIRED   AUGUST 27

"Don't limit yourself. Many people limit themselves to what they think they can do. You can go as far as your mind lets you. What you believe, remember, you can achieve." – Mary Kay Ash

Do you inspire people? Can you inspire people? What inspires you? We all have the chance to inspire and be inspired. It does not take a grandiose action or gesture. It takes heart sometimes to move someone else. It usually takes us being present to be inspired or to inspire others. Sometimes it takes words to inspire and other times a quiet action or gesture. I am inspired by those around me because I choose to be inspired by their actions, their words, their faith. Here is your chance to be inspiring today. Do not wait for someone else to inspire you, go and inspire. When you need to be inspired or when you see a chance to be inspired by someone, then do so. Your life is an inspiration to someone, you may or may not know them. You are inspired by someone that you may or may not know, pass it along to others so that they too can be inspired. I am inspired to help people do what inspires them, so that they may be fulfilled. *This* is my why!

Today, I get to inspire and be inspired.

REGRET   AUGUST 28

"At the end of your life, you will never regret not having passed one more test, not winning one more verdict, or not closing one more deal. You will regret time not spent with a husband, a friend, a child, or a parent."
– Barbara Bush

We have probably spent time in our lives evaluating what we have done and not done. Maybe these thoughts bring up regrets. Learning to live a life that has no regrets is hard to do but it can be possible. I know that I have made mistakes in my life and sometimes I wonder what would have happened if I choose to do something a little different. I would not be the person I am today if I changed one thing or more things in my past. Are you making choices that will lead you to sorrow or joy? What about those that you love? Are you making those decisions with them in mind and how they will be impacted? I have made some of those hard decisions in my life and they sucked! I know that the decisions I made impacted my loved ones and changed the course of my life and theirs. Some of the decisions ended with a positive ending and others did not.

We have to make mistakes in our lives in order to grow. How do we get better at making the right choices with the least amount of impact on ourselves and others? That, sometimes, is the part that sucks! Sometimes the best thing for us hurts others or the best thing for others hurts us. It is very noble to think that we will always choose the pain for us versus others but that is not always the case. I had a decision to make once that I knew had an impact on my family and friends. I felt like I was beating my head against a wall. I could not make progress with the situation, and it was not going to end well. I could have stayed in the situation and continued to feel the pain, which I had done for years. It was an emotional pain that, in my eyes, was no longer bearable. I decided to leave and not live with the pain anymore. It hurt others and that was hard but, in my mind and heart, it was the best for all involved. We can live regret-free if we understand the consequences. It does not mean it will not hurt me or someone else.

Today, I will look at the decisions I make and try to understand the consequences that go along with those decisions.

ANNIVERSARIES   AUGUST 29

"May you live all the days of your life." – Jonathan Swift

An anniversary is a date on which an event happened in a previous year. This can be a good thing, like a wedding, a birthdate, or sobriety. It can also be a tragic memorial, like the start of a war, a divorce, or the loss of a loved one. If you look at a calendar you can find something to celebrate on almost every day of the year. Some are more memorable than others and some have deeper meanings.

I recently celebrated a good anniversary and two weeks later one that was not so good. Celebrations of the anniversaries of my birthday, and the death of my brother all happen within two weeks. Life has a weird way of making sure that you live all the days of your life, as mentioned in the quote above. I get the choice to wake up every day with an outlook of my choosing. I can choose to have a positive or negative outlook on the day presented to me. I get to choose whether I am devastated by the memories and the feelings of grief, or if I will feel the feelings and find the positive impact that was made. We all have choices when it comes to anniversaries. We can choose to ignore them, as some people do with their birthdays saying they are nothing more than another day in the year. I find that tragic. An anniversary is a time to reflect on the past year. To remember where you were and how you have grown during that time. You may have lost a step or two along the way, but I bet it has been one heck of a ride these past three hundred and sixty-five or three hundred and sixty-six days. Filled with laughter, tears, joy, and heartache. *We* get to live and experience all that comes with the days. Part of that is the new memories we get to make along the way. So, what will you do with the next year of your life? What will you start today with that you can celebrate one year from now?

Today, I will look at the anniversaries in my life and find ways to celebrate where possible, and reflect on the changes that have happened over the past year. I will feel what I need to feel and make the most of what I have today.

GRIEVING   AUGUST 30

"No one can tell you what to expect or can offer a guide to grief. Because every relationship is so unique, no two people grieve the same way. And you have no idea how you are going to grieve till you are grieving."
– Alysia Reiner

How do you grieve? Grief has its way of working in you and around you. Do you find it in your own space, whether it is your bedroom or a special quiet place? Do you have a friend or loved one that you reach out to? I have been able to do both, and both served a purpose for the time. I had to learn to sit with the grief and feel the feelings. There is no wrong way to deal with grief, except to ignore it and push through it. I did that when I was younger and did not know how to handle grief.

I struggled when my first grandparent died when I was in college. I learned how to suck it up and not talk about what I was feeling and be strong for others during that time. I was that was for a while. When my daughters were fairly young and we lost both of the dogs that we had within a few weeks of each other, I about lost it. I got to take both of them to the vet to have them put down because their bodies were shutting down. There was nothing we could do to save them or prolong their lives. I cried and felt the sting of loss not only for me but for my kids. That was hard to let the grief run its course. I did the best that I could with what I had at the time. I had to learn how to grieve again years later when I lost my other grandparents, my stepfather, my brother, and my dad. Each one meant something different and needed a different type of grieving. "Grief will come when it wants and go when it wants," said a counselor.

Talk it out and let those close to you help you by just listening when you are grieving. And do not forget to be that person for those that are close to you because they will need it too.

When I go through times of grieving, I will let the emotions flow and do my best to talk to those that can listen, be present, and comfort me.

Humility and Compliments   August 31

"I have been complimented many times and they always embarrass me; I always feel that they have not said enough." – Mark Twain

Getting a compliment can be very uplifting. It can also cause embarrassment and pride. When I was younger, I did not know how to take a heartfelt compliment. I was embarrassed and usually brushed it off with some sort of sarcastic self-deprecating retort. It lost its purpose, meaning, and shine. It takes humility to accept a compliment, especially one that is filled with emotion. I have been brought to tears over a compliment. I have found the best way to overcome my lack of humility in these situations is to say thank you. When I learned of the power of a true compliment, I started to think about how I could give them or how I could be more generous with my praise of others. That also helped me receive them too. I found that the more I was able to express the compliment the better I was at receiving them because I understood the heart that it takes to give a sincere compliment. I understood the emotion behind them and when I was faced with the embarrassment of the person that I was giving to, I would assure them that they are worthy.

When working with a client, can you compliment them? Are you able to find something worthy of praise in your time with others without being cheesy or trying to butter them up? All these come back to character. We can have the character to be humble and offer compliments and even receive compliments. Don't go fishing for compliments either, because that can also be a lack of humility.

Today, I will look for ways that I can sincerely compliment people. And when someone compliments me, I will say thank you. Soaking in the words they have given.

September

One More Step   September 1

"That wall is your mind playing tricks on you. You just need to say, 'One more step, I can do this. I have more in me.' You'll be so proud of yourself once you push yourself past your threshold." – Kerri Walsh

Sometimes, we fall short or stop short of our goal or the end. Have you ever been lost and just cannot get to your location? The GPS is saying you are there, and you are surrounded by nothing but fields? There is nothing. No building, nothing! We drive a little more and still nothing. We cannot see the destination. We get frustrated and feel like turning around and going home. But we cannot. It has to be here or close to here. I was in a rural area about thirty miles outside of Atlanta. I was trying to find a business and my GPS was saying it was ahead on the right. I started to slow down and look for the business. I came upon the location that the GPS said it was located and there was nothing. A field and not a house or a business anywhere in sight. I drove a little further and turned around and drove a little more and still nothing. I had to drive around for another twenty minutes until I finally found the building and my location, which was just beyond where I originally stopped. Sometimes we do not go far enough to find the destination or the thing that we are looking for. When we find ourselves coming up short, do we know how to push ourselves? Do we have the ability to go a little further?

Today, I will find ways to push myself to take one more step.

Watch What You Say   September 2

"Before you speak ask yourself if what you are going to say is true, is kind, is necessary, is helpful. If the answer is no, maybe what you are about to say should be left unsaid." – Bernard Meltzer

Have you ever wished you could take back the words that are coming out of your mouth? Something insensitive, that you thought was funny, but after it came out of your mouth it was devastating. You thought they said one thing and you responded to that something, which was completely off base. Why do we do that? We can get in such a hurry to speak and let people know how smart we are. Sometimes we feel nervous and want to say something that will appear intelligent. If we would take the advice written above it will help us. Pause and ask if what you are going to say is, true, kind, necessary, and helpful. We might not talk as much as we do if we did that. I know of several instances when I said things that were neither true, kind, necessary, or helpful. I have said things that were just one of those and felt the sting of remorse as the words left my lips. Unfortunately, I still struggle with this. I was talking to a new friend the other day and said something about a conversation that I had with another friend. It was a remark about the car that they were driving, trying to be funny. I said it and immediately wished I had not said it. My dad tried to motivate me one time and the words that came out of his mouth hurt me instead of motivating me. It took about six months for us to clear the air on that. Be mindful about what you say because it can and will affect you both personally and professionally.

Today, I will ask myself if what I am saying is true, is kind, is necessary, and is it helpful. The answer may surprise us and cause a pause when we talk.

WHEN WAS THE LAST TIME YOU GOT ANGRY? SEPTEMBER 3

"Anybody can become angry - that is easy, but to be angry with the right person and to the right degree and at the right time and for the right purpose, and in the right way - that is not within everybody's power and is not easy." – Aristotle

In life, we are faced with many different situations. How do you determine when to react and how to properly react? It is easy to just fly off the handle and respond in kind to the situation or the person. There is a time to respond with joy, kindness, sadness, even with anger. We can get angry when someone pushes our buttons again and again. We can get angry when, at the right time, for the right reasons, and in the right way, the situation dictates we show the proper level of anger. When we respond with anger in the proper way, it communicates the exact message that was intended. How do we do it? Should we practice? Probably not, but then again maybe. If you are anything like me, practice will come naturally because situations will present themselves. I can look at my life and find a number of examples when I got to practice responding with anger. Some were the right way and others were not. Did I show too much anger or not enough? I have had situations come up in public that needed to be dealt with in private. I have also had some situations come up in private that needed to be dealt with publicly. Learning how and when to be angry is not always easy, but it is a necessary skill.

Grant me the ability to see when I need to be angry and when to remain calm.

WHERE DO YOU SEE YOURSELF IN FIVE YEARS?   SEPTEMBER 4

"The difference between where you are today and where you'll be five years from now will be found in the quality of books you've read."– Jim Rohn

If I had a crystal ball or a good fortune-telling ability, this would be an easy question to answer. Reading or listening to books, listening to podcasts, or watching instructional videos are all ways to learn and grow as an individual or team. In my younger years, I did not understand the importance of reading or listening to books. As I learned more about leadership and growing as a salesperson, I found that the best way to learn was to read what others had done. Like most things in life, goals, and action plans to fulfill those goals, make it easier to get to where we want to go. Do you have a five-year plan? How are you going to get there?

Do you have a plan that involves reading books, if so, how many? I have read and heard, that a number of successful people read at least sixteen business books a year. I personally have a goal of sixteen business books a year and an additional forty-four books of my choosing, or what I call "fun" books. That is about one book per week or five books per month. Some weeks and months are better than others. Some books are short, and some are really long. There, in lies the balance. Books give me vision, dreams, and goals. They help me to push myself and expand my horizons. When asked where I see myself in five years, it probably has something to do with the books that I have read.

Today, I will look at my future plans and ask myself if books or instructional videos can help to form my future.

CHARITY   SEPTEMBER 5

"I expect to pass through life but once. If therefore, there be any kindness I can show or any good thing I can do to any fellow being, let me do it now, and not defer or neglect it, as I shall not pass this way again." - William Penn

What do you think about giving charity to others, whether it is time given or money was given? What about receiving charity, again whether time or money received? Whether it is money or time from someone else, we could all use some help at various times. That is charity. We may not think about it that way or want to think about it that way but that is what charity is. Help provided to another in a time of need. Why are we so stubborn when it comes to charity, giving or receiving? Some people find it hard to give because they want to put conditions on the time or money they give to another person. They want to make sure that *their* money or time is used the right way. When you give like this, with conditions, you take away the very nature of the word. You strip the kindness and love out of the situation. When you learn how to not control your gift it then becomes an act of love. If you cannot give without control, then you should not give.

I found out I was doing this when I was giving to people. I wanted them to act a certain way or take the "gift" I was giving them and use it a certain way. What I had to unlearn was that I do not get to control how a gift is used and be ok with that. When I learned that giving is all I can do and all I should expect is nothing in return for the gift. If I could not give in that manner, then I should not give. I stopped giving for a time until I was able to learn how to give properly. I continue to learn as I give to others, whether time or money. Time can also by just stopping to talk to someone, give a kind word, or share some wisdom that you have learned. So, what is your view on charity?

Today, I will find ways to give without expectations or desire to control what gift I have given to others. If I cannot give freely, then I should not give. I may need to unlearn some things before that happens.

Procrastination   September 6

Working is one of the most dangerous forms of procrastination."
– Gretchen Rubin

Procrastination can mean a lot of things. Most importantly, you are not ready to do or deal with what's right in front of you. I have found that when given a task that needs to be done, I need to do it as soon as possible so that I can move on to the things that I enjoy doing. It is called "eating the frog." Sometimes though, we are not ready to do that chore, that task, or that assignment until the last possible minute. We use excuses like, I work better under pressure, or I do not have time to deal with that right now. Those may be true. I think about how many term papers or reports could have been done with more accuracy or been written better if I only had done it earlier. What have you been putting off, letting sit on your desk until it was time? Maybe today is the day to get that off your plate and move on to other more interesting things that you really want to put time into.

Today, I will look for things I have been putting off or procrastinating and finish them so I can get to the things that I really enjoy.

Ability   September 7

"We all have ability. The difference is how we use it." – Charlotte Whitton

We are all capable to a certain extent. I have the ability to walk, to talk, to see, to hear, to dream, to live, to laugh, and to love. All these things are gifts that should not be taken for granted. I also have the ability to hate, to frown, to yell, to not listen, to despise, and to be unhappy. All of these are choices that we get to make and when we decide what we want to do in that time and in that place is where we will use our abilities. Will we use it to succumb to the pressure of others? Will we use it to stand for what we believe in? Just because we have the ability to lie does not mean that we should. We have choices in how we treat people and how we will act in situations with friends and family. When we are sitting with a client, what abilities are you using to "get the sale"? Do you treat them with care and respect or with contempt and deceit? What are you going to do today? How will you choose to use your abilities?

Today, I will give more thought to my abilities and understand the manner in which I choose to use them, either for the positive or the negative, with myself and those around me.

What Are You Hiding?   September 8

"Isn't everyone hiding something?" – Jessica Sorensen

We all have secrets. Maybe it is things we are embarrassed about or things that we are ashamed of having done. Sometimes we were just a party to something that happened, but we never said anything about it.

I used to have a few secrets. In fact, I used to believe that I should not trust people because if you share your secrets, they will hold them over your head or against you. I did not know how to trust myself, let alone others. Most of the secrecy came about because I was living a life centered around me and I did not learn how to love myself or others properly. If I wanted something or wanted to do something, I would probably get it or do it. There is nothing wrong with being ambitus so long as you are not intentionally hurting others to get what you want.

As I got older, I learned that if I was doing something I did not want others to know about, then I probably should not be doing that thing. I learned over time to become a serial perfectionist to prevent embarrassment. I did not like to make mistakes, nor do I know many who do. I would overthink things to the point it would take me a long time to make a simple decision or action. As an adult, when asked about my most embarrassing moment, I would share about something that happened in high school or college. I blocked myself to the point where I could not share or acknowledge that I had made embarrassing mistakes. There came a point in my life when I did not think that I was loveable and that my life was too much of a burden. I was not happy, and I could not admit that the life I dreamed of and was currently living, were two very different paths. I did not believe that continuing to live this life was worth it. I was in a bad place, and I was hiding it from everyone. Not even my closest friends or family knew the pain that I was feeling. I could not share that because I did not believe that people would not understand. I found that to be a complete lie. People do and did understand because they have had similar thoughts, situations, and even actions. You can share whatever you want in a loving environment, and they might love you even more because you trust them with these secrets. When we keep these secrets to ourselves, it becomes a burden mostly to us, but also to the ones that we love. We are not being our true selves. We are a shell of the person we can and should be. It can feel like the weight of the world is upon us and it makes simple decisions, like what to eat, feel like monumental decisions.

What are you hiding? It sounds like a simple question, but it can have a powerful impact if we allow it. I was sharing with a friend the embarrassing thoughts that were running through my head recently. They chuckled, not at me but with me because he shared that he had similar thoughts. It was powerful because we became closer friends. You do not have to hide anymore.

Today, I will find a way to share the things I have been hiding. I will begin to trust myself and trust others. Who can you share things with today?

Less is More — September 9

"Less is only more where more is no good." – Frank Lloyd Wright

I went to college to study Architecture. I finished with a degree in Speech Communications. My first job outside of college was in sales. I used to use the "shotgun" approach to sales. I would verbally give every detail I could think about the product and hope that something would get through, and they would buy. I did ok in my first job, but I was not a sales professional by any means. Fast forward to now where I coach people on how not to use that ineffective method of communication. In sales, less is more because most of the time more is no good. When we bombard people with information, we are not looking to meet anyone's needs other than our desire to talk. How much more effective can you be with fewer words? Can you sell if you speak less than 50% of the conversation? This is not just a tool for a salesperson. What about in your personal life? Maybe it is time to find out how to communicate more effectively. Ask the right questions. Give the appropriate answers. Cut to the chase, so to speak. We can be more direct and use fewer words.

Today, I will look for ways to effectively communicate better. Saying less can actually give everyone more from your time together.

CLOSURE   SEPTEMBER 10

"Your experiences are what made you what you are today. So, when tragedy happens in people's lives, and things are left unsaid, it can be very unsettling. The lack of closure can linger." – Michael Pitt

Whether it is the loss of a friendship, loss of a romantic relationship, or the death of a loved one, if you do not have closure, it can take you a while to get over the painful experience. I have lost a friendship, that I had for years, due to a number of things. When you are on a pattern of growth in your life and your friend is not on a similar type of growth pattern then you have to evaluate that relationship. I decided to end a long-term friendship because they were not growing but they were also headed down what appeared to me as a destructive path for them and those around them. I was not willing to go down their path. I was at a point in my life where I needed to be protecting myself and those around me. I lost a romantic relationship because of a similar issue. Now before you make the point that I am the common denominator in these situations, which was true, I was also learning more about what it meant to find my peace and not try to solve other's problems. That is called codependency. I had to realize that my health and wellbeing are more important than others especially if the other people in my life were causing me emotional or psychological pain. I was not able to get the closure that I would have liked, and it took me a while to bring those relationships to a close. Likewise, I have lost friends to suicide and there was no closure, no goodbye, no note as to why they decided to leave. Things like this are hard to deal with. When you can get closure, you can move through these types of things quicker. It does not mean that you get over them, but it will help you get through them. Sometimes you need to forgive them in order for you to have closure. That is not easy especially if they hurt you over and over with their actions and their words. Starting with you is always the best way to work through things like this, or at least it has been for me.

Today, I will find ways that I can bring some closure to the things that have been holding me back.

QUIET   SEPTEMBER 11

"We need quiet time to examine our lives openly and honestly - spending quiet time alone gives your mind an opportunity to renew itself and create order." – Susan L. Taylor

Do you know how to seek out the quiet, daily? The quiet is a deafening stillness. You can hear yourself breathing, the gentle wind, and nothing all at the same time. When I was in my twenties and thirties, I was not as connected to the quiet. I longed for it, and I waited for it when the kids were having a tough time falling asleep. There were days when I just left a particularly difficult client, or one that talked a lot, or one where I had to talk a lot. I would get into my vehicle and turn off all the sounds as I drove away to my next appointment. No phone calls, no radio. Just the hum of the vehicle.

Today, as I sit in my red chair, I can feel the quiet, stillness of the morning, I am able to hear everything and nothing at all. I hear the gentleness of the air being pushed by the ceiling fan. I hear the raindrops outside. The quiet surrounds me. It is peaceful and serene. We all need to have quiet times. To gather ourselves and our thoughts. To leave the world aside for a few minutes and clear our minds. Remove the inner voice that sings a song or tells you how things ought to be. Find the quiet. Find the peace. Find yourself in the quiet. It may take a minute to find it, but it is there, even if you live in a busy city apartment with thin walls. If you need to go out to the woods, take a drive in your vehicle, find the quiet that awaits you.

Today, I will find quiet time and enjoy the peace and stillness surrounding me.

ARE YOU A FOOL? SEPTEMBER 12

"It is better to remain silent at the risk of being thought a fool than to talk and remove all doubt of it." – Maurice Switzer

Do I remain silent or speak? We have probably chosen both paths, to speak and not to speak. We want people to think we are smart. We want people to think well of us. Yet we keep giving them an opportunity to be disappointed. What is it about us that feels the need to fill the empty air with words? I have been proven a fool more times than I care to admit, but I keep learning from most of those situations. I was speaking with a group of friends one day and there was a "sales" question that was posed to the group. Being one of the two salespeople in the conversation, I immediately thought, I have the answer. This is an easy one. I even mentioned out loud how I was eager to answer. I gave my advice and spurred the other, wiser salesperson to give his response. He thoughtfully sat back. Asked a few clarifying questions. Pondered some more. Then thoughtfully and gently gave us his pearls of wisdom. I was so disappointed in myself and even felt embarrassed because I just gave a quick thoughtless answer. I wanted to appear smart when, in fact, I was simply the fool. I spoke without all the facts. My friend was right in his discernment of the situation. I learned from that, again to be slow to speak. When we speak without all the information, we give poor advice. But who is the blame for the poor wisdom? Is it really even wisdom if it is wrong for the person or the situation?

What will it take for us today to learn to listen and ask the appropriate questions? Too often we are the fool, though we think we are being wise.

BUCKET LIST   SEPTEMBER 13

"People talk about this 'bucket list': 'I need to go to this country. I need to skydive.' Whereas I need to think as much as I can, to feel as much as I can, to be conscious and observe and understand me and the people around me as much as I can." – Amy Tan

Do you have a list of things that you really want to see or do before your life is over? Are you adventurous? Are you one that wants to see certain things, or experience what the world has to offer in food and drink? Maybe, you like to see the different types of architecture, or see the beauty of the mountains, lakes, or oceans? Do you have a list of things that you want to accomplish from a sales or business perspective? What is a bucket list for you? Is it your lifetime achievement award or a list of goals? If you have a list, how often do you work on it? If you do not have a list, should you create one?

I have one that changes. I feel like once I cross a thing or two off then I need to add more to it. I have been blessed to do a number of things that people would probably consider worthy of a bucket list. In the past ten to fifteen years, I have focused on the experiences in life versus the places. I would rather go to dinner with friends or family and experience a meaningful conversation and taste some really good food. I like driving to the mountains or the ocean and taking in the view and being present in the experience. Can you experience life now and let that fulfill your bucket list? Can a bucket list be full of things that a lot of people take for granted, like a deep conversation with a friend or a loved one? Cooking a great tasting meal for friends or family. Watching a sunset or sunrise and appreciating the beauty that is in front of you? For some, this is not possible because they see things differently than I do. What about you? What do you want to see or do that flips the emotional buttons that make you pause so you can see the beauty or the serenity? I know people that have a hard time pressing pause. It is a challenge for them to stop and just breathe. They are constantly on the go and that is ok too.

Today, I will look for the things that I find peace in and can create my own list of things I want to do and experience.

Find Your Passion   September 14

"Finding your passion isn't just about careers and money. It's about finding your authentic self. The one you've buried beneath other people's needs." – Kristin Hannah

Do you know what you are passionate about? This is something that can get your heart to swell and be fulfilled. These are the things that you can get lost in and the smile never leaves your face. These are the things that you were made for doing. When you find your passion, you will know. You beam, your heart is content, your true self is coming out. I have a few things that I am passionate about and people around me know that as well. When people ask me about training and coaching others, I light up. My eyes shine brighter, they even get bigger. People have told me they can tell that I love to contribute to other people's success. When I get to help someone, who is genuinely interested in learning about sales, I feel different. I am sure that I sound different and look different too. I lose track of time, though I am careful not to completely lose track of time. When asked, what would you do if you won the lottery, my response is simple, I would do what I am doing now and coach and train people until I could not do it anymore. Then I would go play golf! What is it in your life that makes you feel like this? Do you have something that you are passionate about? Would you do it for free if given the opportunity? That is usually a good sign that you are passionate about it.

Today, I will start to clearly define what I am passionate about. Then I can decide how I want to pursue it if I am not already chasing after it.

BEING TRANSPARENT WITH ONESELF — SEPTEMBER 15

"I love when things are transparent, free and clear of all inhibition and judgment." – Pharrell Williams

We want things to be transparent around us, at our job, with our friends, but when it comes to being transparent ourselves, we clam up. We forget that we should be transparent with ourselves first and foremost. This ties into being honest with oneself. If you cannot be honest and transparent with yourself, then you cannot be that way with others. Why is this such a challenge? More than likely, because we are all listening to the judgment that has been passed on to us over time, and now it is our inner voice. We have been around it so much that we have become it. Are you shaking your head too? The thought of being something like that makes me shake my head and cringe because I want to shake it off and get away from it. I do not want to be a part of it, even in thought. I have learned the value of being transparent with myself first, so I can be the same with others. I was not taught to be this way growing up. I had to learn this over time and through many trials and errors. When I learned about being transparent, I no longer had to hide in shame. I no longer had to worry about what I thought, or what others thought about me. We forget how judgmental we can be with ourselves, let alone others. I know who I am, and I no longer need to make excuses or explain why I am who I am because I have been transparent first to me than to others.

Today, I will find ways to be more transparent with myself and with others. Finding ways to open my heart to the true person I am.

FAMILY — SEPTEMBER 16

"No matter what you've done for yourself or for humanity, if you can't look back on having given love and attention to your own family, what have you really accomplished?" – Lee Iacocca

Some of us grew up in a family environment that was safe and full of love. Others of us grew up in less than ideal family situations where they continued to pass down the bad habits and teachings they received in their home. Maybe it was toxic, and we did not realize it at the time. When we were able to step back and look at it, we got to see how bad it really was. We had rationalized it for years. We may say things like, "it was not that bad" or compare your situation to another saying, "See, it was not that bad." We build up a wall that causes us to not see the reality of that situation or other situations because we are using rose-colored glasses. We only choose to see the good stuff and that is not always reality. I believe that we should look for the good in people and situations, but if we cannot assess the person/situation clearly, then we will become surprised when we get hurt by the reality of it.

When we understand the gravity of what we grew up in, we get the chance to break that chain if we choose. We get the opportunity to love and show how we want to be a part of a healthy family instead of continuing in the disfunction. Family can be a big part of how we view the world. How we act in the world and how we deal with the things that are presented to us. If you grew up in a loving and caring environment, what are you doing to pass that along? Even better still, how can you improve on your family and others? If you grew up in a toxic environment, is that what you are passing along, or are you trying to change that? We all have choices. What are you going to do with yours?

Today, I will look at the family life I have been building and how that has impacted my life and those around me. I will look to make decisions that can positively impact myself and others.

Preparation and Expectation   September 17

"This is the precept by which I have lived: Prepare for the worst, expect the best, and take what comes." – Hannah Arendt

When we are younger, we tend to have great expectations and yet we do not have the foresight to see the potential pitfalls that may lie ahead. There is a certain level of naïveté that we carry with us, and there is nothing wrong with that. As we get older and more seasoned by our experiences, we tend to change our level of expectation and start planning for all the things that could go wrong. If we have high expectations, we can get disappointed. It does not mean that we cannot expect a certain level of professionalism or maturity from some people in some situations. Just remember that others do not have the same standards as you and do not always think the same or act the same way. So, when you have a meeting planned with someone, you have a date or even plans for a vacation, plan what you can so that if things go a different direction, then you know what your options are going to look like. Expect to have fun and maybe even learn something. Anything beyond that is all icing on the cake.

Today, I will look at ways that I can have proper expectations and preparations for myself and others. To not lose hope or be overly disappointed by my expectations or my preparations.

WHAT DRIVES YOU?   SEPTEMBER 18

"Human progress has always been driven by a sense of adventure and unconventional thinking."- Andre Geim

Why do you get up in the morning? Is it simply because you have a job? Is it because you want to get the promotion, so you have to get to work before the other people to prove you are worthy and dedicated? Are you inspired by the work that you do so you cannot wait to get up and start to work? There are all kinds of things that can drive us to do the things that we do. Salespeople may tell you that they are driven by money. Some are driven by helping others. Whether you are driven by money, helping others, or any number of other reasons, you have something that can motivate you every single day. Some people learn that by developing goals, they are more inclined to get things done because it motivates them to see the prize in front of them.

I have been driven by different things at different times in my life. I have been motivated by money, family, friendly competition, and because I want to help others. Each had a place in time in my life. Each served a different purpose and taught me along the way. I needed to have each one so I could learn the importance of each of those things in my life. I have found the most rewarding thing for me has been my motivation to help others. I am inspired to help others do what inspires them so that they may be fulfilled.

Today, I will find out what inspires me or drives me to do the things I do.

What has Broken You? SEPTEMBER 19

"I see a broken shell and I remind myself that something might have needed setting free. See, broken things always have a story, don't they?"
- Sara Pennypacker

In life, we are faced with many challenges. Sometimes we are thrown and tossed about, and we can, like a lot of things, find ourselves broken. In the Bible, Matthew 21:44 refers to falling on a rock and being broken versus the rock falling on us and crushing us. We all have had hard times in our lives, and it can break us. But for some, the brokenness brings about a rebuilding, a strengthening due to the repair. It is hard to allow ourselves to be broken by things that happen in our lives, but the alternative is far worse. If we do not allow ourselves to be broken, then we will get crushed. It is much harder to repair something that has been crushed because the pieces may be too small to gather and put back in place. If you look at your life, you can probably point to times when you were broken, and you can tell of the triumphal repair and what that did for your character or resolve. Great lessons can be taught from being broken.

What has broken you? What has caused you to repair and rebuild? Maybe you have gone through something recently that has you feeling broken. Find all the pieces, talk to people that can help you heal, and then resolve to be a stronger person from the lesson. We all get the chance to learn.

Today, I will find the resolve to fix what may have been broken in me. I can then allow myself to heal.

SAME KIND OF DIFFERENT AS ME   SEPTEMBER 20

"I found out everybody's different--the same kind of different as me. We're all just regular folks walkin' down the road God done set in front of us."
– Denver Moore

We are all different, yet very much the same. We can think differently and act differently, but we are all humans that experience emotion. Some have more education. Some have better features. Some have more athleticism. We all are built for different things. We have highs and we have lows. We have successes and we have failures. We all get the chance to interact with people. We all get the chance to make a choice when it comes to dealing with others as well. Some are kinder. Some are gentler. Some are gruff. Some have been jaded. Some think of no one but themselves. Others think of anyone but themselves. We may look different, act different, and even have different talents. The question is do you see that we are all human?

Today, I will look past the external features and personal qualities that separate each of us while still acknowledging that we are all the same. We are humans.

LEADERSHIP   SEPTEMBER 21

"The task of the leader is to get his people from where they are to where they have not been." – Henry Kissinger

At some point in our lives or careers, we have had a person show us what a leader looks like, and we were willing to go through anything to work for them. I had such a person shortly after I started working in HVAC. He gave me the first real opportunity to lead, and I will be forever grateful for the chance he took on me. He was able to teach me not just how to read a P&L sheet but how to treat people and help them get to where they wanted to go in their careers. I was not very good at it at first but through his guidance, I was able to learn. He was kind and cared about me and my family. He did not want me to say I worked for him but that I worked *with* him. You may have that person in your life now. If you want to be a leader learn how to take care of those you have been entrusted with and help them to become more than you are today. What would that cost you? Being a great leader means you understand how to surround yourself with the right people to make the team better. Being a leader means taking most of the blame if something goes wrong and little of the credit when it goes right. You get the opportunity to affect others' lives whether it be positive or negative. Choose wisely. If you do not want to be a leader that is ok too. However, do not be that person that makes the leader's job difficult because you are constantly in opposition to them.

Today, I get to be the leader that I need or want to be, helping to change the lives of those around me.

INFLUENCE SEPTEMBER 22

"Act as if what you do makes a difference. It does." – William James

There are so many people in the world right now, we often wonder how we can make a difference? It is hard to see how our lives can change people and the world. Yes, there are about seven billion people on the earth today but how many people do you have the chance to influence? If you influence just one person, have you made a difference? Depending on your age, you have been around at least hundreds and even thousands of people. If you are old enough or live in a big city like New York or Chicago, Beijing, or Hong Kong, then you have probably been around millions of people. You could have influence over some of those people as well. Most of us do not realize the impact that we have or can have on those around us. When I played collegiate football, there were little kids that were asking for my autograph. I was eighteen or nineteen and I had an influence over people that I did not realize. With social media today, we can expand our sphere of influence. It is more important now than it has ever been to act as if what I do makes a difference. Whether you want to or not, your life has influence over others. What will you do with that influence today? It does not have to be some grand gesture. It could be a simple smile that brightens someone else's day. It could be a helping hand to a stranger. It could be taking a friend out for coffee or a meal just to check in on them and spend time with them. It could be spending time doing charity work, building a house, or passing out food to those in need. It could be sending money to an organization that helps others get back on their feet after a natural disaster takes away everything they had.

What does influence look like to you? It could be the cute outfit you are wearing, the beverage that you are holding, or the car you are driving. Influence is about impression as well as impact. So, are you interested in just making an impression, or are you willing to make an impact?

Today, I will find ways to influence people in a way that makes difference in their life. It could also bring joy to my heart.

FLEXIBILITY   SEPTEMBER 23

"Blessed are the hearts that can bend; they shall never be broken."
– Albert Camus

How flexible are you? Are you capable of rolling with the punches? Can you be fluid in a situation and not get upset, bent out of shape, and remain calm? For a lot of us, it depends! Maybe someone is dancing on the last nerve. They have been tormenting you all day, and this is the last straw. Can you go from a rigid situation to a more fly by the seat of your pants situation? What has gotten you to this point? What has trained you to be so flexible and not break down when things don't go your way?

I grew up learning to be very flexible because I got to work for my dad at a young age. I wanted to play like the other kids in the summer, but I got a chance to earn a little money and work on my tan. My dad owned a landscape company and when it is summertime, you have to work. I do not begrudge that situation or my dad for choosing to follow his dreams and own his own company. I would not be the person I am today if I did not receive some of those early lessons in life. I got the chance to learn how to be flexible. Some days started at 4:30 am and others at 6 am. Some days we caught a break because it was raining, and we could not work without causing bigger problems. Sometimes we did work in the rain. Sometimes we could make it home in time to play baseball with our summer teams, other times we got home well after dark. Learning how to be flexible with your schedule can help you.

I know some people that feel like flexibility is their middle name and they will show up when they want and if they want. That is also being flexible. Right? When dealing with customers you may have to be flexible too. They may not move on your timetable and that is ok. They may need some encouragement. They may need a shoulder to cry on or an ear to bend. Can you learn to be flexible?

Today, I will see how I can be flexible with situations or customers. It may be a chance for me to grow and flex a little.

KARMA   SEPTEMBER 24

"How people treat you is their karma; how you react is yours." – Wayne Dyer

Do you believe in Karma? Do you believe that your actions, good and bad, have a consequence to them? Sometimes it is easy to see the consequences of our actions. You are driving your vehicle and you are not focused on the road ahead and you hit something. You quit your job in anger, and now you cannot find a job and have no money. You treat someone with love and compassion, and you receive that back in kind. You give money to someone in need, and you are blessed with receiving that amount or more shortly afterward. Sometimes we do not see the immediate hand of Karma. Someone steals from you, and you do not get to see the person get caught or brought to justice. Someone is a bad salesperson, and they get a promotion. I have made comments that were sarcastic and offhanded, only to feel the instant fate of Karma slap me with a bitter and hurt-filled comment from a friend or colleague. I have also tried to shortcut processes in my job only to have it come back and take twice as long and cost more to do it the right way. I have also known the humility of giving and teaching people the right way and having complete strangers tell me I am doing the right thing and I need to keep going. How do you live your life? Are you aware of your treatment of others?

Today, I will look at how I treat others. I will find ways to keep the good Karma and eliminate the bad.

STRENGTH VS. FEELINGS   SEPTEMBER 25

"Your mind has to be stronger than your feelings. Think about every poor decision that you have made in your life. There was more emotion that was involved in it than there was mind. Every single one of them. Think about it. Your feelings, keep you in bed. Your mind tells you, get up!"
– Tim Grover

Do you struggle with making level-headed decisions? Do you let your emotions get the better of you? People tend to make decisions based on emotions. I have seen and heard a lot of sales trainers talk about making the sale emotional. I have talked about that to people that I have coached or trained over the years. Decisions can be good or bad and our emotions can play a large part in them. If we get too emotional it can make things go in a direction that we do not want. I have made decisions that were not very good ones and when I look back on why I did the things I did it had a lot to do with my emotions. If you get too emotionally attached to something you can make a bad decision. When we allow our mind to add logic to the decision-making process it can help out with the emotional attachment that we may have with something and give us clarity in the situation. When you use your mental strength, you can overcome the obstacles that hinder you like procrastination, laziness, and apathy. If we let our emotions take over, we can stay in bed, not go to that meeting, not make that phone call, or even not ask the hard question when meeting with a client. This comes down to mental strength. What does it take for you to take action and gain mental strength each day? Just like working out builds your physical muscles, making decisions builds your mental muscles.

Today, I will find ways to build up my mental strength. I will not allow my feelings to direct me toward laziness or apathy but allow my mind to move me toward strength.

BACKUP PLANS   SEPTEMBER 26

"I am sure that people in life, have told you, make sure you have something to fall back on. But I never understood that concept, having something to fall back on. If I am going to fall, I do not want to fall back on anything. Except my faith. I want to fall forward." – Denzel Washington

Athletes, actors, people from all walks of life have all probably heard this several times in their lives. The people who are saying that, and I have been that person at times, are afraid for you. They do not know the power that lies within, or do they? Do you have a backup plan? Do you have something that you can go back to if this does not work? Do you have a backup if your marriage does not work out? Do you have a backup plan if you do not do well in sales? Do you have a backup plan if your business does not work out the way you think it should go? If you do, then I would suggest one of two things you need to decide on today! Quit playing around with your current plan and take the backup now! Or maybe it is time to throw away the backup plan so you can focus on the present. A backup plan can be an admission of premeditated failure. Maybe you thought, "I knew it was not going to work out, so I made a backup plan." Your only backup plan should be to try again. Try again. Try again. You get better or is it not something you were built for? I was not made to be a wrestler. I tried it and did not like it very much. I was on the team in middle school, once. Then I took my tall, near six-foot frame over to the basketball team. If you are no good at something, then get better at it or move on to something that better suits your talents. Do not dwell on the fact that you are not good at one particular thing. If you are good at sales but you need to improve then find out what you need to do to improve. Practice what you do and let go of the backup plan.

Today, I will let go of the backup plan and move forward with my current plan. Find ways to improve and get better, making my only plan to keep trying.

BEING USEFUL TO OTHERS SEPTEMBER 27

"I've been to the top of all those material world mountains, and nothing makes you happier other than being useful to others. That's it. That's the only thing that ever will satisfy that thing, is that what you're doing is useful." – Will Smith

When some people get to the top of their success, they can find that the things they thought were important were not that big of a deal after all. I have been at the top of my sales team, and it was great, and it was cool to be admired by others for a short time but, people thought I was cocky, arrogant, and selfish. I was all of those things at different times or maybe the same time if that is possible? But once I got there, what was next? To be the best in the region? I was on some level. To be the best in the nation, or the company, or the world? Being the best comes at a cost. You do not typically get to be the best without causing yourself or someone else pain.

I like what Will Smith says, "nothing makes you happier than being useful to others." Some will argue that it is good to be the king, on top, or whatever the best is. But are you helping others? After I became the top salesperson at my company, I got the chance to do more and be more. I got to go on to lead others and I found out very quickly what it meant to be useful to others. I found it hard and stressful at times, but it was way more satisfying than winning the award for being the top salesperson. What would you do with all that money, success, or adoration if you were at the top? If someone gave you ten million dollars, how would it change your life? Would your character be different, or would it get magnified by the amount of money you had? In my experience, I have found that when you work hard, do the best you can, and continue to grow, the money will take care of itself. You will make more than enough to support yourself and those around you.

Today, be the best that you can be in your professional and personal life. Choose to be someone that gives rather than takes.

Ask for What You Need   September 28

"If you don't ask for what you need, the need will keep getting bigger."
– Iyanla Vanzant

Do you struggle to ask for help? When you need something, do you agonize over asking others? Too often we think we are not worthy, or we may think that we do not know them well enough to ask for help. Maybe we have not talked to someone in a while and now we need their help. Maybe, we are overthinking the situation and building up a false conversation in our own heads. There are a lot of scenarios in which we can talk ourselves out of trying to get help. But when we really need something, and we fail to reach out, that need does not just go away.

When I was running a company for the first time, I needed help. I did not have all the answers and situations arose that were not covered in the management training class. Some of the things were quick reminders of things I had seen in the past and others were tougher situations that warranted someone with more experience. I learned that I needed help early on and I was not afraid to pick up the phone or send an email to garner help. As time went on though, I slowly asked for less and less help, thinking I could do this on my own or I should know some of this by now. It made asking for help more challenging because then I would start to overthink things and waste too much time looking for the answers when I could have had a conversation with someone and gotten what I needed much sooner. I let my ego start getting in the way. I learned how to ask for what I needed. Years later, I would get the same opportunity.

There will be plenty of times in our lives when we get to ask for what we need. If we are willing, there are people around us that can and want to help. Will we let them? Sometimes we ask God or the universe for help. Someone appears in our life to give us what we need, and we do not believe this is the right person or the same thing we asked for. We think we know better and yet we are getting just what we need. But we do not like the delivery system or person delivering the thing we need. Do you push them away? Do you keep asking the universe or God for a specific need, not seeing the answer right in front of you?

Today, I will ask for what I need, without angst or trepidation. I will find ways to ask for what I need and believe that I am getting exactly what I need.

SUCCESS   SEPTEMBER 29

"The twin killers of success are impatience and greed." – Jim Rohn

How do you define success? Maybe you see success as having money, selling a million or ten million dollars a year of your product or services. Maybe you see it as being a parent with children that do well in school. Maybe you see it as having certain types of friendships or fifty years of marriage. We all have different goals in our lives.

As I write this, information is given to us instantly. We have handheld computers called smartphones and we have the ability to get our food made for us within minutes because of fast-food restaurants or processed frozen meals.

We all go through the growing pains of wanting to grow up sooner than we probably should. But now we are seeing kids become millionaires. We are also seeing twenty-year-old people become super successful, in the world's eyes, because they are popular, and people are wanting to be like them and buy whatever they are buying. I am seeing people think that becoming successful is just so easy because someone else their age did it. What they do not see is the work that went into helping that person be successful. They do not see the financial backing that was needed to start them on the road to success. We do not see all the planning and failure that happened before the fast-food business became a success. We do not see the sleepless nights spent creating the programming code that went into creating the systems like Facebook, Instagram, TikTok, etc.

People are getting impatient and want things now. We want success without hard work. Sometimes we are in the right place at the right time, and it can speed up our success. Remember that luck is what happens when preparation meets opportunity. It is not often that a salesperson becomes a success story on their first or second try. It is not often that someone becomes a fashion icon on their first or second attempt. It is not often that a person creates a successful company in one or two days or even weeks. Success comes when you work your plan and plan your work. Do not rely on luck to be your plan but be ready to accept it when it comes along, because you were working hard, and someone noticed.

Success can come at any moment, but usually, it comes when we work hard. Do not keep looking for success or it could become a never-ending game of hide and seek.

HUNGER   SEPTEMBER 30

"We have a hunger of the mind which asks for knowledge of all around us, and the more we gain, the more is our desire; the more we see, the more we are capable of seeing." – Maria Mitchell

Are you hungry? Do you know what it is like to go without? There are a couple of ways to look at this. First is the actual hunger for food. The other is a hunger for success. Have you ever fasted for twenty-four hours or more? If you have, then you probably can understand what it means to be hungry. If we miss a meal and we say we are hungry it is like saying I have a paper cut on my finger and I have a major injury. If you go without food for days, then you know what hunger feels like.

When I was in college, I had the opportunity to fast for a week. I decided to not eat food, drink smoothies, take any supplements, or have drinks filled with sugar or high caloric values. I wanted to give up something good for something better. I wanted to learn more and *be* more. When you are learning to be successful you can and should build a hunger within you. A desire for more. What are you willing to give up so you can be more successful? Whether you are an athlete, a business owner, or someone that is learning to be successful in your first sales position, we all can develop that hunger.

What will you give up to become better? If you have not sold anything in a while, do you get hungry or do you give up? If you have not won a game in a while, do you give up or do you focus on the things you need to do to get better? The quote above is true. Once you have gained some knowledge, understood what it is like to win, felt the fulfillment of getting that sale, you want more. You want to do it again and again. What is it that drives your hunger? It could simply be that you love helping people and that makes you more successful at sales. You may need to get better at closing, listening, or answering the customer's questions.

Today, I will find ways to feed my hunger for success. Start to execute the things that I have been lacking and learn how to build a taste for success.

October

Meditating   October 1

"Meditation is not a way of making your mind quiet. It is a way of entering into the quiet that is already there - buried under the 50,000 thoughts the average person thinks every day." – Deepak Chopra

Have you tried to meditate? Can you sit in silence and block out the world and your thoughts? The silence can be incredibly loud at times. There are times when I sit and listen to the noise created by my head, ears ringing or buzzing, the hum of the house. You can think that I am crazy and hearing things, but it is there for me. When I am able to sit in peace and meditate, I can get overwhelmed by the silence. The rush of emotion that I sometimes get just by being silent is hard to handle. But I just sit. I remain in the silence. What about you? Can you sit in silence? I am not talking about reading a book or playing solitaire on your phone or tablet. Can you quiet the thoughts running through your head, telling you about all the things you need to do, or that you are not good at, or the dreams that you have? Try and simply sit, maybe close your eyes, and clear your mind. Why in the world would I do that? I have far too much to do, and I cannot clear my head. I have thought that many times. But when I learned how to sit in silence and clear my head for just five or ten minutes, it became very powerful. I was able to gain clarity on things that I could not before. It is almost like doing a defrag on your mind. It can put things in place and helps clear up the head trash. It took me a while to figure out how to just sit still and be quiet and clear my head of the thoughts. I still struggle with the thoughts at times but that tells me I need to focus more time on meditating, not working on all the other things running through my head. It also does not mean that I meditate to neglect the other things I need to take care of. Take time for yourself and meditate.

Today, I will find a way to meditate for five minutes. I will try and clear my head and listen to the silence.

What Impression Are You Leaving?   October 2

"I've learned that people will forget what you said, people will forget what you did, but people will never forget how you made them feel." – Maya Angelou

Being in sales as an ambassador of information, this quote may dishearten you. You want to make sure that the message is getting across to your customer. Yet, they may be thinking of nothing more than how you made them feel after you have gone and cannot remember what you said or did while you were in their presence. This too is part of your "job" when you are in sales. You think your job is to always "sell" someone on the ideas, products, or services that you and your company provide. But maybe you are there to make someone feel good and that is what makes them use you and your company, products, or services. Are you aware of when this happens? Can you tell when someone needs you to support them, or say what they need to hear to be comforted and feel better than they did prior to you coming into their life? This can help you be a better person and a better salesperson. I had opportunities over the years, during sales calls, to meet people and become friends and we are still friends to this day. They never forgot how I made them feel.

Today, I will find ways to leave a positive lasting impression, one that makes more than a sale and may lead to a long-term friendship.

Straightforward   October 3

"Truth is always straightforward." – Sophocles

Do you know how to be direct and straightforward with others? Some think you must be mean to be direct, and others struggle with getting to the point. Being direct can be refreshing. Even if you are on the receiving side of the direct message. Most people prefer you to be direct with them because they do not like being lied to. You may be thinking, hey I am not lying to them, but you are. If you are willing to "sugar coat" the truth, then you are not willing to tell the truth. Being direct can hurt you and the person you are talking to, but that should not determine if you are direct with them or not.

I had a client that I knew was in financial hardship, they told me that at the beginning of our meeting. I assessed the situation and came back and said that they needed a new HVAC system and she slowly burst into tears. There was no way to fix it, it had to be replaced, yet she did not have the financial ability to change it. We discussed her options and found a solution that would work for her currently. I had another client recently who asked me to assess their business. I asked questions, observed some of their activities, and then sat with them to discuss their current business state. I was direct and said if things did not change, they were going to lose their business. That hit very close to home with them and were nearly brought to tears. They did not want to lose their business. They heard what I said, though it was hard. In both of those situations, I was concerned with how they would take the message, but I knew that I needed to be honest and direct with them so that they could see where they were at. How are you at being direct and taking direct news? Hopefully, you can see the value in the straightforward approach on either side and appreciate that value for what it is. Pain can help us grow if we see the pain for what it is. That is a valuable lesson.

Today, I will see the value in being direct, not to hurt someone or to be hurt. I will find ways to overcome my fear of being direct with myself and others.

Reflections of Self in Others — October 4

"Realize that your world is only a reflection of yourself and stop finding fault with the reflection. Attend to yourself, set yourself right; mentally and emotionally. The physical self will follow automatically." – Sri Nisargadatta Maharaj

Sometimes, we have the ability to see in others what we cannot see in ourselves. Maybe someone made a sarcastic remark, and it immediately bothered us, yet it was not directed at us at all. Maybe someone is insincere or not the least bit empathetic, and it sets us on edge. I have experienced this before and later realized that I struggled way too much with that same issue that I was quick to point out in someone else. Some call it, *you spot it you got it*. This is the ability to see the fault in someone else because you have the same fault. When you realize that you have that issue, are you quick to cover it up and not talk about it to anyone? Do you refuse to see the issue in yourself or want to deal with it? I found that the things in others that bother me the most are probably things I struggle with personally. What do you do when you see this personality trait in yourself? I have found that I become more aware of my character strengths and weaknesses when I take the time to meditate and read. Those two things help me to be more self-aware. When I do that, I am less likely to want to point out the issues of others. If I do, then it is much gentler. I will approach it with the knowledge that I have the same issue or have recently seen that same issue within me and here is what I am doing to correct it. This all comes from humility. This comes back to taking care of ourselves first so that we can help others. Unless you are in leadership, mentorship, or other relationship like these, it is not your job to correct or fix others.

Today, I will look inward before I look outward. Looking to correct myself before correcting others.

MANAGING YOURSELF WITH TIME   OCTOBER 5

"Time management is an oxymoron. Time is beyond our control, and the clock keeps ticking regardless of how we lead our lives. Priority management is the answer to maximizing the time we have." – John C. Maxwell

Time management is hard for most people. But in reality, we are incorrect in thinking that we can manage time. Time continues no matter what we do. It is elusive and will always slip through your fingers unless you learn how to manage yourself with time. If you give yourself thirty minutes to complete this task and you are able to do that then you have managed yourself with time. Are you able to plan your days? How many hours do you need to sleep? How many hours do you need for you, bathing, dressing, spending time with yourself and with loved ones? Then how many hours do you have for work? Too often we think of all that stuff in reverse order. We have to work so many hours a day, then I want to spend this much time with friends or family. Then I have this many hours to watch tv, spend time on social media, or read a book. Then I have so many hours left to sleep. When we do the latter, we rob ourselves of so much joy and fulfillment. We are a slave to our schedule. We get tired or burned out because we do not manage ourselves with time. When we realize we only have so much time in a day and certain things are needed for me to function properly and consistently. If you have a deadline to meet and you need to stay up late and get less sleep, then you need to do that. If you are constantly putting off sleep and food and me time to recharge yourself, then you will not be as productive as if you did do all those things. Time is always moving, but what we do with the time that we have is up to us. Can you make a plan for your time? Start with the small goals and go from there. It will be a challenge because you are having to make a mind shift and that usually does not happen immediately. It comes with time and practice. Eventually, you will become great at managing yourself with time. Let your calendar be your friend that reminds you of your plans for you.

Today, I will learn to start planning my time. My sleep, alone time, family and friends time, and work time. It may not be easy, but I will learn how to manage myself with time.

Spinning Your Wheels   October 6

"It seems to me that the older I get, the more running around I do with less satisfaction, just spinning my wheels." – Paul Newman

Do you feel like you are spinning your wheels? Do you feel stuck in place? You cannot seem to get any traction and the harder you try the more of a mess you seem to be making. Like when our vehicles get stuck in the mud or snow, we tend to floor the accelerator thinking that will free us from the situation. Sometimes the best thing to do is to put your vehicle in the lowest gear and slowly press on the accelerator. This is true with us when we get stuck. We need to slow down to get unstuck. I was talking to a friend the other day about their business and how they realized that they needed to slow everything down so they could speed up. I understood that immediately and thought, how can I slow down my life and my business to get more traction? I have been moving so fast going here and there, meeting after meeting, phone call after phone call. I have been sliding all over the place. Now is the time to slow down, get some traction, and move forward in a purposeful, meaningful direction. When you feel like you are stuck or sliding out of control, take your foot off the accelerator, slow down. Get some traction to move with purpose in the right direction.

Today, I will find ways to slow down where I need to, to get the proper traction in my life so I can move forward and stop spinning my wheels.

Forgiving Yourself   October 7

"It's toughest to forgive ourselves. So, it's probably best to start with other people. It's almost like peeling an onion. Layer by layer, forgiving others, you really do get to the point where you can forgive yourself." – Patty Duke

Learning how to forgive can be hard, especially when you have been in an abusive environment, emotionally or physically. Learning how to take that a step further and forgive yourself can be challenging too. We probably have had the chance to be wronged in our lives and so we have been given the opportunity to forgive someone. They overstepped their role and said or did something that was out of line. We can hold on to that hurtful word or deed or we can choose to forgive them and move on. That is really the purpose of forgiveness, letting go so we can move on. It does not mean that we forget their actions. But how do you handle the things that you say or do to yourself? Have you heard how you talk to yourself? How do you berate or belittle the things that you say or do? We can be our own worst enemy when it comes to criticism. I learned that I was not enough growing up. I could not be enough, do enough, or say enough to be the person I was supposed to be, according to someone around me. That taught me more about how to continually criticize myself and I became not good enough in my eyes. That pushed me to do better, say things better and that holds some merit to bettering oneself. However, that kind of pushing can cause a lot of damage to a person and their ego and self-worth. I have struggled for years to forgive myself for things that I have said and done. I was speaking to a therapist once and they asked, have you ever forgiven yourself? I did not know how to answer that. I think I have forgiven myself for the "big" things, things that I know I should not have said or done. But then I had to think a little deeper and ask, have I really forgiven myself? The issue here is I am an overthinker and I cannot let certain things go until I have thought about it from every possible angle and then looked at it again, and again. I have hesitated on more than one occasion about that question, and I have come to the conclusion that I have forgiven myself, so I can move on and stop asking myself if I really have done that. When you learn to forgive yourself, you can move on. When you learn to forgive yourself, you also learn how to forgive others.

Today, I will look for ways to forgive myself for things I have said or done, so I can start moving forward in my life.

PLANTING SEEDS — OCTOBER 8

"Don't judge each day by the harvest you reap but by the seeds that you plant." – Robert Louis Stevenson

There are people in life that love to plant things and others that like to gather the harvest. For some, it is more fulfilling to see what we have produced each day than to understand the potential of the seeds being planted. Can you see the seeds you have planted? What change you may have affected each day? Maybe you can and maybe you cannot. Are you deliberately planting seeds or are you just hoping that you are? You do not need to teach the world, for no one likes a know it all. Can you see opportunities when they arise? If you are meeting with a potential client, are you looking for ways to plant seeds so that they will want to work with you? When you are giving your sales pitch, are you planting seeds so that the client will become more knowledgeable about you, your product, or your service? When you are with your friends or family, are you planting seeds about the things that you have learned so that they can have similar knowledge or just trying to show how smart you are?

When I was younger, I wanted people to see how wise I was, and I almost always wanted to interject that wisdom when I was in conversations. I was considered arrogant, and rude. I learned that I did not need to be the smartest person in the room, because I rarely ever was, and my comments did not help show my wisdom. I got to learn over time, how to listen and ask appropriate, thought-provoking questions. I learned how I could ask certain questions that would plant seeds. Maybe they grew right in front of me, maybe they did not blossom until later, and sometimes they may not have taken root at all. The words that we speak are like seeds that we get to scatter throughout our lives. If we are lucky, the planted seeds will do what they were supposed to do.

Today, I will find ways that I can plant seeds that I may or may not get to see grow and mature.

Revenge   October 9

"The paradox of vengefulness is that it makes men dependent upon those who have harmed them, believing that their release from pain will come only when they make their tormentors suffer." – Laura Hillenbrand, Unbroken

Have you ever felt like someone owes you because of the wrong that they did to you? Maybe you think they need to be repaid for that wrong? That is the definition of revenge. If you are stuck in your mind and your heart, thinking about how that person wronged you, then you are stuck in a vengeful mindset. That can grab hold of you and set you up for disappointment. Can you let go of things that people have done to you? This is a hard thing to do but when done releases you from their power. As a side note, they probably have no idea that they are still having that kind of power over you and have long forgotten about you and what they may have done to you.

So, how do you get out of the grasp of vengeance? Start by not playing that lopsided recording in your head over and over again. Forgive them, maybe you need to forgive yourself too, and let God or the universe handle it so that you can move on with your life. I know first-hand that is easier said than done, but the amount of relief that you will get from doing that will take the burden away from you. Things that were done to me in my childhood, in sports, in school, things said to me by a boss or co-worker, all caught me off guard and played over and over in my head. They all got to live in my head rent-free because of me, not them. I have taken the time to figure out why it bothers me, forgiven the other person or myself, and then walked away from the situation, in my head and my heart. It does not mean that I have forgotten about the situation but that I have dealt with it so that I can move on with my life without that interference anymore. Inigo Montoya from *The Prince Bride* said, "I've been in the revenge business for so long, now that it's over, I don't know what to do with the rest of my life." Though this is a character in a movie, he was able to move on and figure out the next steps for his life and so can you.

Today, I will let go of the vengeance in my heart and mind to move on to a more peaceful life for me and those I care about.

ARE YOU A GOOD PERSON? OCTOBER 10

"I'm not a believer in predetermined fates, being rewarded for one's efforts. I'm not a believer in karma. The reason why I try to be a good person is because I think it's the right thing to do. If I commit fewer bad acts there will be fewer bad acts, maybe other people will join in committing fewer bad acts, and in time there will be fewer and fewer of them." – Daniel Handler

I was listening to a book the other day and the guiding question was, "are you a good person?" It gave me pause. I thought about the impact of the question. Our knee-jerk reaction to questions of character is usually, well of course I am the positive answer to the question. Upon reflection and deeper thought, is your answer going to be the same? We can get defensive when we are asked personal questions about our character. I have learned the value of being genuine, though there are times I still feel the struggle. When someone asks how I am doing I give thought to it almost every time before I answer because I am not interested in giving pat answers on these types of questions anymore. The same is true about questions like are you a good person. I do not need to overthink this or dwell on it for too long. Can I honestly answer the question? Yes, I can, and I will. For the most part, we can all answer the question with honesty. There are a few times that we do not act properly, think properly, or with good intent. But we generally are good people with good intentions. Allow questions to give you pause and time to quickly reflect on who you are. Be thoughtful and mindful when asked even the basic questions, like how are you today? If you do not allow the time and energy to reflect you become the opposite of the things you want. Thoughtless and mindless.

Today, I will answer questions with truth and heart. Giving enough energy to not be a robot but a thoughtful, mindful person.

PUSHY OR PUSH-OVER? OCTOBER 11

"The question isn't who is going to let me; it's who is going to stop me."
– Ayn Rand

Are you pushy or a push-over? Can you stand up for yourself? Do you set proper boundaries so that others know where you stand? Or do those boundaries fail? Do you have boundaries at all?

While growing up, we all learn different habits, emotions, and things that start to form the ideas that will carry us through our youth into adulthood. We learn to set boundaries or let others set those boundaries for us. The challenge comes when we are confronted with a different thought, belief, or way of doing things. These things can be passed on for generations. We learned something from our parents who learned it from their parents and so on. Eventually, someone gets to decide if they want to keep living this way or change it. We all get a chance to break the cycles in our lives. Some cycles are good, and others are not good at all. We learn how to be pushy by the examples in our lives. Maybe it's the things that we encounter as we are growing up and developing our character. For some, it serves their personality to be a bully, because of how they were treated and were taught to treat others. It is not right to treat others in this way and most get to find that out at some point in their lives. Some people have a meeker personality and do not resist the stronger personality of others. They can be pushed around and bullied until they learn how to use their voice to speak up and set boundaries that serve themselves.

I have lived on both sides of this fence at different times in my life and with different people. Learning to be more consistent and less extreme is part of the lesson to be learned. I was the pusher with some and the pushed around with others. One led to the other. Being pushed around then led to pushing others around because that is how it works right? Wrong! I had to learn that just because I allowed that to happen in my life does not mean that I get to now do that to someone else as a rite of passage. Hazing is an example of this. At one age you are the victim and then later you get to be the bully because that is the cycle. Your parents did things a certain way, that did not make sense to you. Now you are the parent, and you get to say, do it because I said so, knowing in your heart that it is wrong. This is how you get to break the cycle. Be different. Do not pass along the bad things that happened to you. Help others to see that they too get the chance to change the cycles in their lives. You do not have to be pushy or a push-over. Set the appropriate boundaries and help others to do the same.

Today, I will look at the cycles in my life that need to be changed. I will learn to start setting appropriate boundaries for myself and those around me.

KNOWLEDGE VS. WISDOM   OCTOBER 12

"Knowledge comes, but wisdom lingers." – Alfred Lord Tennyson

It can be exciting to learn something new. Sometimes you want to share that newfound knowledge with others because it brought you a new level of understanding. Wisdom is the ability to use that knowledge in a meaningful way. When I started in sales, I got to learn a lot of tips and ideas that would help me be a better salesperson. I became knowledgeable about a lot of things that I was not aware of before. I was young and immature, I spouted off the knowledge that I had just learned and thought that it made me look smarter. It did, but it also made me more arrogant. Just because you know more does not mean you need to start yelling from the rooftop how smart you have gotten. Then I learned about wisdom. Being mature is learning and then dispensing knowledge at the appropriate times. I grew wiser and got better at sales because I was able to learn when it was appropriate and not appropriate to share the knowledge I had been learning. I continue to learn product knowledge, sales tips, and other things that will not only help me but help others get better. Everyone gets the opportunity to learn something new every day. What do you do with the things you learn? Are you able to add that to the things that you can learn or that you can share with others because it has become part of what you do or who you are? Are you compounding all the knowledge, or does it leave your knowledge base after you have seen it or learned it the first time? Building wisdom is like building a house. You must build a foundation then you can build the walls, roof, etc.

Today, I will take the knowledge that I learn and find ways to compile it into wisdom.

Learn to Unlearn   October 13

"The most useful piece of learning for the uses of life is to unlearn what is untrue." – Antisthenes

Have you ever had to unlearn something so that you could learn it again properly? You think you are doing something the right way and you have to teach yourself to unlearn it so that you can learn it the right way. It could be something simple like riding a bike, playing a sport, or learning how to sell. We do things so we can build a process or train of thought in our heads that move to the subconscious. It goes to a place where we no longer have to learn it and it becomes a routine.

When I started in sales, I did not have a lot of experience and so I made mistakes. I let people sell me instead of selling or helping them buy things. I was taught some "old-school" habits of how to manipulate and stretch the truth, a.k.a. to flat out lie to get the deal done. Unlearning can be hard at times. The lying thing was not that hard to change. Teaching myself the proper way to say something was a challenge. The muscle memory that I had with the way I would say things had to change. I had to unlearn so that I could relearn how to say and do it properly. I had to learn how to be comfortable in uncomfortable situations. Being honest with the deliverables of the product, the timing of product availability, and the silence that comes from a pause in a sales conversation because the client is actually pondering your question. What are some things that you need to unlearn so that you can learn them again?

Today, I will see the things that need to be learned properly and start unlearning them, whether they are personal or professional.

INNER PEACE   OCTOBER 14

"True and lasting inner peace can never be found in external things. It can only be found within. And then, once we find and nurture it with ourselves, it radiates outward." – Gautama Buddha

Do you look to external things to make you happy or bring you peace? Maybe it's buying something on sale, eating the perfect meal, finding that ideal relationship. Finding inner peace was like looking for a needle in the haystack for years of my life. I was looking everywhere for it, and it seemed to elude me. I looked at my work, my family, and my friends. I looked in relationships, food, and alcohol. I looked in books, movies, and even sports. I looked everywhere but inside me. Strange, since it is called inner peace, I would look at every external option available. When I looked at myself and what I could control that would help me find inner peace, I was happily surprised. I found the thing that could help me. I had to quiet the voices, external and internal. Being able to calm the inner voice helped me. To not be in constant fight or flight mode but realize that I am safe in my space right now. Look at your feet. Where are they? Are you in trouble or danger where you are right now? If you are reading this, you are probably sitting somewhere safe. Perhaps your own red chair! Taking breaths that go unnoticed because they are so natural. Easily move your eyes across the page to see the words and understand their meaning. Listening to the sounds around you, or maybe the quiet that engulfs you. Your inner peace is a moment away. Waiting for you to call upon it at any time to come and serve you. The world may be in total chaos around you right now, but you are finding your inner peace and nothing else matters. You need it. Find it. Go to it whenever you need it to lighten your stress or to just take a break. Your inner peace is there if you look in the right place. Listen to your inner voice now as it lifts you up for taking time to find your inner peace. Come back soon and often.

Today, I will make time to find my inner peace and let it flow over me. Understanding that it is here and available when I want to find it. I just have to look in the right place.

YOUR PERSPECTIVE   OCTOBER 15

"The severity of your problems is a matter of perspective. Change your perspective and most of them become insignificant. Some of them will no longer exist as problems - but opportunities instead." – Ernie J Zelinski

I have a different perspective than a lot of other people, mostly because of my height. I was with some people, and they were pointing something out that they could see very plainly. I could not see it because my view was blocked by another object because of my height. However, when I moved, I could see what they were talking about. There are times in our lives when we need to change our perspective so that we can see clearly, without obstruction. Sometimes we just need to look at things differently so that we can see another person's perspective, which gives us clarity and understanding. You have probably heard the phrase, walk a mile in someone else's shoes, or something like that. When you do that, you are trying to look at things from another's perspective. I have been stuck in my way of thinking until someone shares their views and it helps me to understand a situation better. When you are in sales, you are asking people to take a different view of things. You are asking them to take a different perspective and give them understanding. Sometimes they need to have someone persuade them to view things from their perspective. When you started working for a company, you needed to be persuaded or challenged to view their product or service from a different perspective.

Today, I will take the time to look at situations differently, not always just from my view because that may be obstructed or tainted.

RIGHT SEAT RIGHT BUS — OCTOBER 16

"It is better to first get the right people on the bus, the wrong people off the bus, and the right people in the right seats, and then figure out where to drive." – Jim Collins, Good to Great

This idea took me a while to understand this concept. When I became a leader/manager it became much clearer to me. If you read the book *Good to Great* the author, Jim Collins discusses this concept. If you have been in sales or any job for that matter, for any length of time you will realize that the company you work for is the bus and we all are in different seats on that bus, sales, marketing, administration, etc. Have you ever felt like you do not seem to fit in a company, whether it was the culture or the atmosphere, but you never felt comfortable? You were probably on the wrong bus. Have you ever felt like you just do not like what you do and would rather do something else, but the company that you worked for felt very right for you? Then you were probably on the wrong seat on the bus. I have felt both and have decided to make the move off the bus, and a few times, it was made for me because I was not seeing it. All of this is critical to your success and ultimately the company's success. What are you doing to make sure you are on the right bus and then in the right seat?

I learned that I was on the right bus, I knew this from the day I started researching the company and what they did and what they believed, etc. What I had to figure out was, I was on the wrong seat. That was hard to realize because I am good at my "chosen profession". I have been doing it for decades and have been highly successful at it. Recently, I found that I did not really enjoy this profession like I used to. I did not get the same joy and excitement from the successes as I did in the past, and I wanted to do more and something different. Sometimes you may find that you are frustrated and not really understand why. It may be time to check your ticket and see if you are on the right bus and in the right seat.

Are you on the right seat on the right bus? If not, what can you do to get on the right bus and find the right seat?

When You Survive This   October 17

"When you survive this, it will not be because someone said you could - Although it's good to be reminded from time to time. And when you survive this, it will not be because you had money in the bank or a roof over your head - Because there may come a time when you have neither, and still, you will survive this." – Peter Chiykowski

This title could be a mantra, a reminder of what you want or need in your life. It could be a speech given by a coach or a mentor that inspires you to push through the tough times or the grief. It could be something that you say to yourself over and over to help remind yourself of the great things to come. It is a short story, and the above is only a small clip of the total short story.

I found out a couple of days ago, that another best friend of a best friend of mine lost his battle with mental illness. It reminds me that the struggle is real on a daily basis. My friend talked to him the morning of his death. Shared what he could but it was not enough to overcome the demons.

We all have our own unique struggles. Just because your struggle is not a matter of life or death does not make it less important. It is the reality that you are living in right now. When we take on the mindset that, "When you survive this..." we will have a stronger chance of getting through whatever we may be dealing with. It could be a job loss, a relationship that did not turn out the way we wanted, or even a test in school that we failed. We all have a story to tell. Stories of how we survived this or that. Some are more dramatic than others but what a great story to tell. This is how I survived that! What are you struggling with right now? Can you tell yourself, "When you get through this?" You will have a great story or strength to tell and maybe it will help someone else survive this.

Today, I will remember the phrase, "When you survive this," so I can look to the future and see the strength that I will have as a result. I will see the person I will become and know that I will be able to share with others how I survived.

WHAT ARE YOU CAPABLE OF?   OCTOBER 18

"We are all capable of infinitely more than we believe. We are stronger and more resourceful than we know, and we can endure much more than we think we can." – David Blaine

There are things that motivate us and things that do just the opposite. If you hear this often enough you get tired of the question. Like a couple that has been dating a while getting asked when are you getting married? Similarly, the salesperson that is busting their tail is getting asked what have you sold today? This can be a great question or one that annoys you because you know you can be doing so much more. How do you know what you are capable of? You typically make mistakes or run up against obstacles. Sometimes your crush a goal or fall short. Have you seen someone that had talent and was not really using all that talent?

They had skills and abilities that seemed natural, but they only seemed to be scratching the surface. Younger me did not always understand how to step outside of what I saw I was capable of and press on to see what I really could do. There are still times when I see something that seems out of reach, but I now try a little harder or look at the situation from a different angle to see what more can be done. You may not see what you are capable of, and you may need someone else to show you the possibilities. This is where a mentor or a coach comes in to play. We all need a little help in our lives to reach out further, run a little harder, have more patience, or just make one more phone call. Sometimes we need to love a little more, have more compassion or empathy, or just stop and look around to appreciate the little things, so that we can see what we are capable of doing or feeling.

Today, I will ask myself, what am I capable of? Looking at the bigger picture and seeing how I can grow and be better than I was yesterday.

Pain   October 19

"He who learns must suffer. And even in our sleep pain that cannot forget falls drop by drop upon the heart, and in our own despair, against our will, comes wisdom to us by the awful grace of God." – Aeschylus

We are all familiar with pain, physical and emotional pain. When we work through the pain in our lives, we tend to come out stronger on the other end of it. When an athlete is working out it usually can cause pain. The muscles are getting worked in different ways and they are made to grow, which is painful. You are tearing down the muscles when you lift weights or run long distances. You are asking your body to adjust to the requirements that you desire, stronger and faster. There is a negative side to physical pain as well but that is mostly due to unwanted bodily abuse. If you have that kind of physical pain, you may need to get some help from someone else that can help you leave a situation of abuse. It is not our place to abuse others, whether emotionally or physically.

Emotional pain can help us to grow, or it can set us back. When life gets difficult, it can emotionally wear us down. Learning how to overcome the emotional challenges in our lives makes us stronger mentally. There are other times it can cause us to doubt ourselves, and we can get caught up in our insecurities, and that becomes harmful. If you continue to doubt yourself because of the emotional pain, then it is time to get help from someone that can get us through the emotional pain. Some emotional pain, like the death of a loved one, is not something you simply get past. You have to work through the pain, which can lessen over time if we allow it. It does not mean that we do not love that person or that we have forgotten about that person. We have a different life now without that person, which can be more difficult, but missing that person or mourning them does not make the situation better or help us. We can get stuck in the emotional pain of the loss of that person. You still need to process the feelings but getting entangled in the loss can be like a whirlpool in an ocean. If we hang out near the whirlpool, we are going to get sucked into it. If we acknowledge that it is there and we respect its strength and power, we do not need to go near it.

Today, I will look at the pain that I can learn from and accept the change that needs to occur to help get me through that pain. If I need to get help with a situation, I will ask.

The Gap   October 20

"As you grow, you lose certain homies because it's called closing the gap. How do you close the gap? When you come back down you lose. So, you gotta keep going up. That's why closin' the gap, gotta be them, catching up to you. And if they don't catch up, you gotta leave 'em behind." – Snoop Dogg

If you have experienced any type of growth in your life or have watched others grow, you understand the gap. I am speaking about emotional or spiritual growth. Sometimes you are on the lower side and sometimes you are on the upper side. What can be difficult is when you or a friend is on the lower side and the lower side is holding the upper side back. When I was in my twenties, I had a friend that was about ten years older than me, and he was at a time in his life when he needed to be more professional. I was still learning what that really meant to grow in my maturity and professionalism. We had a conversation where he said that we could not be friends anymore because I was not a good influence on him. I was hurt by that conversation. I have never forgotten that conversation and the impact it had on me. I understand it now more because I have felt like this with some people in my life too, over the years. When the gap between you and someone grows, it is obvious to both parties. Some people get mad at the person that is growing emotionally or spiritually and that feeling is the responsibility of the one getting mad. I have found that when I grow in maturity, I am no longer drawn to spending time with those that are not moving in the same direction as I am. That is hard for me because I may genuinely like them and want the best for them, but they are not ready to grow. Whether you are on the upper or lower part of the gap, what are you going to do to either close the gap or remove the relationship? Do you see it happening? If you do not get mad or determined, you may be apathetic toward the other person and that shows you something too. If you are on the upper side of the gap and you keep trying to help people catch up to you, then you might be getting sucked back down to them. Sometimes, like when I was in my twenties, people have to let you go so you can grow!

Today, I will see if there is a gap in my relationships and, if there is, decide what I want to do about it. It may be time to help someone or ask for help. It may be time to let go.

THE FUTURE   OCTOBER 21

"The best possible preparation for the future is a well-lived present."
– George H. Brimhall

If you could see into the future, how would that affect the way you live your life? Would you work as hard or just give up? Would you resign yourself because you saw something that is less than what you had hoped for? Would you work harder because you saw some success, but it was just shy of what you had hoped for? Or you saw that you were able to do a certain amount and now you want to do more? There are probably so many reasons that we cannot see into the future with certainty, though we can create an image or idea of what we want our lives to look like. Accomplishments and even failures can be seen in our mind's eye. We have the ability to see into the future and it is that vision that pushes us or tells us to slow down. Our mind is powerful. The reason we cannot see into the future is that it is not right now. We live in the present and sometimes in the past, but it all leads to the future. Who we are and who we will become is up to us, the decisions we make and the actions we take now will affect our future.

So, what does your future look like? Do you want to change it or are you ok with the direction you are headed? We all get a chance to change our future. It is not predetermined for you. As we decide and act each day our future is changing.

Today, I will get to decide on what my future looks like by the decisions and actions that I take.

I AM SORRY   OCTOBER 22

"Never ruin an apology with an excuse." – Benjamin Franklin

"I'm sorry" can be one of the hardest things to say. You have made a mess of a relationship or a situation and there is nothing else to say but, I am sorry. You feel it in the innermost part of your being. The sorrow, the pain, the sheer disappointment that you have caused. You try to make amends, but you keep feeling worse. You keep feeling like I could have done so much better. You go back and try to explain how you messed up. You try to make excuses, yet it only makes it worse. You have probably been on both sides of this conversation before. You felt the angst, the pain, maybe even the disgust as the words come out of your mouth or others. Why do we feel like this?

Sometimes we just need to acknowledge that we made a mistake so we can apologize and then move forward. Making amends sooner rather than later can save you and others a lot of sorrow and heartache. When you realize you made a mistake, are you capable of setting the record straight now or do you try and move on without dealing with it to others? When I have tried to smooth it over or act like I never said or did those awful things, it makes the situation or relationship much worse and completely awkward. When you make your next mistake, because we all will, start with recognizing it. Then move to deal with it, not pushing it aside first. Then, if possible, get back to where you need to be so that you and others can move past it. Some things are more difficult than others to move past. Find the appropriate amount of time to work through the hurt and the other feelings that you may have caused.

Today, I will see my mistakes and where needed I will apologize without any excuses. Acknowledging my part in the situation and taking responsibility and finding the ways in which I can make amends.

What Scares You? October 23

"Figure out what scares you the most and do that first." – Steven Pressfield

There are a couple of ways to look at the question, what scares you? There are some things that frighten you and you avoid them, haunted houses, cemeteries at night, a scary movie, etc. There are some things that frighten you because they are too hard, will take too much of your time, or might bring unknown success or failure. Being afraid is typically centered around knowledge or lack thereof. If we do not know enough about a situation, we might be hesitant to move forward. What if we have a friend, mentor, or coach, who tells us it is ok to do the things that we do not understand because they can bring knowledge, wealth, and success? What if they teach us some of the unknown? Do you want to make the leap and take a new job with more responsibility, or start your own company? I have felt a lot of these feelings, thought a lot of these thoughts. I know what it feels like to have my heart racing or pounding so hard it feels like it is about to come out of my chest. The sweaty palms, the butterflies so intense, I feel like I am going to be sick. Yet here I am. "Still standing, better than I ever did! Looking like a true survivor!" Thank you, Sir Elton John, for the inspiration!

It takes some work on your part to understand or overcome those feelings. Get some help, find a friend or a coach. Spend some time understanding what scares you and then move forward to overcome that fear where possible and necessary. We all can overcome the things that we are scared of, especially when we understand that we are not alone. We have help if we want it. Most of the time, we simply need to ask for it.

Today, I will find those things that scare me and start to address them. Overcoming the fear of what I do not know so that I can overcome those things that frightened me in the past.

LIFE IS SHORT OCTOBER 24

"Life is short, Break the Rules. Forgive quickly, Kiss slowly. Love truly. Laugh uncontrollably. And never regret ANYTHING that makes you smile." – Mark Twain

What a powerful phrase, *life is too short!* Some people use this as an excuse for their bad behavior or their arrogance. Some people use this as an excuse not to try things that intimidate them. Does it inspire you? Does it make you pause and reflect? What comes to mind when you read this or hear this? Life is too short to live someone else's dream. Work for someone else's goals. Live in a poor or toxic relationship, whether romantic, family, or friend. Life is too short to work at a job that you hate or that does not bring you fulfillment. Life is too short to worry about who is talking about you behind your back. It is too short to not see the things you want to see, try the foods that you want to try, or experience the life that you want to live. This is not a license to be irresponsible, but it is an opportunity to see your life from a different perspective. This is a time to say, "why not?" I have been blessed to be able to travel, which is something that I really enjoy doing. I have been to forty-nine of the fifty United States. I have been to most of the lower provinces of Canada, been to Mexico, a number of Caribbean countries, and China. I would like to see more and do more. What about you? Where do you want to go? What do you want to see or experience?

Today, I will remember that life is too short to do things that do not serve me or fulfill me. I will find ways to start doing or planning for things that I want to do because life is too short.

Your Words are More Than Just Words   October 25

"If you want your children to improve, let them overhear the nice things you say about them to others." – Haim Ginott

If you want to know how powerful your words are, then say something nice about someone to another person, or to their face. Tell a third person how beautiful you think a friend is. Share about their heart for others or animals. Say something of substance and meaning that you appreciate about them. Watch their face light up. See how their body perks up in reaction to the things you have said.

Your words are like choice morsels, according to the Bible. Think about how you feel when that happens to you. Words can wash over you like a refreshing shower on a stressful day, or a cool breeze on a hot day. When you take responsibility for the things that you say, you begin to understand how important those words are that come from your heart and your mind. You can then understand the impact that they have when you just throw them around without thought or care. Words can pierce the heart for good or for bad. When you are upset with someone and you lash out with words, you intend to hurt them, maybe the same way they hurt you? Do you think about the impact of the kind, loving, or uplifting words that you say about others? When I coach people, one of the biggest shortcomings I see in people is their ability to communicate with others. Using your words is so important, and using the right ones is even more important. Words are more than just words.

Today, I will look at the words that are coming out of my heart and mind. I will ask if I am communicating what I want to or need to communicate to others. I will find ways to lift others up using just the words that I speak.

YOU ARE NOT ALONE   OCTOBER 26

"We're all in this together. It's okay, to be honest. It's okay to ask for help. It's okay to say you're stuck, or that you're haunted, or that you can't begin to let go. We can all relate to those things. Screw the stigma that says otherwise. Break the silence and break the cycle, for you are more than just your pain. You are not alone. And people need other people."
– Jamie Tworkowski

We all run the risk of getting stuck in life. We hit a bump in the road, and we feel like we are the only ones that go through this. We see others go through it, but when it comes our turn we think, who else could understand what I am going through? We forget that others go through things just like us. They have similar struggles. They have similar thoughts and heartache. I've been through tough times. I thought that if I just had an accident that would be an easy way out of the pain that I was going through, and I would not have to explain the struggles that I had. I decided to share it with a couple of friends, thinking they would not understand, but I did not want to just end everything either. Those friends did not totally understand my situation, but they listened, and it helped me talk about it. I shared it with a few other people years later and still no one really understood. It did not deter me from talking about it because I knew that what I was feeling was not normal. It also helped me to talk about it and when I shared it with people, we were able to grow closer because we had felt similar struggles. I spoke with a counselor years later and was able to talk openly about the situation. I have since spoken to others who had a similar story. Friends that I have had for years and that I never would have thought would have a similar struggle. There are people around us that feel some of the same types of things that we feel and when we open up about who we are, we find that we are not alone. Whether it is a bad day at home or a bad day at work, we all have things to share with others and we will find that we are not alone in the thoughts and feelings surrounding the good and the bad days.

Today, I will find people that I can learn to trust if I do not have them already. I will learn to be open about the good the bad and the ugly. I know that I am not alone, and neither are they!

ORIGINALITY   OCTOBER 27

"I did stand-up comedy for 18 years. Ten of those years were spent learning, four years were spent refining, and four years were spent in wild success. I was seeking comic originality, and fame fell on me as a byproduct. The course was more plodding than heroic." – Steve Martin

Too often we find it difficult to be original. We see everyone doing the same thing, saying the same thing, thinking the same thing. If we are not careful, we end up in some sort of herd mentality. Looking and acting alike. In sales or business, if you are like everyone else then that is not necessarily a good thing. Though the ideas may not be new, the way you tell them needs to be new. The way you present it needs to be new. In sales and business, it comes down to differentiation. If you can be just a little bit different, in a good way, from the other people providing the same product or service then you will probably get the business. How can you be different? Most of the time it comes down to your own originality. Imitation is a good thing, and we need to learn to emulate the good things that people are doing. But that will only make you a follower of someone else. Can you take the good things that someone else says or does and figure out how to make them yours?

I learned how to cook at a young age, and I found the idea of following the recipes to be super important for any success in the kitchen. Later, I also found that when I add my special twist on things it makes it a little bit different, sometimes better sometimes not. Now, when I coach people, I talk about adding your own seasoning or flavor to a presentation or client meeting. We all learn how to say and do things from others, but you must do it with the way you do it or say it the way that you say it. It must be the authentic you and not some representation of someone else.

Today, I will learn more ways to perfect my craft, I will then learn how to adapt them to my ways and enhance my personal way of doing things. I will continue to find the authentic me.

NEWNESS   OCTOBER 28

"As children our imaginations are vibrant, and our hearts are open. We believe that the bad guy always loses and that the tooth fairy sneaks into our rooms at night to put money under our pillow. Everything amazes us, and we think anything is possible. We continuously experience life with a sense of newness and unbridled curiosity." – Yehuda Berg

You may have heard it said that every day is a new opportunity. Each client meeting is a new opportunity. Do you view things that way or is it just another meeting? How do you feel when you see or get something that is new? Are you excited about seeing this new thing or are you just ok with it, keeping your emotions in check? As a child we would get excited at the new things, as adults, we can get hardened to life and new things are just something else, we have to deal with. I get excited about the little things. I get excited about the newness of things I get, whether it is something new I get to pick up at the store or have delivered to my home. I get excited about taking a new road, seeing new things. I get to travel a lot, especially in the major metropolitan areas where I have lived. I try and use every on and off-ramp for the highways in my area. If it is new to me, I make a mental note to look around and see the new perspective that I get to have. I know that may sound childlike, but it is something I actually enjoy. When I play golf, I try and enjoy the views that I get to see at the different times of the days from the high or low spots, with the water and the rolling green fairways. I like the newness. It gives me a mental rejuvenation. We all get the opportunity to do this every day. The sun comes up and you get to see things from a different perspective. The fresh start you get to have with friends, family, and even new people you will meet today. These are all opportunities to do something new. A fresh perspective, a new thought, a new solution.

Today, I will look at the opportunities that I have as new. A chance to start fresh, with a clean slate. If I need to clean things up from mistakes I made yesterday, I will do it with a newness at heart. I get to start a new day today!

Labor of Love   October 29

"Before the reward, there must be labor. You plant before you harvest. You sow in tears before you reap joy."– Ralph Ransom

You must work to receive the reward. Yet, for some reason, there are a number of people that believe they can get the reward before they put in the work. They get the prize without running the race. What allows people to believe that you can have the flowers without planting and nurturing the garden? Why do you believe that you can win the sale without asking the tough questions or doing the work? Early in my sales career, I got a few wins. Call it dumb luck or someone was just ready to buy, and I was in the right place at the right time. I did little to make them happen but just show up and take the order. That was not sales, that was taking orders. I then went on a dry spell. I could not sell. I thought I was doing all the right things, but I was not.

I can look back now and say that I was not willing to put in the time to the work that needed to be done. I did not make the cold calls, I did not nurture the leads, there was no email or system to help remind me of the activity needed to do that day or week. I had to learn how to do all of those things to work on the relationship with the customers that I wanted. I know now that if I do the work the results will happen. If you are willing to put in the time, do the work, and finish the work the results will be amazing. The results will be more than you imagined.

Today, I will focus on the work that I need to do and less on the results. The results will come when I do the work every day consistently.

WHAT ARE YOUR LIMITS?   OCTOBER 30

"Everyone has limits. You just have to learn what your own limits are and deal with them accordingly." – Nolan Ryan

What are your limits? How far will you go before you hit a hard line? If you are a runner, do you only go a mile or two before you say, I cannot do anymore? Every one of us has limits. We learn how to push them to get better, do more, be more. Some of us are afraid to push past what we know we can handle. Fear holds us back. Fear can rob us of a lot of things not the least of which is joy. When we set limits in our lives we miss out on a lot of things. I have a friend that will not get on a plane. I do not know all the reasons behind it, but that is her limit. I know people that are afraid to learn another language, yet they work or live in a situation that would be much better if they would learn another language. I know people that are afraid to learn more skills so they could advance in their chosen career, doing the thing they love. They are on the verge of losing that career, or they bounce from employer to employer because they will not learn to develop themselves. Everyone has morals and ethics, and it is very important to understand your limits. But you will come into situations that will test those limits. What are your limits and how are you setting boundaries?

Today, I will find out what limits I currently have and which ones I need to push, and which ones I need to strengthen.

OBSERVATION   OCTOBER 31

"To acquire knowledge, one must study; but to acquire wisdom, one must observe." – Marilyn vos Savant

Do you ever simply sit and observe people? Do you ever analyze how they walk, how they speak, and the gestures that they are making with each other? I was at a stoplight and observed a couple on the corner waiting for the light to change. The woman was intensely speaking to the man with some grand gestures and animations. She was clearly not happy, and he looked sheepish as if he was being corrected or at least admonished. I did not hear the conversation as I was too far away, my windows were up, and I had some music playing in my vehicle. But I could tell there was an intense conversation happening. When you are sitting with a client and you are engaged in the conversation, are you able to pick up on the things that they are trying to communicate through body language and vocal inflection? Can you see the angst or the fear they have when you ask certain questions? How about the uncertainty, the doubt, and the fear? How observant are you?

If you are able to see what is happening in your life and what is going on around you, you will be better at seeing what is happening with others. We can get too caught up in our own world, our own scripts, our own thoughts and miss what is happening right in front of us.

Today, I will find ways to be more in tune with the things that are happening around me and more aware of what someone is saying without words.

November

NEGATIVITY

NOVEMBER 1

"Negativity is the enemy of creativity." – David Lynch

Negativity will always creep into our lives. We all have negative thoughts that slip into our minds. We all have the people in our lives that look at everything from a glass-half-empty perspective. How do you handle the negativity in your life? Are you like some that act as if it is no big deal, choosing not to acknowledge it or ignore it? Are you like others that can see it and react to it, wreaking havoc on your day? I got used to living in pain every day. I remember waking up every morning and doing a mental body scan. I would ask myself as I sat up on the edge of my bed to put my feet down, "what hurts today?" I did that for years! I do not recommend starting your day off with that question. When I realized what I was doing to myself, I decided to change a few things in my life. I figured out why I felt the need to ask myself that question every morning and I decided to do something about my health so I would not wake up feeling that way every single morning. I also decided to start my day with more positive thoughts. Ones of gratitude. Ones that gave me hope rather than despair. Now my morning routine is far different, and I never ask what hurts today! I have a different mindset when it comes to negative thinking now too. I no longer say I *have* to do something. I *get* to do things in my life, even if it is not my favorite thing. I try to put a positive spin on things that people say to me and help them think differently as well. I do not expect them to change but I offer a different perspective and sometimes it helps them too. I also choose not to be around people that are negative most of the time. I had a friend that was like that a lot. Looking at the negative side, always waiting for the other shoe to drop. Filled with bitterness and rage. I thought I could help them to change but I could not, and most of us could never help someone like that. They need to want to make the change before anyone can help them. I am not some super positive, fake smile kind of person, that goes around trying to push positivity on everyone. But I do choose to not let the negative thoughts get a foothold in my day. It may not always work. But I refuse to be the person that people do not want to be around because of their negativity. How about you? What can you do to push the negativity out of your life, your thoughts, or your speech?

Today, I will take steps towards being more positive. I will look at myself, my situations, and the people around me to see where I can be more positive.

WHAT ARE YOU RESISTING? NOVEMBER 2

"Resistance is a psychological reaction to change." – Michelle Rees

There are things that we are resistant to in life. Most of us have an immune system that works in our bodies to fight off disease or illness. We are also resistant to change, whether it be a new job, place to live, or a new romantic relationship. Most of us just do not like to turn our lives upside down just because we have nothing better to do. So, we become resistant to that thing or idea. Ask yourself, what are you resisting? What is happening in your life that seems to be calling you again and again? Is it a promotion or a new career? Is it starting over with a relationship or relationships because you are toxic together? Is it a relocation because there is or has been too much negative emotion or energy where you are living now? Sometimes we need a gentle nudge to get us to see what we already know is there. We have been afraid that the next chapter is too much or not enough.

I have had several crossroads in my life. I knew I needed to change my relationship, my career, and my location, and I did not want to do any of those things independently or collectively. Each was a hard decision to make but all together they were the best thing for me and those around me. I needed to start new. I was spiraling downward, and looking back now, I know I was not a good person to be around, though I thought I was "covering" it well. Putting my best foot forward and a smile on my face, all while my insides were in turmoil. I remember the conversations I needed to have and having them. How difficult they were at first but then the overwhelming relief that followed. I stopped resisting and it opened up opportunities that I never thought possible. It allowed me to grow, and more change came as a result. When we stop resisting there can be good or even great things awaiting us on the other side.

Today, I will look at the things I have been resisting and determine why I have been resisting those things. Then, I will determine if it would be better for me and those around me in the long term to make the change.

Manipulation   November 3

"Genuine sincerity opens people's hearts, while manipulation causes them to close." – Daisaku Ikeda

Do you manipulate people or are you manipulated by people? An answer other than neither is not a good thing. When I use the word manipulate, I mean it in the negative controlling sense of the word, not in the persuasion of people. In sales, part of your job is to persuade people not to manipulate. Often people think that they can and should manipulate when they are in sales and that is one reason why salespeople have a bad reputation. A manipulation is a form of control. When you are on the receiving end, you get controlled. That can lead to mistrust and anger on your side. When you manipulate, you do not care about the other person's feelings, you just want to get something from someone. You want a desired result or outcome. If you are trying to use this type of communication when you are selling you will lose every time, in the long run. Short term, you may get the sale, or you may not. When you treat people, and yourself, with respect and genuinely care it not only shows but you also open yourself up and become vulnerable. If you find yourself trying to manipulate a person or a situation, ask yourself why and what is the end game? You rarely genuinely win when you try to manipulate.

Today, I will look at how I am treating people and situations. I will identify the signs of manipulation and stop them. Whether I am the one manipulating or someone else is trying to manipulate me.

Softening   November 4

"Give others their dignity by opening and softening in your heart to them." – John de Ruiter

How have you been hardened by life? I know I have been. We get burned, rejected, or abused and it can make us hard-hearted. A romance gone wrong turns to not trusting the other person in a relationship again. One foot in and the other ready to run as soon as you think you will get hurt. A job that sucked the very life out of you because of harsh co-workers, or even worse, a toxic manager. You feel like you have no choice, you have a hard time giving your best at work because it is never good enough. Why do we treat people this way? Why are we so horrible at communicating that we push people away instead of telling them what we want and need in the relationship? I had been in several failed relationships. I thought I wanted to be close to my significant other, best friends even, but I did not know how to do that or be that person. I had tried, or so I thought. I finally found someone that I connected with. Someone I could be real and vulnerable with, but I had one foot pointed in the other direction just in case. When the time came, I ran, and so did she. I had to soften. I had to realize that I did not have all the answers and I was not going to be perfect, and neither was she, and that was and is ok. We were able to recognize the shortcomings in our previous relationships and put them aside. If you are waiting for the perfect relationship, then you are probably waiting for something that might not happen unless you soften and open up to others.

Today, I will look at the things that have hardened my heart and see how I can soften and be more open for the right situation. Not to be a stepping stone for someone to use or to not have one foot out the door in every situation.

Connecting Through Listening — November 5

"The most basic and powerful way to connect to another person is to listen. Just listen." – Rachel Naomi Remen

Often when we try to connect with other people, we think we need to have some sort of deep conversation. Where both of us share about things that we would not normally share with just anyone. There is truth in that, but it also comes about because we are listening intently to the other person. We get caught up in trying to tell our story or our side of things and we do not connect with people because we did not listen to what they said. Some of the best conversations I get to have with people is with me doing a lot of listening and not with me talking a lot. When we listen, we can make more of an emotional connection. Understanding where people are coming from and what they want, can all be done if we listen. Remember what it feels like to be heard, to be understood, to be listened to completely, without judgment or repercussions. When you listen, you can respond completely. You can respond with the intent to understand not with the intent to be heard.

Today, I will find ways to connect with people through listening.

Being Part of a Team — November 6

"The things you learn from sports - setting goals, being part of a team, confidence - that's invaluable. It's not about trophies and ribbons. It's about being on time for practice, accepting challenges and being fearful of the elements." – Summer Sanders

Flying solo is hard. Some people think they were born to be alone. The majority of us need and want to be a part of something bigger than us. We want to be on a team. Being part of a team does not have to mean that you are in sports. It could mean that you belong to a team of friends that always looks out for each other or has each other's back. That you work with a team of people that you really enjoy, and you help each other out to the success of the larger part. Being part of a team means we learn to work together; give and take. We learn our strengths and weaknesses. We learn how to communicate. We learn how to feel our feelings and share that with others as well. When we are not good at being on a team it usually is because we are not good at being open. Open about who we are, good and bad. We may not be able to express ourselves and that leads to trust issues. We can appear to be selfish or closed off.

A sales profession is the same way. If we are part of the sales team, we help each other out. Too often management sets up the sales team to be uber-competitive and that destroys the team. I am not saying you should not be competitive in sales. You need to be in order to be successful. But not when you are pitted against each other in a sales environment to the point where management is just throwing a piece of meat in the middle of the room and only the strong will survive. This is not the way to build a healthy sales team or sales environment. You are setting it up so that people are deceitful, they do not take care of the customer but rather their own needs and wants. I have been a part of a healthy sales team and one that was all about the survival of the fittest. The latter proved to be a horrible culture and provided all kinds of mistrust not just amongst the salespeople but also about management. Being part of a team is hard work because you have to share about things that may make you uncomfortable. When you learn to be a part of a team, you learn a lot about yourself and others.

Today, I will find ways that I can be a better teammate. I will support others and do what I can to build them up.

Order vs. Chaos   November 7

"Chaos is merely order waiting to be deciphered." – Jose Saramago

Chaos is viewed by some as problematic, and others as Zenlike. Some look at order in a similar way, problematic or Zenlike. We are all built differently and view things from different perspectives. I like order but I understand chaos. I do not thrive in chaos as some do but I have learned to manage the chaos and find the order in it. I can then see what I need to see and work on what I need to work on to make sense of the situation. That is how my brain works. If there is too much happening, I can also shut down as I do not want to deal with the amount of chaos happening. What is it like for you? Where do you thrive and where do you shut down? Are you all about the order or all about the disorder? We all have strengths and weaknesses. We can work on each side and improve them where we see fit. We can also turn aside from them and ignore them because we do not want to deal with them. Either way, we make a choice. A choice that can impact us for a short time or a long time. Sometimes we can change our hearts and minds and decide that the order is too much, and we need more disorder, or we can want more order in our lives. Just because you do something one way does not make it right for everyone else.

Today, I will choose to see the order and disorder in my life and decide which makes the most sense for me. I will also learn how to view both sides and understand that one may affect me more and then I have to work on it.

Trust   November 8

"I think we may safely trust a good deal more than we do. We may waive just so much care of ourselves as we honestly bestow elsewhere." – Henry David Thoreau

Trust is something that most of us must work on all the time. People have stolen our trust, it hurt, and we are not sure we can do that again.

It usually happened more than once and that is why you are not sure you are ready to go back and try that again. It could have been a family member, a friend, a coworker, or another relationship that took that from us. The sad thing about this is that we do not know how we got here, and they probably do not remember doing that to us, but it happened. But here we are at a point in our lives where we do not want to just trust people because, they remind us of someone who hurt us, or the situation is like the one that hurt me before. What will it take for you to trust again, a fresh start, an apology, or you take a stand against the people that stole your trust? Sometimes, it takes drastic measures to get drastic results. One of the things that I had to learn was to forgive those that took it from me, then I could start healing myself. Forgiving someone can be as simple as stating to yourself and the universe in the privacy of your own room. For others, it may take a face-to-face to relieve the burden from you. Find what you need to forgive and take the next steps. You did not get here overnight so do not expect to find relief overnight. But you owe it to yourself to start the journey of healing.

Today, I will look for ways to build trust for me in others and forgive those that took it from me.

Digging Deeper   November 9

"It is moments like these that force us to try harder, and dig deeper, and to discover gifts we never knew we had - to find the greatness that lies within each of us." – Barack Obama

We have all been in a situation that called for us to dig a little deeper. We thought we were giving it our all and then we found that next gear. Our heart kicked in and offered another level of fight or determination that was the key to our success. Sometimes we give all that we have, and it still is not enough. That hurts. The failure stings the heart and the psyche. It makes us wonder if we have what it takes to do whatever it is that we are trying to do, an athletic event, a relationship, a career? I have felt it in each of those situations, at least once! I remember playing sports and feeling like, am I enough? Do I have what it takes to compete at this level? Not wanting to give up, I would push myself just a little bit harder. I was able to do it, make the block, catch the pass, make the basket. In relationships, I was told I was not a good communicator. I was not given more specifics than that. I have learned that my love language is touch and acts of service. What I believed was love was not loving to them as they had a different love language, and I did not know how to "speak it."

In my work, I had to learn how to drop my defenses and be humble enough to learn from others. It was hard because I grew up learning how to do things myself, self-taught because I would not listen, or others did not want to teach me. I had to learn how to dig a little deeper and let go of my ego to say I do not know how to do that instead of powering through. Learning how to dig deeper within you to find the courage, the strength, or the humility can allow you to grow beyond what you thought you were capable of doing. My sports career is over, which is ok. My relationships are better than they have ever been, and my career is providing a level of fulfillment I never could have imagined. What about you? Are you able to dig a little deeper to get the things that you need and want?

Today, I will look at situations that will require me to dig a little deeper. Then I will find a way to do just that to see what I am capable of doing or becoming.

HEALING A BROKEN HEART   NOVEMBER 10

"There is something beautiful about all scars of whatever nature. A scar means the hurt is over, the wound is closed and healed, done with."
– Harry Crews

When your heart gets broken, it can feel as if there is nothing more emotionally painful. Maybe the love of your life has told you they are done. Maybe a loved one died. We all have scars on our heart where it was cut or torn. An emotional scar can hurt just as much if not more than a cut we get on our hands. I recently cut myself while chopping a jalapeno. I know it sounds painful, but it caught me by surprise more than anything else. My thumb felt weird for the next couple of days, not in a pain kind of way but in a texture kind of way. I felt things differently over the next few days because of the cut. It got me thinking about how when my heart has been broken. I feel things differently for days or weeks after that happens. I see things differently than I used to after it gets broken because I am more in tune with my heart. I am more aware of the feelings I have and am more aware of what is happening around me, at least emotionally speaking. Like my thumb, my heart heals. It takes some time, some extra tender loving care, and some more time.

I have some physical scars on my body. There are stories for each of them and lessons that were learned as a result of them, but the physical pain is gone. My heart has some scars as well. Most of the pain is gone but some of it lingers. I am tearing up just thinking about some of the emotional pain that still exists. But for the most part, the scars on my heart have been healed. My broken heart has mended and yours can too. It will probably take some time and some tender loving care, and then some more time. Find the time to let the healing begin.

If my heart is broken, I will take the time today to feel the feelings and allow the process of healing to begin. I will allow myself to be loved and cared for by myself and others. Then I will give myself more grace and time to heal knowing that it can and will get better.

NEEDS   NOVEMBER 11

"When you are with the wrong person, who doesn't really love you, all you want is to be adored. It makes you more inward and needy. Gross."
– Marina and the Diamonds

Some people can be in a relationship and not need much from their partner. You do not need the conversation, the spiritual development, the physical touch, the intimacy. Are you the type of person that can be left alone and you will do fine because you do not need much interaction? That can work for some but most of us need to be interacting with other humans. Giving and receiving on different levels of intimacy. My job usually allows me to interact with people all day, and some days I need to unwind and decompress before I can interact with family or friends. I have also found that in a love relationship I need to be needed on several different levels. I also want to be in a relationship with someone that feels needed by me as well. That may sound like a selfish thing, but I like to know that I am needed in a relationship and that helps me to be connected to that person, it makes me take my role as a partner seriously. I am not saying that I am needed to survive, or I am there to solve all your problems. I need to be a part of an active relationship on both ends of the give and take. I want to give and get from the relationship in intellectual conversation, spirituality, and intimacy.

In business, I have similar wants and needs. I want to be needed and I want the people I do business with to know that I need them as well. Are you someone that can give and take to be fulfilled and to fulfill others? If you give all the time and do not receive that causes imbalance, much like someone that receives or takes all the time. Relationships like this usually do not do well whether in business or personal life. They can work but there is a purpose to that relationship being one-sided. A transactional relationship has a defined purpose, you have a tool that I need, and I want to buy it from you.

Today, I will look at my relationships and see if I am in balance or not and if not find ways to correct that if needed.

Your Attention   November 12

"Give whatever you are doing and whoever you are with the gift of your attention." – Jim Rohn

When you speak to someone do you notice when they are distracted, and their attention is clearly somewhere else? Do you know how to give your full attention to the situation or to someone that you are having a conversation with? I have been in conversations with someone when I feel the tug. Something else more interesting is grabbing my attention, or worse something else has distracted me from giving this person or situation my full attention. How you keep your focus on a conversation can determine what you are able to get out of it. I can be fully immersed in a conversation, asking interesting questions, giving genuine responses, but never feeling fully engaged with the person I am speaking to because they appear not to be present. How frustrating! When I am engaged in a conversation and notice that the other person is not, whether, through body language or clearly thoughtless answers, I ask if this is still a good time to meet. How important is this meeting or conversation? Giving of yourself and your time can be a lot. It can drain you emotionally, even physically. I have given presentations for a couple of hours and felt the need to sleep afterward. I have also felt very energized and ready for the next event. So why the difference between the two? Is it the attention that was given by myself or the audience? It was probably a mixture of both. I find that when I feel that I am having the carry the load of the situation or the conversation then I am more drained. When I am giving and the audience is giving, then I am much less drained and actually feel more energized. Can you feel that and do your clients feel that when you make a presentation or are meeting for the first time? What kind of energy are you bringing to the meeting? Are you feeling drained or energized? When I do not give my attention, I am robbing everyone.

Today, I will remember that everyone has a gift to give, it is your attention. When presented it can be a great gift. When your attention is not in the present situation or conversation you are stealing from yourself and others.

BE KIND   NOVEMBER 13

"Be kind whenever possible. It is always possible." – Dalai Lama

How is your day going? No, *really*, how is your day going? Did you hit your toe on the bed or did you just get a wake-up call from a family member with some devastating news? Did you just get that promotion or raise that you were hoping for? I have experienced all of these, and all felt very different. We just do not know what kind of a day a person is having just by looking at them. Being kind costs you nothing, in fact, I find that I usually feel better when I simply smile at people. It makes me think of the kinder and more pleasant things that are good in my life. The warm embrace of a friend, the kind words of those you love all conjure a smile that can be passed along. It is hard to be kind when you are struggling with anger or fear in your life. What does it take to be kind to others? Sometimes it is as simple as a smile or a kind word of encouragement.

Today, I will find ways to be kind and give to others because you never know what kind of a day that they are having.

WHAT INTERESTS YOU?   NOVEMBER 14

"But what I mean is, lots of time you don't know what interests you most till you start talking about something that doesn't interest you most. I mean you can't help it sometimes." – J. D. Salinger

What are your interests? How did you discover these interests? Do you take time to try different things or are you too old for that? Do you take time to develop yourself by reading books, watching videos, or asking different questions? When my kids were much younger and they were trying to figure out what foods they liked and did not like, I gave them only one rule: They must try everything once. They cannot say that they did not like something simply by name or appearance. I did that because I did not want them to miss out on something that they may like because it sounded bad, or they only wanted chicken tenders and french fries. They would have missed out on risotto and a snickers cheesecake, among other things. Can you find something that you have not tried? Maybe it is time to take a chance.

Personally, I have almost all types of music in my music library. From classical to rap, country to jazz, and nearly every other genre that is out there. I will try making different types of foods though I know a couple of items that I will not add to my dishes when I make them because I have tried them several times and I am not a fan. What about how you work? Are you open to learning and trying different things? Do you like research? How about working with numbers? Do you like to write or read? Do you like to work with your hands? Do you like to lead others or teach others? Just because you tried it once ten years ago does not mean that you will not like it now. Give it a shot. Try something different and see what interests you. Maybe you do like the energy you get when you are trying to persuade someone. Maybe you do like speaking publicly or playing a musical instrument.

Today, I will take the time to discover what interests me. I will ask more and try more and not stay stuck in the things that I have been doing for years out of habit. I cannot wait to see what lies ahead and what I will discover.

BE TRUE TO YOURSELF   NOVEMBER 15

"For the past 33 years, I have looked in the mirror every morning and asked myself: 'If today were the last day of my life, would I want to do what I am about to do today?' And whenever the answer has been 'No' for

too many days in a row, I know I need to change something." – Steve Jobs

Do you ever hear your inner voice telling you to do or not do something? I am referring to a constant message of confirmation as the quote above mentions, "for too many days in a row." We tend to ignore the "You should do this!" message, especially if it is something risky or out of our comfort zone. How do you respond to something that is possibly right for you? A relationship, a job change, something that moves you in the right direction to follow your dreams or aspirations. We can forget that we know ourselves best and we need to be true to who we are. For some this is difficult and for others, this is something they have worked on for a while and they understand how to set boundaries for themselves and others. They know the truth about themselves. They sense the right situation from the wrong.

I had been working in a job for a couple of years and I had tried to convince myself that I was in the right situation for me. I kept telling myself I was happy when I was not and each day it was tearing me apart little by little and I did not see it. I was not being true to myself. I did not love my job, though I loved the clients I worked with and even most of my co-workers. It was the right place for me to be for a while because of other circumstances but it was not the right place for me to be myself and deep down I knew that, and so did my boss. When I stopped working there, I realized how much of a burden was lifted and I took the time to figure out what was best for me. I then found the perfect job for me and what I wanted and needed to do. I am being true to myself, but it took a while to figure that out. I have asked this of others, and I think it is important to ask ourselves this from time to time, "What do you really like doing?" If you could remove all other obstacles in your life, what is it that really speaks to you and that you are good at? Sometimes we think we cannot do something because we will not make enough money, or we do not live in the right situation for this or that. Are those just excuses or are they just obstacles that need to be overcome?

Today, I will ask myself, "If today were the last day of my life, would I want to do what I am about to do today?" Find what inspires you, speaks to you, and drives your innermost being, then you will be true to yourself.

Are You Making a Living or Making a Life?   November 16

"We make a living by what we get, but we make a life by what we give."
– Winston Churchill

Too often we focus on the wrong things in our daily lives. We look at the task in front of us instead of the road ahead. We are taught to work hard so we can make money to do the things that we want to do. We forget to stop and relieve the tension of the daily grind.

Yesterday was one of those days for me. I could feel the emotions building. The sadness, maybe even depression. I needed to cook. I had several meetings that took me until 6 in the evening, but I still needed to cook. Cooking for me is a stress reliever and somewhat relaxing. It puts my heart and soul into what I am doing. I was making apple butter and if not done properly it can create bigger problems. I needed to focus on the cooking process. The mind-numbing process. I have done this for several years now and I almost have the recipe completely memorized. I have the process down for sure. I am making memories. I am living my best life and I get to do the things I want to do because I am living my life and not always worried about making a living. I am not irresponsible or shirking my responsibilities. But I *get* to live my life and cooking is a part of that. Working for a living binds you up and makes you think there is nothing but work. Today, I get to see a friend that I have not seen in years. A project that I have been working on for months is near completion, and it is going very well. I get to see my family next week and celebrate the lives of those we have recently lost. Life is good because I get to choose my life. What will you get to do today? Make a living or make a life?

Today, I will find ways that I can start living my life or continue to make decisions that will help me live my life. I get to do things today.

Resentment   November 17

"Resentment is like drinking poison and then hoping it will kill your enemies." – Nelson Mandela

Resentment is a nasty thing. Most of us have struggled with this during our lives. It can get inside you and takes up residence in your head. It can do so much damage to you and your psyche. It creates all kinds of discussions in our heads, most of which is not true. We arrived here because we were probably mistreated, skipped over, or not thought about enough, at least in our minds. Resentment then turns you into someone or something else! Rational thinking is probably out the window and heading for the fields. I have had situations where I thought I was mistreated and it caused me to have all kinds of fun and exciting, totally lying here, conversations in my head. It took my time and my energy. It took away any kind of joy or happiness that may have been coming. One thing that has helped me to move away from resentment is the understanding that I get what I get because of the life I am living, basically karma, or it is not my turn. It is ok for it to not be my turn at times. When it happens too often, I have to ask myself, what can I do to not let that happen again? Sometimes I get more than I deserve. Without explanation, I receive an abundance. Sometimes we need to ask ourselves, why were we mistreated? Without knowing it, we can bring on the storm by what we say or do. Maybe we did know it and we did it to manipulate the situation or get attention. Instead of resentment maybe we should take a step back and look at our part in the situation and see where we need to improve. Then we can move on to happier more fulfilling times. Stop drinking the poison thinking it will harm someone else!

Today, I will look at why I am feeling resentment and what I need to do differently to not let that happen.

THOSE THAT HEAL   NOVEMBER 18

"Nobody escapes being wounded. We are all wounded people, whether physically, emotionally, mentally, or spiritually. The main question is not, 'How can we hide our wounds?' so we don't have to be embarrassed, but 'How can we put our woundedness in the service of others?' When our wounds cease to be a source of shame and become a source of healing, we have become wounded healers." – Henri Nouwen

Do you believe that people come into your life to heal you? I am not just talking about medical professionals that you go see when you are sick. Do you know of people that you have in your life that actually heal you? Are you aware of them? Sometimes people come into our lives and help us to heal, repair our brokenness, and feel whole again. Do you feel that from others or do others feel that from you? Your best friend might be that person that was brought to you to heal you. It may be a stranger.

Who is in your life for you to get healing from or for you to heal? You do not have to go looking for deep conversations or try to make it happen, just be aware. The moments will present themselves.

Today, I will be more aware of the people that are in my life to help me to heal or me to help them. Maybe someone needs to hear the words from me that will help them to heal.

GRATITUDE FOR FAILURE   NOVEMBER 19

"I even feel grateful for the failures." – Tom Hiddleston

This may be hard to understand for some but when you think about it this makes sense. Do you have an appreciation for the failures in your life? Do you see the learning opportunities that come from your failures and be grateful instead of being hurt, bitter, or even put out by your shortcomings? I have been fired from jobs, I have been through failed romantic relationships, I have lost more games and sales deals than I can remember. Through all of it, I have become the person I am today. Without any of those failures, I would not be the person I am. Each one has taught me something and I am now more grateful than ever to have had those failures. I am not proud of them. However, I am thankful that I had them and was able to come out on the other side. I did not always see the beauty in the failure or the understanding that would come because of the failure, but I can see now how important they were to the development of my personality, my character, and my gratitude. Holding on to failure and the feelings that can go with it can help and hurt us. Holding them as a reminder can help us to not make that same mistake. Holding it for too long can imbitter us, sour us, and prevent us from moving forward.

In sales, you have the opportunity to learn from failure. You said it one way, now you need to try it another way. You did not ask the right question. Your timing was off, and you missed the opportunity to ask a certain question or mention a particular benefit that would solve their current problem. What do you do with failure, and have you learned to be grateful for the lessons that come from them?

Today, I will see my failures for what they are and try to be grateful that they are they to help me to grow and learn how not to do things.

What Are Your Terms? November 20

"Do not engage an enemy more powerful than you. And if it is unavoidable and you do have to engage, then make sure you engage it on your terms, not on your enemy's terms." – Sun Tzu

We all have heard the phrase about terms and conditions. We have to accept them to get on websites, make a purchase, or even apply for a job. We all have them for ourselves, though we may not know it. When we learn what works and does not work for us, we set boundaries and create terms and conditions for others or situations we will engage in. Being in sales, I learned that I have created terms or standards for myself and my clients. I make sure that I make them clear when I am engaging with clients. I have to do that, or I get frustrated working in conditions that I am not willing to work in. I engage in sales negotiations that become uncomfortable all because I never set the terms. I worked for a company where I was willing to go on sales calls whenever the customer wanted to see me. The problem with that was that customers wanted to "kick the tires" on Saturdays and Sundays, some even on Friday around five or six in the evening. At first, I thought I was helping people by accommodating their schedules. I learned that people were just using these times as a convenience for them to check a very cheap price they had gotten from someone else. When I set my terms by not taking calls at certain times of the day, those types of calls disappeared, at least from my schedule. The company was willing to send me or someone else to these calls because they believed that we could move them from clients to customers. That was not the case because most of them already decided on whom they wanted to do business with. They were making sure it was a good price. They were buying a commodity and we were not selling commodities. Setting terms is not a bad thing. It can help you focus on what you need and want without causing you and others unnecessary pain. What are your terms?

Today, I will figure out what terms I need to establish in my life and continue to figure out what works best for me and the life I need and want.

Learn It, Until You Earn It   NOVEMBER 21

"Fake it 'till you make it." – Mary Kay Ash

We all know the phrase fake it 'til you make it. We have used it to describe a situation in which we did not have the proper education, understanding, or credentials to carry out a certain level of expertise. We get a new job or new responsibilities, and someone says, just fake it 'til you make it.

I was speaking to someone a few months ago and they described to me how they were learning how to do certain skills by watching videos or reading papers on how to do that skill. It dawned on me that we should not fake it 'til we make it, but we must learn it until we earn it. Often, we do just that, we learn it. We take the time to figure out how to obtain a certain piece of knowledge or a certain set of skills. Once we learn it, we earn the ability to do that skill. We earn the credentials necessary to do that skill, and maybe even teach it to others. We are in an age now where almost everything we need to learn is at our fingertips, literally. So why not learn it. I know it takes time and we live in an instant age, but we have the ability to use the tools at our disposal to make ourselves better. I know plenty of people that said they learned something simply by pulling up a video on their phone. We all have the chance to learn it until we earn it. What skills do you lack? What sales technique do you need to improve or just learn? Now is the time to learn it and stop faking it.

Today, I will find ways to learn what I am lacking so that I make it and not fake it.

THINGS BEYOND YOUR CONTROL   NOVEMBER 22

"For the rest of my life, there are two days that will never again trouble me. The first day is yesterday with all its blunders and tears, follies, and defeats. Yesterday has passed away, beyond my control forever. The other day is tomorrow with all its pitfalls and threats, its dangers and mystery. Until the sun rises again, I have no stake in tomorrow, for it is still unborn." – Og Mandino

Maybe you started your day with a positive mindset. Maybe you woke up on time and were able to get your stuff together and get to work on time, in fact, you were early for your first appointment. Then you got a phone call, or your internet goes down right before your meeting, your dog runs out the door and takes off into the neighborhood. All things that can ruin your day in a heartbeat. Some days are just like that. How does that make you feel?

I was driving to see my family and the drive was going to be about 6 hours. I left at about 9 in the morning so I could arrive by no later than 4 and pick up my nephew from soccer practice at 5:30 and take him for his birthday dinner that we had planned. Two hours into the drive, traffic started to slow and eventually came to a complete stop. I could not get off the highway, in fact, I found out that not only was the highway blocked off, so was the next exit with another accident. I had nowhere to go. I watched time pass as my GPS was telling me my arrival time was getting later and later and now, I was going to arrive around 6 pm. It was hard to sit on the highway not moving for that long. What do you do? I used to get frustrated. Now was not the time to get frustrated about something that was out of my control. Someone else was having a much worse day than I was, and I was not going to be stuck in this forever. When it finally cleared up, there was no sign of an accident. Nothing to show for the cause of the delay. It was clear and so was the remainder of my travel that day. Sometimes we just need to ride out the wave. This too shall pass.

What can you do to not get uptight or angry when things happen that are out of your control?

Today, I will be more mindful of my reactions to things that are truly out of my control. If I have a choice, I will avoid them but if I cannot, then I will let go of fear and anxiety that may come as a result.

VICTIM MINDSET   NOVEMBER 23

"Leadership is a mindset that shifts from being a victim to creating results. Any one of us can demonstrate leadership in our work and within our lives." - Robin Sharma

I would bet that most of us have been a victim at one time in our lives. What did you do? How did it make you feel? Most of us probably got upset or determined to never let ourselves get into a situation like that again. We open our eyes and had become more aware of people and their actions. Some of us may have chosen to not act that way or were not able to become aware of the ways of others. We may have gotten used to being a victim because of the feelings attached to that. We may have enjoyed the attention that people gave us by becoming a victim or being portrayed as a victim. We learned to accept the fact that we were stuck in this place or this role. The black cloud seemed to be stuck right over our heads and we could not get away from it.

In sales, we can play this game too. We probably know someone right now who is playing the victim on the sales team. They say things like, I do not get the same leads that the others get. My territory is smaller or larger than the others. I make the calls and send the emails and they do not respond to me. The list goes on as to why they are not getting the results. Maybe you are that person. I have been that person! I learned that no one is responsible for my sales results except for me. Nobody else is in my shoes. They may be similar but not exactly the same. We get to make the choices that impact us and will affect us and our future. We can be the victim or the hero. It must be up to us to act on our lives and not wait for others to step aside or give us the helping hand. The question is, what are you going to do? Will you play the victim, or will you step up and refuse to allow that to happen to you?

Today, I will look at my behavior and no longer allow myself to be a victim. Things may happen to me, but I get to choose whether or not I will be the victim or the hero in my own story.

MEASURING UP NOVEMBER 24

"Any form of measuring yourself by the unkind action of another towards you is like looking into a badly fractured mirror... and then blaming yourself for the shattered image you see therein." – Guy Finley

Too often we can get caught up in measuring ourselves against others. Sometimes that is a good motivator but other times we are so competitive that we forget we only need to be better than ourselves. When we constantly try to compare ourselves to others, we forget that we may not have all the training and abilities that someone else has. They may have a certain look, charm, or ability to speak to people that we do not have or have never learned. We should learn what we can from them, but some things we cannot learn. We cannot learn how to change our natural features. Changing character flaws is ok but measure how you are today versus how you were yesterday. If we make progress from day to day, we win. Sometimes we lose a step and that is ok too, but then we move forward to the next day so we can get better. The only way to measure up to someone is physical height.

Today, I will remember that being competitive is ok just as long as it does not dictate how I measure myself against others. I get to work on the best version of me today.

CRITICISM   NOVEMBER 25

"Criticism, like rain, should be gentle enough to nourish a man's growth without destroying his roots." – Frank A. Clark

We also have been critical of ourselves and others. We understand how to pick out the good and the bad. Too often we pick out the bad over the good because we are insecure. Seeing the issue in others is one thing, saying something about it can be another. Do you know how to help others without being overly harsh?

I was out at dinner with my family recently and they brought us some water. My daughter tasted it and got a sour face immediately. Her husband tried it and then I tried it. We all got a great surprise when the overly salty water hit our tastebuds. It was almost like getting water from the ocean in our mouths. We could have made a big deal about it but when the waitress came back to take our order, I mentioned that the water was a little salty. She immediately knew what the problem was, apologized, and said she would get us new waters. There was no big to-do about it because it was a fixable problem that she had no knowledge of. When we made her aware she fixed it and all was good again. When someone needs some correction, can you gently instruct them, even if it is the second, third, or fourth time you have had to tell them? Someone was gentle with you now go and do likewise.

Today, I will learn to be gentler when correcting or criticizing people. I do not know what someone is going through and that gives me more patience for them.

Wellness Versus Illness November 26

"If you do not make time for your wellness, you will be forced to make time for your illness" – Anonymous

Too often we can get caught up in the business of our day and our life. If we do not take the time to take care of our own wellness, we can find ourselves getting sick physically or emotionally, or both. What does self-care look like? Eating properly, meaning not fast food all the time, or eating out every meal. For some, this is a challenge. When you are a person that travels all the time, you may not have a choice of home-cooked meals. Try to find healthier alternatives. When I was on the road every day from seven in the morning to six or seven in the evening, it was hard to find good options. I chose to not eat fast food because I was seeing and feeling the effects. Can you pack a lunch or find healthy choices at local restaurants? Take time to improve yourself, whether it is through reading, meditation, or prayer. Take time to focus on yourself every day. If you let this go for too long, you can start to feel the weight of the world you live in. Do some exercise that you enjoy. There are so many options out there, that even a walk around the neighborhood can help you feel better.

I had to learn most of this the hard way. I gained about forty pounds, I was not eating healthy, I was not exercising, and I was not taking time daily for myself. I was having regular gout attacks and they were increasing in intensity and duration. This caused me to take time out of work to deal with my illness. The stress was building up, the weight was slowly killing me, and I was not a happy person to be around. I was battling the illness that was building in my life and my body. I am not perfect, but I have gotten better. I am a healthy weight, I read, pray and/or meditate most days, and I get to exercise a few times a week. Do the best you can and learn to make progress for yourself. If you do not, and maybe you are feeling this now, you will be dealing with an illness.

Today, I will find a way to start making healthier choices for my overall well-being. If I take time for my wellness, I will not have to take time for an illness.

Guilt   November 27

"Guilt is not a response to anger; it is a response to one's own actions or lack of action." – Audre Lorde

Guilt has a strange way of helping us and hurting us at the same time. It helps us to see that what we did or did not do was not right. It hurts us when we cannot let it go. Sometimes we feel the need to carry the guilt with us for much longer than we need to, and it becomes this looming cloud. Guilt is a mechanism we use to help us to see the thing our conscience knows is right or wrong. I have carried guilt a lot farther than I needed to in my life. I carried it for things done or said in my past that have been long forgotten by others that may have been harmed by my actions or words. Did I say enough or too much? Did I not get involved when I should have or did I overstep my boundaries? I get this pit in my stomach that just will not go away, then my mind gets to thinking about what I should have done or said. Then I feel shame when I am around the people that I think I hurt by my words or actions. What I have found is that people do not think about me as much as I think they do and the situations, unless completely over-the-top, have been pushed aside or even forgotten. I can allow myself to learn from the guilt, make the changes I need to, and then let it go by forgiving myself. I can then grow from the situation.

Today, I will accept guilty feelings in my life for what they are, a signal to myself to stop or start doing something. After I have started taking corrective action, I will forgive myself so I can move forward without the guilt.

Decision Making   November 28

"In any moment of decision, the best thing you can do is the right thing, the next best thing is the wrong thing, and the worst thing you can do is nothing." – Theodore Roosevelt

We all have things that we get to decide on every day. What to eat, what to wear, or who we are going to meet with today. Some decisions are easy to make, and others are really challenging. What practices do you find helpful when you are trying to make a decision about important things? Hopefully, you are counting the costs when it comes to very important items in your life. You are looking, as best you can, to the impact that this decision will have on you, your loved ones, and your future with all involved. I have used what I call the 'Gideon Test' on things like this before. The story is from the bible, where Gideon needs help making an important decision. He asks God for some very specific things, one thing to happen one day and another the next. He was trying to get out of a situation, but I use it to help me decide. I would ask for specific things to happen and point me in the right direction. It has proven helpful when I have really needed it in making these heavy decisions. A few months after I started my business, a friend of mine said some things that pointed me in a direction of being more focused on a certain type of clientele. I mentioned it to a few other people who agreed. I then spoke to a new acquaintance, and I ran the scenario by them. He thought it was great that I was going to do that, and he wished that he was able to do that with his business but had not, as of yet. I knew that was my green light to go ahead and focus my business. It was the right decision and now I knew it. I have stuck with it and am not looking back. Do not let hard decisions get in your way of moving forward. Find what you need to do to make them and then move forward.

Today, I will search for the decisions I have been putting off and see what I can do to push them forward. Whether it is asking God or the universe for help or gathering your trusted advisors.

TIME TO MOVE ON — NOVEMBER 29

"Don't cry because it's over. Smile because it happened." – Dr. Seuss

Too often moving on can be a challenge. We want to stay longer. We feel awkward for some reason. We know we should just go but something is not letting us. We know when to leave a class, yet some of us linger after class. We know when to leave a video conference, yet we are all waiting for everyone else to say goodbye before we leave, so we do not miss anything. We know when a business is closing for the day that it is time to leave, yet we linger because we deem ourselves more important than the store employees.

Do you know when the right time to leave a relationship is? What about a job? If you are managing people, do you know when to let them go so they can move on, whether for a promotion or to release them to work for someone else? What or whom are you trying to save? What are you trying to fix? We know that things have a beginning, middle, and end. Why are we afraid to apply the same idea to things in our lives? Why are we so afraid to let things go or end them? We probably have had that person in our life that was toxic. What did you do in that situation? Did you let them hang around or did you set boundaries, so their toxicity no longer affected you? People come and go in our lives, even close relationships, for a reason. Have you had someone come into your life for a time and then move on?

I have had people that I felt a close connection with, and we became close friends. I started to change my priorities and realized I was being codependent. I also wanted people to fix people and I was afraid to let go because that is who I was. I learned to take care of myself, and my well-being became a priority. I still want to help people, but they have to want to help themselves. I cannot fix people. I can only share what has helped me along my journey. They must do the work. I have found that people have been in my life so that I could learn, or they could learn something. It was appropriate for them and/or me to move on. Some people bring good lessons and others hard lessons that can turn into good if we allow it. Let people come and go in your life. It does not mean that you need to become shallow or disinterested in making deep friendships. It means that you have a level of maturity that allows people to come into your life, make an impact, and you can let them go because they have fulfilled what they came to do. You still get to live your life and they get to live theirs.

Today, I will do some soul-searching and find out if there are situations or relationships that I need to move on from. If so, I will find out why I have been holding on to them so that I can move on and create space.

SIBLINGS   NOVEMBER 30

"Where would you be without friends? The people to pick you up when you need lifting? We come from homes far from perfect, so you end up almost parent and sibling to your friends - your own chosen family. There's nothing like a really loyal, dependable, good friend. Nothing."
– Jennifer Aniston

Some of us have siblings and others do not. But we can end up making our own family. We have friends that are closer than a brother or sister. We adopt or bring people into our "family" as we draw close to them over time. Some of us grew up in a situation that was less than favorable, and we made the most of it for as long as we could. Now we have found or maybe created the family that we wanted and needed. If you are close to your siblings then that is a blessing. Not everyone is able to make the same connection as you. I had someone in my extended family tell me that I needed to be closer to my brothers because they were close to their sibling, and we should be just like they were. They wanted to force their situation on us. The idea was great, but the reality is harder. I love my family and we get along fine, but I have learned that I have different wants and needs for my "family." I have learned that we all have different personalities, different wants, different needs, and do not always get along or work well together. And that is ok, that is normal. You cannot force people to love you or even like you, and that means family too. Siblings can be great as trusted friends or confidantes, but not everyone experiences that and so we go outside the family to find that type of relationship. What do you look for or expect from your siblings and yourself?

Today, I will look at the family that I have and the one that I have chosen, friends that are like family. I will do what I can to love and give of myself where I can to make sure my family can be as close as I need and want them to be.

December

GIVING AND RECEIVING — DECEMBER 1

"Always give without remembering and always receive without forgetting."
– Brian Tracy

We cannot properly receive until we properly give. We often want to change the order of that statement. We want to receive in order to give. We use excuses like, "if only I had the money to give to others" or "If only I had the time to help others.

Giving properly means that you give without expectations of a return. Other than the joy in your heart, you should expect nothing in return for your gift of giving. If you expect a return, it is no longer giving, it is an investment. Giving to invest is not the same. When we receive properly, we do it without expectation. When we think, you need to give me this or give me that, you owe me this or that, or even I deserve this or that, are we not expecting to get something for something we did or think we did? When someone gives us a gift and we try to reciprocate or return the favor of the gift, we are negating or removing the object of the gift. It can be hard to receive a gift from someone, especially when you feel like you do not deserve it. But that is the idea of a gift, a thing given willingly to someone without the expectation of payment. Humility allows us to receive a gift properly.

Today, I will find ways to give and receive properly and respectfully.

CRISIS — DECEMBER 2

"The measure of a country's greatness is its ability to retain compassion in a time of crisis." – Thurgood Marshall

We all go through times that are more difficult than others. We get to choose how we handle those hard times. Most of the time we are reacting and not conscious of the way we are acting. When we realize how we are handling crises, we get the chance to continue or change. If things are going well and we are handling the crisis properly, then what is there to change? If we are not handling it well, we can make the appropriate corrections. Crisis can bring out the best and the worst in people. Maybe it is a bad car accident that causes you to spend whatever savings you had, and you were already living paycheck to paycheck. Then there is the death of a friend or family member that rocks your world because they were not that old. Each of these could be and usually is a crisis where our hearts and our actions get tested.

I remember details of the first job I lost, well maybe I chose to get fired. I was a cocky teen when I chose to walk away from one of my first jobs because the district manager made a snide comment to me. He was not wrong about what he said. He gave me an ultimatum about changing my appearance before I came back, but I did not handle the situation very well and I chose not to return.

I was driving home the evening my mom called me with the news of my brother's death. I felt the weight of the world and went into autopilot as I drove. Trying to support my mom and seeing the calls coming in from my older brother and my dad, felt very surreal. I knew I needed to find my strength for my family at that time. I also knew I would feel the impact of the feelings later.

My heart was tested on these occasions and some I handled better than others. We all get the chance to show our true selves when there is a crisis, whether it is one that we are dealing with personally or that others are dealing with, and we are on the outer edges of that crisis. Some people go into autopilot and fix everyone and everything. Other people fall apart during a crisis. Others do not know what to do or how to handle a crisis and are therefore paralyzed by these stress-filled situations.

Today, I will check my heart when I find myself in crisis. Can I handle the crisis and retain compassion for myself and others?

Turnback Moments   December 3

"Everybody has a turnback moment. You have a moment where you could go forward, or you can give up." – Steve Harvey

Throughout our lives we have opportunities to keep moving forward despite our pain or we can give up. We are playing sports and getting knocked down. We can get up or we can stay on the ground. We are going through life in our relationships, and we hit a rough patch that seems insurmountable. We can find a way through the rough patch, or we can give up. Sometimes it may seem like we are giving up but we are finding a way around the mountain instead of trying to climb the mountain because we are not equipped to climb a mountain. We are working in our careers, and we can no longer find joy in what we are doing. We have been doing this thing for years and this is what we went to college for, trained for, and have been working for years to master. But it is now just a job, not a passion. There is nothing wrong with waking up one day and saying why am I doing what I am doing? Steve Harvey goes on with the quote above to say that if you give up, it will never happen. Turnback moments can be defining moments in your life.

I decided to try out for the University of Illinois football team, against the advice of my high school football coach. I could have walked away because I was told I would not make the college football team. I was able to play for four years and was a varsity letterman for two. I was given the opportunity to make a career change. I chose to not take a job in the Midwest and was later offered a better job in the Midsouth. I was not ready for one opportunity and another one that was better came along. I did not give up and kept working towards my goals and was presented with the right opportunity. Sometimes you are faced with a turnback moment, and the timing is not right, and you may have to let go of the one to find the right one.

Today, I will look at the turnback moments that come my way and do what I can to keep going and not give up. It may mean that the timing is not right to push forward but I will not give up on my goals.

Value   December 4

"Do not value money for any more nor any less than it's worth; it is a good servant but a bad master." – Thomas-Alexandre Dumas

When we purchase things, whether it is a meal at a restaurant, furniture, or a vehicle you determine what you are willing to pay for the product or service. We do this every day. We figure out what something is worth and assign a value to it. Do we want to pay twenty dollars for the pizza, or will you pick one that does not cost as much because you are just hungry, and you just need some food? Do you want to pay $400 per month for that vehicle or can you get the same needs fulfilled from a vehicle that only costs $250 per month?

Because we do this, we also understand that we have value too. We bring value to most things that we do or participate in. Do you bring value to your friendships? If you do not, then do you have a good friendship? If you are in a romantic relationship, you bring some value to that relationship. You provide security, emotionally or financially. You can provide emotional or physical support. But if you do not provide some sort of value to the relationship, is it a solid relationship? In business, if you do not provide value for what you are being paid, will you have a job with that company very long?

I have been in relationships where I have not provided enough value to the relationship to overcome my shortcomings. I had to learn how to be a better listener, communicator, and how to express my emotions clearly. I have had jobs where I was not providing enough value for the money I was being paid. The decision was easy for my employer, and I understood their logic, maybe not at the time but later. I had to learn how to get better at sales. I had to learn more about business and the bigger picture so that I could improve at sales and operations. I got to read books, watch videos, and have discussions with people that were able to teach me how to improve.

You should not have to prove the value that you are providing in relationships or in business. It should be evident. If it is not evident then you may not be able to stay in the relationship or the job. We all have a value that we bring to the table. When we know what it is, it is easy for us to show that value by the things we do.

Today, I will continue to work on the things that bring value to who I am, in life, relationships, and business. I will learn how to be a better listener and learn how to communicate clearly and concisely. I will learn how to add to the things I know about business by reading books, going to seminars, or watching videos of people that can teach me how to improve.

WHAT ARE YOU SEEKING? DECEMBER 5

"Do not seek to follow in the footsteps of the wise. Seek what they sought."
– Matsuo Basho

Every day we wake up and chase our dreams or we build someone else's. We get the chance to learn from others that have been successful before us. Maybe they made mistakes and learned things that we did not see, but we hear about their success and want to take the same path they took so we can get the same results. We want to emulate that success by following in their footsteps or even by trying to skip ahead of them. Following someone's footsteps is good if you are walking in deep snow. But if your gait is not the same as the person that you are following it can be harder to follow in their footsteps. Business can be like this as well. We do not know what challenges others faced unless we ask, and we may not have the same obstacles that they encountered. We can learn from them if we want to listen. Our path is likely going to be different and our own experience, not someone else's.

Seek what they sought. Your wisdom will grow with time. You can help people. Make a plan and execute that plan. Drive yourself to do things that you did not think were possible. As you grow in your wisdom, you can make choices that will impact your financial future in a great way. Build upon your dreams and see how far you can fly. If you want to start a business, write a book, become the top salesperson in your company, then how do you get there? Grow in wisdom!

Today, I will find ways to seek what the wise have sought so that I may grow in my wisdom and reach my dreams and goals.

ARE YOU OFF CENTER? DECEMBER 6

"We all have something that centers us in our lives. That linchpin is something that when we don't do enough of it, we start to feel off-center."
– Agapi Stassinopoulos

Have you ever been in your vehicle driving somewhere and the steering wheel feels like it is pulling to one side? It is not a lot but just enough that when you take your hands off you start to drift into the other lane. This can happen to us too. How do you know when you are off-center? Can you feel it? Most of the time we know because something in our head tells us that we are not right. We are missing the mark and we cannot seem to put our finger on the problem. It nags at us until we make a mistake, or we shake it loose. It comes because we lack sleep or maybe we ate something that did not agree with us. Maybe we just cannot get rid of this cloud that is hanging over us because we are wrapped up in unimportant thoughts. We do not feel as sharp. We cannot seem to think clearly. We want to press on and we do the best we can, but we are just not right. Maybe it is time to take a nap. Maybe we just need to sit in front of the TV and aimlessly watch some sports or something else that does not require our full attention. Sometimes we do not have those options. We are in the midst of a day full of meetings. We are heavy into a project that we must finish. I find myself in these situations and I just need to get my feet moving. I need to walk around and get my blood pumping. Maybe I can actually put my sneakers on and head out for a walk around the neighborhood for thirty minutes. What do you need to do to get out of the fog and get back on course?

I was in Indiana and preparing for a big charity golf event. There was much to do before everyone else got to town in the next twenty-four hours and some uncertainty was still looming about the event. It was the first time I helped coordinate a big event like this. I had done almost all of my work on this from my home state of Georgia and the event was being held in Indiana. The stress of putting together a charity event in my brother's honor, in his state, and with a lot of people that I did not know, was overwhelming. I could not have regular face-to-face meetings but had to do everything virtually. When I arrived in town and could see everything coming together, I could take a breath. I had some downtime before things were going to be in full swing. I was feeling off-center because I had been driving for the past couple of days and I was not in my normal surroundings. I needed to ground myself and get back on track. I went outside where there was plenty of sunshine. I sat by the pool facing the sun so I could close my eyes and sit back in the chair. I even took off my shoes and socks so I could feel the ground with my feet. As I closed my eyes and rested my head on the back of the chair, I could feel this wave come over me. It was calming, and I could feel myself being filled up. I sat and meditated for about ten minutes and felt the Zen of being centered. It did not take much but it was exactly what I needed at that moment. I probably sat in the chair for another fifteen minutes before I had to get up and get going again but the first ten minutes were the most important to me getting centered. The weekend event went extremely well, and I was able to be centered and present for all of it.

Today, I will find what can help center me when I feel a little bit off. Whether a walk around a building, or neighborhood, or just a few minutes of sitting peacefully in the sun, meditating.

PATIENCE AND TIME — DECEMBER 7

"Patience and time do more than strength or passion." – Jean de La Fontaine

Sometimes, I do not have the patience or the time to deal with people or situations, but I have to ask myself why? Did I do something to give away my time to something different, probably? So, can I slow down now and take the time to do this thing? A dear friend of mine told me more than once, "Some people need to learn how to be early, and others need to learn how to be late." That was hard for me to learn because I like to be on time or early. But sometimes I need to be ok with being late, especially when it comes to my mindfulness and mental health. When I have an agenda, I want to do it with purpose and in my time. I have struggled with people or situations that deter me from my plans. Learning how to be patient and more flexible with my time has allowed me to find peace of mind. How do you react when someone or something gets in the way of your plans? Do you try to push through them to make your plans work? Maybe God or the universe is trying to tell us that we need to slow down. Maybe someone else needs our help or attention. Strength and passion will do little to no good at that time and place. Can you find compassion and empathy for others?

Life can throw us curve balls at times, and we can react in a couple of different ways. We can get mad and say that it is not fair that I am being treated this way. The alternative is we can understand that things happen for a reason and maybe this curveball saved me from something else. Maybe it is giving me a chance to see things from a different perspective. How do you handle the curveballs? If you have ever played baseball and seen a curveball thrown and then tried to hit it, it can be hard. You must have the patience to connect with it.

Today, I will find ways to be more patient and give myself and others more time. It may be the thing that saves me or others today.

Passing Through   December 8

"Every person passing through this life will unknowingly leave something and take something away. Most of this 'something' cannot be seen or heard or numbered or scientifically detected or counted. It's what we leave in the minds of other people and what they leave in ours. Memory. The census doesn't count it. Nothing counts without it." – Robert Fulghum

We have an agenda, and we are just passing through on our way to do what we think we are there to do. We pass by some people to get to others. If you have been to New York City, or another large city, you have probably experienced this. Passing hundreds of people every day, just to get to your destination. We can get caught up in taking care of our business and not noticing the people we pass by in life. Do you offer a smile or are we caught up in our own world and thoughts? Will a smile, warmth, and kindness from you make a difference in someone else's life? Probably. Think about how you feel when someone does that for you. You get the chance every day to make a difference. Some of us feel like that is a huge responsibility and some cringe at the thought. Others are filled with joy at the idea of helping just one person. While others do not give it a second thought. What about you, today? Will you make a difference, or are you just passing through?

    Today, I will ask myself, "What can I do to make a difference in other people's lives today?" Can I afford to give a smile? Can I afford to look at others with compassion? Yes, I can!

That's Never Happened to Me Before   December 9

"Nothing happens to you that has not happened to someone else."
– William Feather

When things happen for the first time to you are you taken aback by them or is it like a feather in my cap scenario, you got to experience something new? I know when I travel to new places and see a picturesque view for the first time, I am in awe. I feel lucky to have experienced it. I do not think that way when I experience something on the negative side of the scale. I used to think, why did this happen to me, but then I can look back on the choices I made and see how I ended up in the situation with the results that I got. When I stopped thinking about myself as a victim of circumstances and saw myself as an active participant, I realized that things happen. Things happen for the good and for the bad. Have you ever found some money on the street and no one around to give it back to? Have you crashed your bicycle because you were not paying attention? I know people who are constantly looking to blame anything or anyone but themselves for things that happen. People get mad at a tree or signpost because they ran into it. Who are you mad at, really? Who is the subject of that anger?

Looking at the worldometers.info, world population clock, the world population has more than doubled in my life so far and we are somewhere around 7.9 billion people on this planet, as I write this. Our experience is unique because it happened to us in a certain city or country, but if we fall down, break a bone, or go through a hard break up, we are not the only one that this has happened to. In fact, I am willing to bet that you were not the only one to have any of those scenarios happen to them today. Have you ever shared a struggle with a friend, and they say yeah, I am struggling with the same thing? We all have a chance to learn from others and share with others. We can say, I got to experience something that I have not experienced before. Now, I get to figure out how I am going to handle it. I can do that with the help of friends and loved ones or I can try to handle it myself.

Today, I will see the things that happen as experiences. I get to handle them the way that best suits me and those around me.

It is Hard Having to be Right All the Time   December 10

"Our addiction to always being right is a great block to the truth. It keeps us from the kind of openness that comes from confidence in our natural wisdom." – Stephen Levine

Have you been around someone that has to be right all the time? Have you been that person, or are you becoming that person? Being right is addictive. Our brain gets a shot of dopamine when we are praised for being right. Whether the praise comes from outside of us or we tell ourselves how awesome we are for being right. Then we want to do it again. We start to get influenced by the dopamine injection that we are getting, and we crave it more often. When people act like this it is probably not their fault, though they were the ones that got hooked on the feeling from their brain. We gain confidence when we are correct as well. That confidence though can be off the mark if we are just trying to please the dopamine rush in our heads. There is nothing wrong with being right and wanting to be right, the problem comes when this is all we want to do, and we hurt others in the process.

   I found myself feeling this need to prove myself and show how smart I was. It was like I needed to prove something to everyone else around me. The truth was I was not proving anything to anyone but to me. I remember being in a situation where I asked myself, how important is it for me to be right? Someone else was doing the same thing I had been doing and I felt very strange, almost dirty listening to this person. I was that person spewing information or trivia just to be right. I realized that if I did not feel the need to be right, someone else could feel good about themselves. I no longer had to one-up someone. Someone else could be right and it did not take away from who I am. I do not need to be the smartest person in the room. I did not have to be right!

   Why do you feel the need to be right all the time? Are you trying to prove to someone else that you are worthy or smart, or are you trying to prove to yourself that you are smart? We all have a chance to prove to ourselves that we are smart, good, or worthy, and we do not need an audience to do that.

Today, I know that I am worthy and do not need to prove to anyone that I am right. Remember this proverb when you wonder if you should share your thoughts just to be right, a wise man once said nothing.

TRUTH   DECEMBER 11

"When you want to help people, you tell them the truth. When you want to help yourself, you tell them what they want to hear." – Thomas Sowell

A lot has been said about the truth, the importance of it in life, relationships, even at work. The truth can be elusive, and it can be in your face. We have an opportunity to face it every day. Yet sometimes we want to run from it because it hurts too much. We do not see the healing properties of it. We shy away from it. We are afraid to share it with others because it will hurt them. Sometimes it is not easy to share with others, and at times should not be shared with others because it is not ours to share with them. When you learn to be honest with yourself that is a good thing. The truth is a good thing to know and keep with you at all times.

There was a time in my life when I could see pretty clearly the truth in situations and people. I was proud of this talent and so I found it necessary to share this as much as possible. I learned how short-sighted I was with this newfound wisdom. Sometimes I felt the need to share that with people and it was not mine to share, or there was no real value in sharing what I knew because it would cause more harm than good. Yet I felt the need to share it anyways. A close friend of mine shared a saying with me that is very insightful and now helps me when I speak with people. I ask myself three questions: "Is it true? Is it kind? Is it necessary?" The origin of this is and has been open for debate. The last question is the one that holds the most weight now when I speak to people. I find that some of the things that I know are not really necessary to share. It may make me feel better than someone else and therefore is not necessary. It also fails the second question, is it kind? There is another question that I need to add which I recently found and says, "Does it improve upon the silence?" Just because I know the truth about something or someone, does not mean that I need to be the one to share it.

Truth is a strange thing. When you know it, you want to share it, but it is not always the right thing to do. I find that odd. This is where maturity and truth come together.

Today, I will see the truth for what it is. Share it where I need to, and not run from it when presented. It can cut and heal when used properly on myself and others. When I get the opportunity to share it, I will try to incorporate the "Is it true, kind, and necessary" questions.

Positivity   December 12

"Just one small positive thought in the morning can change your whole day." – Dalai Lama

Think of something positive. Maybe it was something that made you smile, brought you joy, or made your heart swell. What prevents us from doing this multiple times during the day? We often let thoughts or ideas creep in and push away the positive thoughts. They seem to get lost in our day and before you know it your day is almost over, and you feel nothing but the negativity that came from it. Starting the day with thoughts of positivity and gratitude helps frame the rest of your day. If you have a journal, do you mention the things you are grateful for each day? If you are not doing that or even journaling, do you spend time reflecting on the ways that you are grateful for people or situations daily? We all have a chance each day to make a choice, actually several choices. We can choose how we start our day. How are you doing? What are your first thoughts when you wake up? Are you happy to have another day? Are you thinking about all the negative stuff that has happened or might happen in your life today, tomorrow, or even next week? Positive thoughts are not hard to find sometimes but we have to do work at them regularly to get better at finding them consistently.

Today, I will start the day with a positive thought. It may be a grateful reminder of loved ones, for friends, a career that you love, or to just have another day here on earth.

THE ILLUSION OF PERFECTION   DECEMBER 13

"Perfection is not attainable, but if we chase perfection, we can catch excellence." - Vince Lombardi

Most of us strive for perfection knowing it is not attainable, but it gives us something to push towards. We have heard the expression that if we shoot for the stars and hit the moon then we have made progress. Putting very large goals out in front of us gives us the drive to hit something further than if we did not set a goal at all. Perfection is a lofty goal. Some of us actually can be hypnotized by it as we strive for it daily in the things we say and do. We think that we need to be perfect so that we do not make mistakes. If we do not fail or make mistakes, then how can we grow? Growth happens when we fall short, not when we win. I am not saying that winning is bad. Winning feels great and looks great on your resume. When was the last time you won and asked yourself, what could I have done better? Some people do that regularly because they know they can always do better. They are looking to improve, always. We look at sports figures typically for this type of driven personality. There are many business people that have pushed for perfection as well. Madam Currie and Thomas Edison are examples of people that strove for perfection. What is it that drives you and pushes you to do your best? The goal should be for progress, not perfection.

Today, I will find a way to shoot for the stars knowing that I will hit the moon or beyond, reaching further than I thought possible.

PROCESSES   DECEMBER 14

"If you can't describe what you are doing as a process, you don't know what you're doing." - W. Edwards Deming

We live each day and do not realize that a lot of what we do is a process. We have our morning routine, typically a process. Getting ready in the morning, shower, get dressed, head out for work or school, all processes. Yet most of these are just in our heads, never written down. Is writing it down important? If you have a child or a pet and you ask someone to watch them, do you write down what they need to do and when they need to do it? You are giving people a process, a step-by-step way of doing things. When you get a new computer, do you follow the step-by-step process that they send you to start up your new computer? If we have these processes for the routine things in our lives, how important do you think a process is? Processes can be good, helping us to establish normalcy in our lives. Some people are very process-driven, and it has to be done exactly to their way or it messes them up. Sometimes it helps us to write the process down so we know how to do things or how things will work. In your work life, a process can be very helpful.

For those in sales, you should have a process for how you sell. If you do not or are unsure, write the steps that you take when you meet with a client. Write down what works and what does not work. See if there is a pattern. I believe what you will find is that there is a process that will help you sell. You need to find it, follow it, and write it down. It will provide you with consistency. It can provide you with more success too. You will start to see how having one improves your communication skills. If you cannot write it down, do you really know what you are doing?

Today, I will find my processes and understand how they can help me get through my day.

REACTIONS   DECEMBER 15

"Life is 10% what happens to you and 90% how you react to it." - Charles R. Swindoll

How do you react to things outside of your control? Do you get upset, mad, happy, even dumbfounded? Every situation can bring a different thought to our mind and therefore a different reaction. When I was younger, I know I reacted much more out of impulse no matter what the situation. It could have been happy, sad, or excited. When you let your emotions control you it is hard to not react to things that happen in your life without emotions. There is nothing wrong with showing emotions or having emotions. The problem comes when we let them control our lives. When you react emotionally to a situation, you may miss out on the facts of the situation, or you could miss out on the depth of the situation. When I emotionally react to a situation without letting it sink in for a minute to try and see the situation as a whole before I say anything or react, I usually am missing something. I usually am not listening properly and letting my emotions dictate my reaction instead of hearing all the facts. As I have matured, I have learned to delay any sort of reaction and do my best to listen to everything, ask questions to help me understand the entire situation the best I can, and assess the situation and my feelings before I reacted. Some situations call for anger, frustration, or disappointment. While others dictate joy or excitement. Reacting with the appropriate emotion can make all the difference to all involved. Have you ever reacted with anger to a child that was scared before they opened up to you? I have and it took a while for me and that child to reconcile. I am not perfect and luckily, still learn from situations when they arise. Some people are better at this than others, but we can all learn how to grow in this area of our lives. Listen, ask more questions, then assess the situation and react.

Today, I will learn how to react to situations by asking more questions and gaining more understanding.

INTENTIONS   DECEMBER 16

"Live with intention. Walk to the edge. Listen hard. Practice wellness. Play with abandon. Laugh. Choose with no regret. Appreciate your friends. Continue to learn. Do what you love. Live as if this is all there is." - Mary Anne Radmacher

Do you live with specific intentions? For a number of us, living with intention is a bit of a foreign concept. We were never introduced to the concept and maybe we are just hearing it now for the first time. Maybe we have been doing it and now we have a name for what we have been doing. Living with intention means that we are thoughtful and deliberate about what we are doing. It means taking responsibility for the actions we take. Too often, it is easier for us to go right into autopilot. We go through the motions of the daily routine. We get up, we make our coffee, we make our breakfast, we eat, and before you know it, we are out the door for work or some other regular activity that we can mindlessly go through until it is time to come back home, make dinner, watch TV, or read and then off to bed. Living with intention means we do not have to do that anymore. It means that we take responsibility for the things we do. Now, this can be exhausting at first because it requires us to think about every little thing that we are doing. When we learn to live with intention, the little things become thoughtful things. When I am making my breakfast so that I can be fueled up for the day, what am I putting in my body? I spend time reading and meditating in the morning so I can be present and mindful of my actions today.

It took me a while to figure this out. When I learned about living with my why, I learned that I was able to start living with intention. Writing my intentions down, saying them out loud, or making decisions based on the intentions. Learning to start my day with intent changed the way I approached the day. It changes the things I do or do not do. It changes the people I "hang out with" and the things I watch, read, or listen to.

Today, I will start my day with intention. If you are reading this later in the day, then start an intention now. A vision, goal, or something you want to accomplish today, tomorrow, or this week.

Doing the Best You Can   December 17

"Are people doing the best that they can? I don't know. I really don't. All I know is that my life is better when I assume that people are doing their best. It keeps me out of judgment and lets me focus on what is, and not what should or could be." – Steve Alley

Are people doing their best? My immediate response was, NO! I know plenty of people who are *not* doing their best. This was my judgmental side speaking on my behalf. I have said the very words that others have said when confronted with the question, why are you not doing better? I am doing the best that I can, with what I have. The last part of that sentence is what really hits home for me, with what I have. This is part of the boundary setting that we all need to be doing. You are probably doing the best that you can. I say probably only because I probably do not know you. But you are doing the best you can with what you have. With what you have been taught, with all the other things that you are dealing with in your life right now. I am doing the best that I can. You are learning to set boundaries when you say that. You are learning that it is ok to push back when you do not meet someone else's expectations. They are not there for others to live up to, nor are your expectations. We are responsible for ourselves. Maybe we are in the custody of someone else for a time, but we are responsible for ourselves and our own decisions and actions. The person that stands on the street corner begging for money is doing the best that they can, right now. The college student, the entrepreneur, the corporate CEO, the person that is working at the grocery store stocking shelves are all doing the best that they can, with what they have. Some people are not capable of thinking or being like you. They do not have the experiences that you do and vice versa. When we look at people and realize that they are probably doing the best they can then we get to go back to things like love and compassion, the things that are and not what should or could be.

Today, I will put aside my judgment and assume that people are doing the best that they can.

THERE IS ALWAYS SOMETHING — DECEMBER 18

"Our opportunity now is to decide to change what we want, to seek what we actually came here to experience, rather than what we've been told by our culture that we are supposed to be experiencing." – Neale Donald Walsch

There always seems to be something. Something to do, something to see, something that needs to be changed. I was having a conversation with a friend and the phrase, there is always something, popped up. I felt tired just hearing it. An overwhelming sense of dread, one more thing for me to do, worry about or overcome. When do I get a break?

I have been working on my health for a few years now and the healthier I get the more there seems to be that I "have to" worry about. The more I learn about things the more there is to avoid. I am not one of those people that is afraid to breathe or walk down the street because of all the stuff that could go wrong. The phrase this morning got me thinking about how when we learn something new, we have two choices. We can either accept that and make a change or we can choose to ignore it and move on in ignorant bliss. Sometimes not knowing is better than knowing. There may be some truth to that but when you are working on your health, and you are trying to improve to the best of your ability it can be hard. Sometimes you do the best you can with the information that you have. Sometimes it is ok to say, I cannot do anymore right now. Mentally, physically you can only handle so much. Accept that and move forward. If and when it comes up again, you get the chance to decide again if you can and want to make a change. Every day we are faced with choices to change. We take steps forward or backward, but we never stay the same because we cannot. Ignoring a decision does not mean you stay the same. You have the knowledge or some of the knowledge and you are choosing not to move forward. That is ok too! You have to do what is right for you today, right now, at that moment in time. It does not mean you cannot change later today, next month, or next year. Some people are changed by circumstances out of their control, but most of us decide to change or not. What will you do today because there is always something?

Today, I will see the choices that I have and consciously decide to move forward or not, knowing that it is my choice.

RESIGNATION   DECEMBER 19

"Acceptance of one's life has nothing to do with resignation; it does not mean running away from the struggle. On the contrary, it means accepting it as it comes, with all the handicaps of heredity, of suffering, of psychological complexes and injustices." – Paul Tournier

When you hear the word *resignation* does it mean something negative to you? Growing up competitive most of my life, I do not remember resignation being referred to as a positive thing. Most of the time it was a term used when you give up and giving up was not usually a good thing. As I have gotten older, a.k.a. more mature, I have found that resignation is not always a bad thing. It comes with maturity and understanding. You are resigned to the idea that you are no longer capable of running that far for that long. You are resigned to the fact that you can no longer lift that much. You are resigned to the fact that you have grey hair, and it is a sign of wisdom. Resignation is the acceptance of something undesirable but inevitable. We may not like the situation but why are you fighting so hard against it? You are going to slow down, not be as strong, or not be as sharp as we used to be. That is totally fine. Sometimes we fight until our body tells us no! Resignation is not a bad thing. It can be our way of realizing that sometimes we need to move in a different direction.

When I was playing football in college, I had to come to the realization that my dream of playing football was coming to an end. I was good with that. It took me a while to figure that out, but I knew that my time was limited, and that was ok. What are the signs for you that it may be time for a change of direction? When do you know it is time to resign from a post or change the direction of a lifelong dream?

Today, I will look at the things in my life that are not going the way I would like them to go and ask myself, is it time to let go and move on, or is it time to push a little harder? Knowing the difference will help me to move on mentally.

WHY ARE YOU IN A HURRY TO GROW UP? DECEMBER 20

"My mom told me, 'Don't grow up too quickly; once you're an adult, you're an adult.'" – Camilla Belle

Some people grow up in an environment where they are forced to deal with adult things at childlike age. They have to take care of themselves or other siblings because the parents work, or they are in a single-parent household. Some are just born older. Most children do not need to be adults before they should, yet there are some that just want to be older and have the ability to make the hard decisions.

I grew up in a single-parent household. We learned how to cook, clean house, and do laundry at an early age. My preteen and teen summer years were spent working with my brothers and father in the family landscape business. I learned a lot of valuable lessons during those years. I missed out on a lot of fun kid summer activities too because I was working. Some need to grow up and take on responsibilities earlier than others. Some need to enjoy being a child and having the childlike summers. Being an adult is something you will do for the rest of your life. We can have our childlike moments as adults but not nearly as often. Let the children be children. Do not make them grow up too early lest they miss out on the joys of being a child. Do not make them be in a hurry to grow up either. Like a tree that needs time to grow and produce shade or fruit, we all need time to grow and mature.

Today, I will find ways to let my childlike moments come to light. I will play in the rain, play video games, or just enjoy something youthful. I will learn to relax and allow my kids to be kids as well.

DESIRE, EMOTION, AND KNOWLEDGE — DECEMBER 21

"Human behavior flows from three main sources: desire, emotion, and knowledge." – Plato

Today, you woke up and got out of bed. Maybe you already got cleaned up and dressed for the day. Maybe you already got some exercise, read something inspirational, prayed, meditated, or made some coffee. What made you do all or any of those things? You have a desire to get out of bed and start your day. You know that your morning routine is just what you need to get off on the right foot. You know that, emotionally, you need to sit in stillness first thing in the morning to allow your mind to settle down and give things over to God or the universe. You have previous experience with yourself and the world. You know what it takes for you to make it through the day, a normal day. Imagine waking up with the knowledge of all that would happen that day. We need to spend time in the morning to arise and prepare for the day, even if it is just a cup of coffee or tea. Understand the source of the behavior that flows from you today. It is a desire, to be you or the best you can be. It is emotion, that powers us through or slows us down to grasp the depth of the day. It is knowledge, things that have taught me in the past that will prepare me for today. Now go and have a great day!

Today, I will acknowledge the desires I have to improve myself, work with and through the emotions before me, and know that my behavior will be a result of my desires and my emotions.

Encouraged to Fail   December 22

"My dad encouraged us to fail. Growing up, he would ask us what we failed at that week. If we didn't have something, he would be disappointed. It changed my mindset at an early age that failure is not the outcome, failure is not trying. Don't be afraid to fail." – Sara Blakely

Have you encouraged people to fail? That sounds counterproductive, when in fact it is very productive. When you are encouraged to fail, your mind takes on a different method of thinking. You are encouraged to learn from your mistakes. You are encouraged to share your failures to the point that you no longer are embarrassed by them. You also get to learn the meaning of joyful success. When you succeed, and you will, you will have pure joy in your life. One that people cannot take from you because of the journey it took to get there.

I was not encouraged to fail. I believe it has something to do with why I tend to overthink things now. Not blaming anyone but me, because I developed that over time, and it lived, rent-free, for a long time in my head. Now, I get the chance to change that in me. I did learn from those lessons that failure has taught me over time. I have been able to see things and do things that I never would have thought possible. I have been to almost all fifty states, traveled to almost all of the provinces in Canada, and traveled to several other foreign countries. I have started my own business. I am writing a book and will have written a book by the time you read this. I have been able to work for the top companies in almost every industry I have worked in. I was able to play American football at the collegiate level in some of the most prestigious American football stadiums. I have been blessed because I allowed myself to fail.

What have you done, or are you doing, in your life to encourage yourself to fail? Not in the negative way but in a way that says go out there and try your best today. If you are not failing, then you are not trying. The only failure we truly have in our lives comes from not trying.

Today, I will find ways to allow myself to fail. I will give my best shot and if I fall short of my goal or intended outcome, I will learn from it.

WHAT IS NONSENSE? DECEMBER 23

"Life humbles you as you age. You realize how much time you wasted on nonsense." – Unknown

Life is full of choices. Some may see your choices as nonsense and others as a wise decision. When we get older, we look back on life with a clearer vision of the things we can remember. We think this was good or this was not good. We think that as we mature, we can look at the things done that were not helping us make progress on our life goals were a waste of time. However, we needed that downtime. We needed to let our minds escape and recharge. We need to relax at times so that we are not so uptight or rigid. We need to breathe. It is humbling to look back on our lives and see all that we have been able to do and see. To understand that we lived through things that are taught in history books. It is humbling to see the growth around us and within us. How did we get so lucky? What are you doing that may be considered nonsense to some but to you, in the present time, it is a needed departure from all that is happening around you or even to you? I hope you enjoy that movie, that book, or that video game. Do the work that you need to do and take the breaks that you need. Life is hard enough with all the choices that we have not to stop and look around every once and a while.

Today, I will make time to allow for some nonsense in my life. I will work hard and find the time to celebrate that work with some downtime.

ACTIONS VERSUS WORDS   DECEMBER 24

"A thousand words will not leave so deep an impression as one deed."
– Henrik Ibsen

We like to talk about taking action but when we take action it needs no words. Our actions speak on our behalf. You can talk about supporting a person or a cause through donations which is helpful and needed. You can also go out and support that person or cause by giving your time to them and lifting them up through deeds of love. It is one thing for me to monetarily support my daughters and it turns into another level when I am in their presence, spending time with them. It is the same with words of encouragement via social media. We all need to support each other and sending your thoughts via text is nice, but will you show up for them when things are hard?

My best friend in college and I had graduated and moved to different cities. We were still in touch when he called to let me know he was going through a rough time. I felt the need to support him with more than just words. I needed to be there for him. I arranged to go and spend the weekend with him. I was not the only one that showed up either. He was surprised at the outpouring of love and support, but he was very grateful that we were there for him.

Life is hard and when we have the chance to act on things instead of just feeling bad and saying supportive words, we can act on our words and show up for people. When was the last time you decided to show up and act upon the conviction in your heart? Have you ever made a meal and taken it to a friend or neighbor because they were going through a rough patch? When was the last time you wrote a card and sent it via mail? We all get a chance to show up and we can show up, it all starts with the first step. When you show up for people, they will show up for you as well. It is easy to show up for people on social media, but do not forget to show up in actions as well.

Today, I will find ways to let my actions speak louder than my words. I will pick up the phone and call or go out of my way to stop by and visit someone. I will take action.

Want vs. Need — December 25

"You have succeeded in life when all you really want is only what you really need." – Vernon Howard

What is the difference between want and need? Too often the lines get blurred, and we think that we need something and yet it turns out to be the worst thing for us because we just *wanted* it. A want is something that when taken away causes manageable unease, a need when taken away creates a void in your life. If you have kids, you can see this more clearly when you take something away from them. They think that the world is going to end when you take it away but that goes away after they calm down and find something else to focus their attention on. If it were something that they needed you as a parent would have made sure that they had it.

When you want something, it can be for the wrong reasons, or we do not fully understand why we want that thing. We may be trying to fill a void in our lives that we do not understand. Filling a void just to fill a void is not necessarily a good thing. We are like a puzzle and there are things that fit into certain places in our lives. There is a void for love, relationships, work, etc. and we must learn how to properly fill those spaces in our lives. When we improperly fill those voids, we get frustrated, we are unsatisfied. Understanding how we can patiently find what we need in our lives can be one of the greatest feelings in the world. We can feel full or even complete in the right way.

Today, I will look at the wants in my life to see if I really need them and learn the difference for me.

WE ARE ALL CONNECTED   DECEMBER 26

"I do believe we're all connected. I do believe in positive energy. I do believe in the power of prayer. I do believe in putting good out into the world. And I believe in taking care of each other." – Harvey Fierstein

Have you ever considered how connected we are to others? You have neighbors, whether you speak to them or not, that are connected to you. You have family, coworkers, friends, classmates from years gone by. We are meeting or connecting with people every day, within our local communities and family units. Even if you do the same routine every day, you encounter new people. There is a connection to others when your city's team wins a championship. There is a connection when there is a tragedy in your community. When you go to the store to get groceries, get gas, or just go shopping in general, you are making a connection. It may not be a deep life-changing connection, but there is a connection if only for a brief time.

Your life has an impact on others whether you realize it or not, whether you want to or not. We cannot escape it even if we stay home and do not interact with anyone, we have a connection. What will you do with that connection today? Will you show kindness or are you in a place where you need someone to show you kindness? Will you smile, hold a door open, or say hello to someone you encounter today? You get to choose every day in those moments, the type of connection that you are willing to give to others. That is all that you can do.

Today, I will look around at the connections I have and will decide to give to that connection what I am able to give. It is my choice, but there is always a connection.

WHAT IS YOUR WHY?   DECEMBER 27

"He who has a why to live can bear almost any how." – Friedrich Nietzsche

Understanding why we do something can seem easy at first; however, several of us do not understand why we get up every day. Are you getting up with your family in mind, spouse, kids, something other than the paycheck to drive your actions? Sometimes money is a motivator to get us through this next spot in our lives. We need to make money to get the debt paid off so we can get to the thing we really want to live for. Your why, or purpose, is what makes you passionate, full of life, and drive. When you have your why, you will be able to get more passionate, especially if your why is to help others. What will it take for you to find your why and start living accordingly?

Today, I will start with finding my why and if I know what it is, I will find ways to live according to my why so that people will understand my why and see it in what I do.

Victim of Circumstance   December 28

"The conflict between what one is and who one is expected to be touches all of us. And sometimes, rather than reach for what one could be, we choose the comfort of the failed role, preferring to be the victim of circumstance, the person who didn't have a chance." – Merle Shain

There is a strange mixture of emotions being the victim of circumstance. On the one hand, it is not our fault. The situation caused me to fail, I never had a chance. On the other hand, why did I let that happen to me? I allowed myself to stay in that situation that caused me to fail, I had a chance, but I let it go. Playing the victim is no fun no matter what the circumstances are. It might feel good at times to blame others or a situation for our failures but deep down, we know that is not right. Sometimes we allow ourselves to be a victim and other times we see the situation developing and get out of the way of the proverbial moving train that is headed our way. Sometimes we allow people to victimize us and other times we set boundaries so we will not fall victim to others. It may seem hard to see how we can change our situation. We are living in a place that is not good with people that are hurting us, and we have no money to move or nowhere to go. We are in a relationship that is toxic, and we cannot seem to find a way out due to our circumstances. We are in a job that we do not enjoy and are afraid to start overdoing something we love because of the financial hardship the change will bring. Some people want to help if we just ask.

I have been in each one of those situations and was terrified of moving away from what I knew because of the emotional strength and hard work that was going to be needed to make the change or changes at the time. Every time it has worked out for the positive. I worked in a job with a toxic boss. I was in a relationship that was also toxic and felt like there was nowhere to go because of our financial situation. But when I asked for help, I was able to find it. Sometimes it was not in the places that I thought I would find it. Yes, it has been hard each time but when you see the reflection of yourself in the mirror and you see a better, happier, more peaceful version of yourself, you know you did the right thing. Do not allow situations or people to dictate your happiness or your growth. Worse yet, do not allow yourself to be a victim of your own mind. You got this!

Today, I will see if and where I have let myself be a victim and make changes to create boundaries to protect me in the future. It starts with small steps sometimes and I get to start today making small steps.

WEAKNESS   DECEMBER 29

"My attitude is that if you push me towards something that you think is a weakness, then I will turn that perceived weakness into a strength."
– Michael Jordan

When you are sitting in an interview and someone asks you to tell them about your weaknesses, do you break out in a cold sweat? When you hear about your weaknesses, do you cringe or get defensive? Do you push back and feel the need to show that person, or the world, that your weakness is not a weakness at all. We all have weaknesses, and some are more apparent than others. Sometimes we need an outsider's view of our life or our business because we cannot see the things that are holding us back. Outside perspective is key.

I was talking to a business coach the other day and she pointed out a couple of things that I needed to work on. But she was able to do it in a way that worked for me and caused me to act immediately. I was able to see what she was pointing out and made simple changes. The changes produced the desired effect and results. What do you do when someone points out your weaknesses? There are some things that we can change and others that we cannot. I am tall and I usually get to hit my head on something because of that height. I cannot change the fact that I am tall, nor can I change the fact that I get to hit my head, every once in a while, because I am tall. I have to be more mindful when I am in situations where I might hit my head. I can change the sarcastic things that come out of my mouth. I get to choose what I say and how I say it. That is a weakness that I can work on and do something about. Can you put aside your feelings to make the changes or are you willing to live with your shortcomings? Most of the weaknesses in our lives are caused by us not wanting to change. It comes because we learned something and now, we are unwilling to unlearn it.

What is one weakness that you can change today, this week, or this month? You probably have something in mind, if not, go ask a friend for that outside perspective.

PRIORITIES   DECEMBER 30

"The key is not to prioritize what's on your schedule, but to schedule your priorities." – Stephen Covey

How do you prioritize your life? How do you determine what your priorities are? Can you only see the trees and not the forest? Sometimes it is hard to look forward and figure out what is a priority versus what happens to be urgent at the time. Deadlines can make things a priority for the time but then you are left with what are the priorities in your life. Find out what really matters to you. Maybe it's family, friends, work, or play. Make your plans for each of those things so that you can address the priorities as you want them. Work is important and needs to get done but so does spending time with yourself and making sure you are healthy. Priorities are a part of life, and how you choose to deal with them will make a huge difference in your life.

Today, I will look to the priorities in my life and start to make the necessary adjustments to my life so that my priorities are where they need to be for me and my life.

YEAR-END   DECEMBER 31

"The studio is a laboratory, not a factory. An exhibition is the result of your experiments, but the process is never-ending. So, an exhibition is not a conclusion." – Chris Ofili

At end of anything is the time to conclude, summarize, and evaluate the process, program, or whatever you are finishing. Some people look at the end of a calendar year as a chance to do just that, evaluate the previous year and make some decisions and even goals for the upcoming year. We can look at the end of the year as a chance to beat ourselves up over the lack of progress or lack of goals achieved in the past year. Year-end should be simply an evaluation of did this get done or not, without any judgment. That can be hard to do. Simply review the year prior to gain understanding or an assessment of where things are so that you can make plans for the upcoming year. It should be a time marker, progress check-in. Goals are good and we should all have them, and you need to check in with the progress against the goal. Otherwise, you do not really have a goal, correct?

Do not put a lot of pressure on your year-end other than to check-in. I usually like to make goals and see where I am at against them. When you have disruptions appear in your life, they can pause your goals or even shift your goals. I have had a few of those in the past couple of years. I started working for a company and had big plans and goals to do things. There were expectations on me as well from my new boss and the company. In the two years I worked for the company, a few things happened along the way. I had just gotten a divorce, my daughter got married, my physical health needed some serious attention. My brother died, I got to focus on my mental health, and my family relationships. Finally, a pandemic started and lingered. I got the chance to focus on the things I needed to without even knowing I would need to focus on them. Being with that company gave me the chance to focus on those things. I was not as successful with my job as I wanted to be, or they wanted me to be. I did get to learn a lot during that time and my goals got adjusted. I became aware of the shifting of goals during that time. I learned from them and learned to be less judgmental during that time.

Today, I will look at my goals and my life and make sure that I am checking in with the goals but not being overly critical of myself because of the progress, or lack thereof, toward those goals. Life happens and sometimes we need to allow ourselves to be a part of it and not fight against it.

Index

A

Ability – September 7	264
Ability to Love – February 21	60
Acceptance – April 29	120
Accepting Change – April 26	117
Actions Versus Words – December 24	381
Adaptation – March 15	79
Adversaries – April 30	121
Advice is Just That, Advice! – February 11	52
Affirmation – May 1	125
All the Small Things – January 18	29
Anger – January 9	21
Anniversaries – August 29	253
Answers – May 3	126
Anxiety – February 27	64
Are You a Fool? – September 12	269
Are You a Good Person? – October 10	300
Are You Broken? – August 10	234
Are You Making a Living or Making a Life? – November 16	340
Are You Off Center? – December 6	362
Are You Ready? – July 12	200
Ask for What You Need – September 28	283
Asking for Help – July 31	220
Awareness – May 8	130

B

Backup Plans – September 26	281
Bad Days – August 9	233
Balance – May 5	128
Basic Needs – March 28	89
Basking in the Moment – May 6	128
Being Direct – January 10	22

Being Part of a Team – November 6	329
Being Transparent with Oneself – September 15	272
Being Useful to Others – September 27	282
Be Kind – November 13	337
Be Present – January 6	19
Be True to Yourself – November 15	338
Blindness – May 9	131
Boundaries – July 11	199
Bucket List – September 13	270
Building a Foundation – June 27	182

C

Can or Cannot, Do or Do Not – May 4	127
Can You Speak Metaphorically? – February 1	45
Chances – May 10	131
Change – April 2	95
Character – January 23	33
Character vs. Reputation – April 7	100
Charity – September 5	262
Children – March 21	84
Choices – May 11	132
Closure – September 10	267
Collaboration – January 17	27
Commitment – May 12	133
Common Sense – March 20	83
Compassion – May 15	136
Competition – May 16	137
Compliments – May 18	138
Confidantes – May 20	140
Confrontation – May 19	139
Connecting Through Listening – November 5	329
Connections – August 2	226
Contributing – May 22	142
Control Issues – May 23	142
Coping – May 30	149

Counting the Costs – April 12	105
Courage – February 12	53
Creativity – August 16	241
Crisis – December 2	357
Criticism – November 25	348
Curiosity – January 31	40
Customer Service – April 6	99

D

Dealing with the Source – June 8	161
Decision Making – November 28	351
Decisions – July 10	197
Delayed Dreams – March 18	82
Denial – February 16	56
Desire, Emotion, and Knowledge – December 21	378
Desperation – May 17	138
Devotion – May 24	143
Difficult Times – March 1	69
Digging Deeper – November 9	332
Diligence – June 5	159
Directionv – May 13	134
Disappointment – July 1	189
Doing the Best You Can – December 17	374
Do You Know Better? – July 25	214
Draw Without an Eraser – April 1	95
Dreams vs. Reality – July 4	191

E

Earning Trust – January 28	37
Educate Yourself – February 26	64
Encouraged to Fail – December 22	379
Energy – May 21	141
Enough is Enough! – August 8	232
Entitlement – March 16	80
Equality – August 26	250

Expectations – April 8	101
Experience – February 2	45

F

Failure – February 3	46
Fairness – January 8	20
Fame – February 19	58
Family – September 16	272
Fear of Death – June 20	175
Fear vs. Understanding – January 12	24
Finding Fault – February 15	55
Find Your Passion – September 14	271
Fix the Unfixable – July 30	219
Flexibility – September 23	278
Focused Plans – April 3	96
Focus – January 13	24
Focus on the Right Things – July 28	217
Forgiveness – July 7	194
Forgiveness vs. Permission – July 27	216
Forgiving Yourself – October 7	296
Freedom – April 4	98
Fresh Start – March 19	83
Frustrations – August 12	236
Fulfillment – May 26	145

G

Gains – April 18	110
Gambling – January 15	26
Garbage In, Garbage Out – August 5	229
Giving and Receiving – December 1	357
Giving – April 9	102
Go With the Flow – August 22	246
Grace – April 11	104
Gratitude – April 25	116
Gratitude for Failure – November 19	342

Grief – January 11	23
Grieving – August 30	255
Growth – April 22	114
Guilt – November 27	350

H

Happiness – July 17	205
Harmony – August 11	236
Healing a Broken Heart – November 10	333
Healing – January 19	29
Healing Words – February 6	48
Helping Others – February 25	63
Honesty with Oneself – February 18	58
How Are You Doing? – July 26	215
How do You Measure Yourself? – August 4	228
How do You See Things? – February 23	62
Humility and Compliments – August 31	256
Humility – March 3	70
Hunger – September 30	286

I

I am Sorry – October 22	312
Ideals – June 6	159
Imagination – April 5	98
Inadequacy – June 11	165
Influence – September 22	277
Inner Peace – October 14	304
Inspiration – April 17	109
Inspired – August 27	252
Intentional Gratitude – June 4	158
Intentions – December 16	373
Intimacy – June 29	184
Isolation – June 3	157
It is Hard Having to be Right All the Time – December 10	367

K

Karma – September 24	279
Kindness – February 7	49
Knowledge vs. Wisdom – October 12	302
Know Your Strengths – August 23	247

L

Labor of Love – October 29	319
Leadership – September 21	276
Learning from Loss – May 27	146
Learning Lessons – February 8	50
Learning Through Others – April 28	119
Learning to Let Go – June 9	162
Learn It, Until You Earn It – November 21	344
Learn to Unlearn – October 13	303
Legacy – January 26	35
Less is More – September 9	266
Let It Out – August 21	245
Life Events – March 8	74
Life is Short – October 24	314
Listening – April 23	114
Live Deliberately – January 29	39
Look Around – January 7	19
Looking Ahead – March 29	90
Love Is… – August 3	227
Love – January 16	27
Love the One You Are With – February 14	55
Love What You Do – May 29	148
Luck – June 15	170

M

Make Time for You – July 18	206
Making a Difference – July 16	204
Managing Yourself with Time – October 5	294
Manipulation – November 3	327

Matters of the Heart – April 16	109
Measuring Up – November 24	347
Meditating – October 1	291
Mentors – July 13	201
Messages and Messengers – August 20	244
Methodology – April 10	103
Mind Control – April 14	107
Miracles – February 22	61
Mistakes – June 7	161
Mistakes vs. Wisdom – April 19	111
Motivation – April 21	113
Music for Your Soul – March 12	77
My Path – June 25	180

N

Nature – June 13	168
Needs – November 11	334
Negativity – November 1	325
Negotiations – January 27	36
Networking – May 28	147
New Beginnings – January 1	15
New Chapter – June 2	156
Newness – October 28	318
Next! – May 7	129

O

Observation – October 31	321
One More Step – September 1	259
Open to Experiences – June 24	179
Opportunity – March 30	91
Order vs. Chaos – November 7	331
Originality – October 27	317
Over Promise and Under Deliver – June 12	167
Oversharing – June 30	185
Ownership – July 2	190

Own Your Decisions – March 4   71

P

Pain – October 19	309
Parenting – July 24	213
Passing Through – December 8	365
Passion – April 20	112
Patience and Time – December 7	364
Patience – February 5	48
Perseverance – March 7	73
Persona – April 27	118
Personality – April 24	115
Personal Pride – June 18	173
Perspective – March 13	78
Planning – March 24	86
Planting Seeds – October 8	298
Positivity – December 12	369
Powerless – June 19	174
Preparation and Expectation – September 17	273
Preparation – June 17	172
Priorities – December 30	386
Proactive vs. Reactive – June 14	168
Processes – December 14	371
Procrastination – September 6	263
Pushy or Push-over? – October 11	301

Q

Questions – June 16	171
Questions Versus Answers – July 15	203
Quiet – September 11	268

R

Random Acts of Kindness – February 17	57
Reactions – December 15	372
Receiving – August 17	241

Reflection – July 21	209
Reflections of Self in Others – October 4	293
Regret – August 28	252
Reprogramming – July 14	202
Reputation – January 21	31
Resentment – November 17	341
Resignation – December 19	376
Responsibility – August 6	230
Results – January 25	35
Revenge – October 9	299
Right Place – July 9	196
Right Seat Right Bus – October 16	306
Rituals – July 19	207
Rough Road – June 28	183
Routines – February 13	54
Rules – January 24	34

S

Sales and Sports – January 4	17
Same Kind of Different as Me – September 20	276
Saying and Doing – March 27	89
Secrets – July 3	190
Self-doubt – July 22	210
Selflessness – June 21	177
Self-Respect – March 9	75
Serial Perfectionist – June 1	155
Siblings – November 30	353
Simple Life – January 14	25
Simplicity – February 24	62
Smile – February 4	47
Sobriety – July 5	192
Softening – November 4	328
Spinning Your Wheels – October 6	296
Spirituality – April 13	106
Straightforward – October 3	292

Strength from Distress – June 23 — 178
Strength vs. Feelings – September 25 — 280
Struggles – March 2 — 69
Stuck – July 29 — 218
Success – September 29 — 285
Surrender – June 26 — 181

T

Take a Chance – January 22 — 32
Team – July 8 — 195
Teamwork – August 15 — 240
That's Never Happened to Me Before – December 9 — 365
The Future – October 21 — 312
The Gap – October 20 — 310
The Heart – March 11 — 76
The Illusion of Perfection – December 13 — 370
The Path – January 5 — 18
The Pessimist, The Optimist, And The Realist – May 25 — 144
The Price of Love – March 14 — 78
There is Always Something – December 18 — 375
The Scattered Pieces Will Come Together – March 31 — 92
Things Beyond Your Control – November 22 — 345
Those That Heal – November 18 — 342
Time – June 22 — 177
Time to Explore – January 3 — 16
Time to Move on – November 29 — 352
Time to Reset Yourself – August 19 — 243
Timing – February 10 — 51
Today – July 6 — 193
Tolerance – March 22 — 85
Toxic People – June 10 — 164
Transparency – January 30 — 39
Trials – January 20 — 30
True Friendship – February 28 — 65
Trust – November 8 — 331

Truth – December 11   368
Turnback Moments – December 3   359

U

Unlearn What You Have Learned – July 20   208
Urgent Versus Important – March 23   86

V

Value – December 4   360
Victim Mindset – November 23   346
Victim of Circumstance – December 28   384

W

Wait for it! – May 14   135
Want vs. Need – December 25   382
Watch What You Say – September 2   259
Weakness – December 29   385
We Are All Connected – December 26   383
Wellness Versus Illness – November 26   349
What Are You Aiming for? – August 13   238
What are You Capable of? – October 18   308
What Are You Hiding? – September 8   264
What Are You Resisting? – November 2   326
What Are Your Limits? – October 30   320
What Are Your Terms? – November 20   343
What Are You Seeking? – December 5   361
What Are You Working For? – March 5   72
What Do You Deserve? – February 9   51
What Do You Know? – March 10   75
What Drives You? – September 18   274
What has Broken You? – September 19   275
What Impression Are You Leaving? – October 2   292
What Interests You? – November 14   337
What is Nonsense? – December 23   380
What is Your Value? – March 25   87

What is Your Why? – December 27	383
What Scares You? – October 23	313
When Was the Last Time You Got Angry? – September 3	260
When You Survive This – October 17	307
Where Does the Time Go? – February 29	66
Where Do You See Yourself in Five Years? – September 4	261
Which Path – August 14	238
Who Are You? – August 18	242
Who Needs to be Taught? – August 1	225
Why Are You in a Hurry to Grow Up? – December 20	377
Why Is This Happening to Me? – August 24	248
Willpower vs. Surrender – July 23	211
Withholding – April 15	108
Words of Love – March 17	81
Words Speak Volumes – March 26	88
Worry – August 7	231

Y

Year-End – December 31	387
You Are Not Alone – October 26	316
You Can Be Vulnerable – May 2	125
You Can Never Go Back – January 2	15
Your Attention – November 12	336
Your Best – March 6	72
Your Past – May 31	150
Your Perspective – October 15	305
Your Story – August 25	250
Your View – February 20	59
Your Words are More Than Just Words – October 25	315

About the Author

Chris W. Michel is a son, a brother, a father, and now a grandfather, who grew up west of Chicago, IL. He was raised in a single-parent household, played three sports through high school, played college football, as a walk-on, and lettered twice. He began his spiritual journey while in college and continued to learn and grow over the years. Like most, he has had his ups and downs during that journey. His spiritual walk has led him to develop a desire to not only work on his own ethical, consultative sales and business path but to also help others in their mindful, virtuous journey in sales and business.

Chris has worked in sales for over 30 years. Throughout his career, he has been in management, a sales and business consultant, and now has his own sales and business coaching firm. He has developed training programs over the years and continues to work with companies and individuals contributing to their improvement and success. When he is not working, he has developed a passion for giving back to his community, focusing his volunteer efforts with Habitat for Humanity, where he can be found most Saturdays.

Chris can be reached for sales coaching, events, and media appearances at www.coachchrisconsulting.com

CPSIA information can be obtained
at www.ICGtesting.com
Printed in the USA
BVHW030732300422
635802BV00015B/508